TURNING STRATEGY
INTO ACTION

THE BEST OF LONG RANGE PLANNING

Series Editor: Professor Bernard Taylor, Henley Management College

The aim of this series is to bring together in each volume the best articles on a particular topic previously published in *Long Range Planning* so that readers wishing to study a specific aspect of planning can find an authoritative and comprehensive view of the subject, conveniently in one volume.

Titles in the *Best of Long Range Planning Series:*

Strategic Planning — The Chief Executive and the Board (Number 1)
Edited by Bernard Taylor

Entrepreneurship — Creating and Managing New Ventures (Number 2)
Edited by Bruce Lloyd

Making Strategic Planning Work in Practice (Number 3)
Edited by Basil Denning

Planning for Information as a Corporate Resource (Number 4)
Edited by Alfred Collins

Developing Strategies for Competitive Advantage (Number 5)
Edited by Patrick McNamee

Strategic Planning for Human Resources (Number 6)
Edited by Sheila Rothwell

Strategic Service Management (Number 7)
Edited by Denis Boyle

Strategic Management in Major Multinational Companies (Number 8)
Edited by Nigel Freedman

Turning Strategy into Action (Number 9)
Edited by Ken Irons

Forthcoming volumes will deal with other topical themes:

Creating Shareholder Value through Acquisitions and Divestment (Number 10)
Edited by Christopher Clarke

Strategic Management in Japanese Companies (Number 11)
Edited by Toyohiro Kono

Strategic Planning for Public Service and Non Profit Organizations (Number 12)
Edited by John M. Bryson

Each volume will contain 10 – 12 articles, and about 120 pages. In due course they will provide a comprehensive and authoritative reference library, covering all important aspects of Strategic Planning.

A Related Journal

LONG RANGE PLANNING★

The Journal of the Strategic Planning Society and of the European Strategic Planning Federation.

Editor: Professor Bernard Taylor, Henley — The Management College, Greenlands, Henley-on-Thames, Oxon RG9 3AU, UK.

> The leading international journal in the field of strategic planning, which provides authoritative information to senior managers, administrators, and academics on the concepts and techniques involved in the development and implementation of strategies and plans.

★Free sample copy gladly sent on request to the Publisher.

TURNING STRATEGY INTO ACTION

Edited by

KEN IRONS
Ken Irons Associates, London

PERGAMON PRESS

OXFORD · NEW YORK · SEOUL · TOKYO

U.K.	Pergamon Press plc, Headington Hill Hall, Oxford OX3 0BW, England
U.S.A.	Pergamon Press, Inc, 395 Saw Mill River Road, Elmsford, New York 10523, U.S.A.
KOREA	Pergamon Press Korea, KPO Box 315, Seoul 110-603, Korea
JAPAN	Pergamon Press, 8th Floor, Matsuoka Central Building, 1-7-1 Nishi-Shinjuku, Shinjuku-ku, Tokyo 160, Japan

First edition 1991

Library of Congress Cataloging–in–Publication Data
Turning strategy into action/edited by Ken Irons — 1st ed.
p.   cm. — (The Best of long range planning: no. 9)
1. Strategic planning. 2. Strategic planning — Case studies. I. Irons, Ken. II. Series.
HD30.28.T82 1991 658.4′012 – dc20 91 – 14450

British Library Cataloguing in Publication Data
Turning strategy into action.
1. Corporate planning
I. Irons, Ken II. Series
658.4012

ISBN 0-08-040666-1 Hardcover
ISBN 0-08-040667-X Flexicover

Printed in Great Britain by BPCC Wheatons Ltd, Exeter.

Contents

Page

INTRODUCTION: Turning Strategy into Action   1
Ken Irons

PART 1   MANAGING STRATEGIC CHANGE

Successfully Implementing Strategic Decisions   9
Larry D. Alexander

Strategy in Action — Techniques for Implementing Strategy   17
Richard Reed and M. Ronald Buckley

Bridging the Awful Gap between Strategy and Action   25
Roy Wernham

Managing Strategic Change: An Integrated Approach   35
Colin A. Carnall

Linking Organizational Effectiveness and Environmental Change   47
Frank Shipper and Charles S. White

Managing Change   55
Robert M. Worcester

PART 2   PUTTING PLANS INTO ACTION

Strategic Planning and Participation: A Contradiction in Terms?   63
H. J. Kloeze, A. Molenkamp and F. J. W. Roelofs

How Planning Works in Practice — A Survey of 48 U.K. Companies   75
Shawki Al-Bazzaz and Peter M. Grinyer

Human and Organization Problems in Corporate Planning   89
A. C. B. Wilson

Participation in Planning   95
H. H. Berschin

Strategic Planning for Public Affairs   101
Thomas G. Marx

PART 3   CASES IN SUCCESSFUL IMPLEMENTATION

Creating a Productive Culture at Shell Chemicals   111
Ian A. Thornley

Planning for a Rapidly Changing Environment in SAS   117
Olle Stiwenius

Changing the Corporate Culture of Rank Xerox   125
Paul Chapman

Successful Strategies — The Story of Singapore Airlines (SIA)   131
Karmjet Singh

Turning Strategy into Action

Ken Irons, Ken Irons Associates, London

This book consists of fifteen exceptional articles which have appeared in *Long Range Planning*. They provide a comprehensive insight into the difficulties of turning strategy into action, and some valuable thoughts on how to avoid them, or at least on how difficulties can be reduced to manageable proportions. It is clear that turning strategy into action is always going to be a difficult task. Few people welcome the disturbance change brings, even when they acknowledge the rightness of the objectives, and for many it can be traumatic, as Colin Carnall shows in his effective analogy between organizational change and bereavement.

Maybe because it is such an emotive subject, stirring up passions and prejudices, few planners are prepared to write about it. Certainly, what looked in prospect like a difficult task, selecting a representative sample of good articles on strategy implementation, turned out to be just that — a difficult task! Although more recent issues of *Long Range Planning* have shown a tendency to redress this balance, the absolute number of articles on implementation is still low, and the insights provided are few.

However, the editors found this an exciting challenge and the end result is a tour-de-force of the thinking on issues affecting implementation and change. In particular, the first five articles on 'strategy implementation' deserve a place in any planner's library.

The Shift to Services

It is hoped that future years will see greater attention being paid to implementation. We are in the middle of a steady — some might say head-long — move toward a 'service society', and this has significant implications for the creation of action out of strategy. Obviously, services are about people but the impact goes beyond the cliché to more fundamental points; first, the true implications of service, and secondly, that services are not confined to a few, identifiable, sectors of business.

To take the first point, there are five elements which are generally held to distinguish services:

(1) *Services are transient* — they are 'consumed' then and there. They have no lasting material being and may only leave memories.

(2) *Services are mainly represented by people* — they cannot be separated from the person of the provider, whose personal characteristics and perceptions of themselves are 'on show' to the consumer and indeed form an important part of consumer's perception.

(3) *Services are only finally made face-to-face with the consumer and at the time of consumption.* They are perishable — you cannot have a production run and store services against future demand.

(4) *Services are, therefore, essentially a series of 'one-off' production runs.* It is difficult to achieve standardization or exercise the same controls over production as you would with a product, for example through 'quality' controls.

(5) *Services are open to influence from the consumer* — not just in some indirect way, as through research or even the exercise of choice — but directly, since they participate in and help make the final activity.

In a service, creating action out of strategy — that is action you intended! — involves the willing participation of a large number of people, who must not only believe in your aims but must act them out, effectively! This is a lesson which could not only be learnt with good effect by many planners, but equally by many Chief

1

Executives — and Government ministers! Even the best strategy is unlikely to have much credit if those most involved feel hostile or threatened, or even worse feel that it devalues their contribution, leaving nothing to replace it as hope for the future.

Nor, to take the second point made above, is the service revolution confined to the few. Government statistics show that about two-thirds of the workforce are in 'services', but the real figure is closer to 90% because, even in major manufacturing organizations, many provide services to others. Increasingly such services are being subcontracted, but they may still be classified as manufacturing. However, even this understates the true breadth of 'service', for as manufactured goods become more and more alike, so service becomes the difference.

Manufacturers of cars increasingly emphasize service and seek to ensure a good experience over the life of a vehicle, not simply the sale of a tin box. Oil companies seek to differentiate from each other through superior service to specific segments of the market, rather than just sell price-sensitive petrol. Suppliers of business equipment, such as computer software, are more concerned to emphasize their support for a customer in its business than to simply sell them some programs. The illustration in Figure 1 graphically demonstrates this shift in emphasis. Whilst drawn for an insurance company, you could substitute a car, or petrol, or a software package for the pieces of paper.

The old way

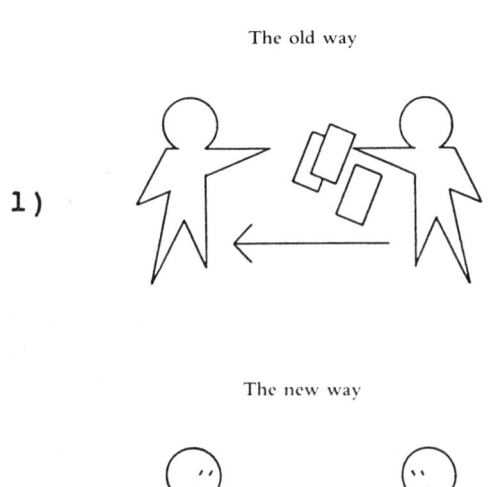

The new way

Figure 1 Selling Customer Service

Putting strategy into this context, we can see how **much we will** need to emphasize the importance **of getting** action in the future.

In this volume, Part 1 includes five articles which tackle this aspect in an analytical way and outside the strict corporate planning framework. They highlight the key issue, that 'problem avoidance' must be a primary objective. This can be achieved by considering implementation needs with the plan.

Then there is an article on 'Managing Change' published twenty years ago. Sadly, it could have been published in 1991 with little amendment, but it serves to show the complexity of the problem which planners face in bringing about change.

Part 2 includes five articles which discuss attitudes that planners need to have to be successful, that is taking successful planning as being successful implementation. What emerges is that a sound plan is simply the 'price of entry', and that without consideration of people and the environment, planning is meaningless.

Finally, Part 3 deals with four cases of successful strategy and successful implementation and, although each case is unique, clear recurring themes and issues emerge: people, organizational culture, communication, harmony with the environment and market place, and leadership.

Part 1 Managing Strategic Change

Successfully Implementing Strategic Decisions
Larry D. Alexander (*LRP* Vol. 18 No. 3, 1985)
A review of a questionnaire evaluating the implementation of one recent strategic decision by ninety-three company presidents. It not only highlights key issues but casts doubts on some traditional views of the barriers.

Strategy in Action — Techniques for Implementing Strategy
Richard Reed and M. Ronald Buckley (*LRP* Vol. 21 No. 3, 1988)
The authors suggest some tools and techniques which provide a means of avoiding many of the problems that can beset implementation.

Bridging the Awful Gap Between Strategy and Action
Roy Wernham (*LRP* Vol. 17 No. 6, 1984)
Based on studies within British Telecom, the author demonstrates that strategy does not always follow the lines intended.

Managing Strategic Change: An Integrated Approach
Colin A. Carnell (*LRP* Vol. 19 No. 6, 1986)
A thought-provoking article which takes an objective view of an approach to the management of strategic change. As the author observes, it is not a question of 'being nice to people' but 'hard work'.

Linking Organizational Effectiveness and Environmental Change
Frank Shipper and Charles S. White (*LRP* Vol. 16 No. 3, 1983)
The authors examine the conflict between internal reactions and external awareness. The lessons for manufacturing and service businesses are strong.

Managing Change
Robert M Worcester (*LRP* Vol. 3 No. 1, 1970)
Based on U.S. research, the article identifies some key areas of change management that persist today.

Part 2 Putting Plans into Action

Strategic Planning and Participation: A Contradiction in Terms?
H. J. Kloeze, A. Molenkamp and F. J. W. Roelofs (*LRP* Vol. 13 No. 5, 1980)
The authors pose a crucial question and their article will help managers to think through this very real conflict.

How Planning Works in Practice — A Survey of 48 U.K. Companies
Shawki Al-Bazzaz and Peter M. Grinyer (*LRP* Vol. 13 No. 4, 1980)
Surprisingly the only example of its kind. Still highly relevant.

Human and Organization Problems in Corporate Planning A.C.B. Wilson (*LRP* Vol.5 No. 1, 1972)
A short but valuable article which emphasizes that strategic planning cannot be a science.

Participation in Planning
H. H. Berschin (*LRP* Vol. 6 No. 4, 1973)
Based on both research and experience, this article shows the need for balance between a centralized and a decentralized approach.

Strategic Planning for Public Affairs
Thomas G. Marx (*LRP* Vol. 23 No. 3, 1990)
This article from General Motors deals with the 'politics' of planning and emphasizes the need to anticipate, plan for and manage conflicts with pressure groups, government agencies and community interests who might otherwise prevent the implementation of the company's plan.

Part 3 Cases in Successful Implementation

Creating a Productive Culture at Shell Chemicals
Ian A. Thornley (*LRP* Vol. 21 No. 3, 1988)
This article shows how, faced with a crisis the solution of which required dramatic cutbacks, Shell was able to productively turn the situation around by successfully affecting a change in the culture of the organization.

Planning for a Rapidly Changing Environment in SAS
Olle Stiwenius (*LRP* Vol. 18 No. 2, 1985)
With inspiring leadership, SAS successfully implemented a turnaround strategy, transforming a functionally product-oriented company into a market-oriented service company by relating the corporate culture and the organization to a more competitive commercial environment.

Changing the Corporate Culture at Rank Xerox
Paul Chapman (*LRP* Vol. 21 No. 2, 1988)
This article describes the implementation of a new 'systems strategy' at Rank Xerox. This involved a radical change of culture, including the use of 'Competitive Benchmarks', a Leadership Through Quality Programme, and changes in the organization structure.

Successful Strategies — The Story of Singapore Airlines (SIA)
Karmjet Singh (*LRP* Vol. 17 No. 5, 1984)
SIA's rapid growth can only in part be attributed to the strategic position of Singapore. The new airline has succeeded largely because of the high commitment, high performance culture that has been developed — and the determination to provide a superior service. It sums up the problems of strategic planning and implementation in a situation which is self-evidently successful and provides a fitting conclusion to this book.

Impacts on Implementation

Successful implementation continues to elude the majority of companies. Maybe this is owing to the nature of planning and, even more, the style of the planners.

For many people in planning, abstract ideas and objective thinking are of critical performance. So long as the plan is being developed, these values are a virtue. However, during the implementation we are dealing with more than an 'art', with the 'style' of the approach. It is clear that the human factor involved in this is not easy for planners to adapt to.

In general, the authors of this book recognized six broad factors which had an impact on implementation.

(1) Communication

An overworked word, which is used to cover:

☆ communication of goals and strategy throughout the organization,

☆ lines of responsibilities, and

☆ feedback procedures.

Although communication was a factor in every article, these problems are particularly highlighted in the first two articles.

Alexander carried out research on 93 companies, had 49 interviews with CEO's and he concluded that in order to:

● prevent problems occurring

● take corrective action, and

● promote success,

the development of strategy needs:

● a sound, and thorough, planning basis,

● the involvement and commitment of employees in the process,

● sufficient resources,

● clear and communicable objectives, and

● an implementation plan which is practical.

In their article, Reed and Buckley suggest the use of various tools to improve communication of the benefits and risks of strategy, throughout the organization. To avoid problems and running risks:

☆ *performance appraisal* should evaluate individual input not organizational output;

☆ *goal setting* should translate long term strategic aims into measurable portions;

☆ *critical success factors*, i.e. intermediate goals, should be determined and then tied to action plans.

They stress the need for a proactive approach to the environment, with the organization structure being multifaceted, flexible and constantly modified, and with the emphasis on 'prevention rather than cure'.

(2) The Human Factor

This is another recurring theme, captured most eloquently by Carnall, who suggests that only by bringing together the managerial skills required for strategic change with the methods individuals use to cope with change, can strategy be implemented successfully.

He compares the process of coping with change to that undergone by individuals during bereavement, and suggests they need help in the form of communication, new skills, support and overall 'empathy', with empathy meaning an understanding of the struggle an individual faces, rather than simply making assumptions about what that individual needs.

(3) Organization Change

Wernham, in his research within British Telecom, suggests that avoiding unnecessary change should be a prime objective. The strategy should be made to fit the organization rather than changing the organization to suit the strategy.

A position attitude to change needs to be encouraged. Success breeds success, and an organization needs to ensure that the decisions to be implemented are relevant, both technologically and for the market. This will create a track record which will inspire confidence, and this confidence will in turn create a positive attitude to implementation and change.

This is also an important part of Shipper and White's article.

(4) Involvement

This is an area of obvious ambivalence for planners. Worcester's article shows clearly the need for involvement but many writers see it as 'necessary but unfortunate'!

Of course, involvement brings its own problems. Kloeze, Molenkamp and Roelofs believe that strategy cannot be realised without cooperation at all levels, but they also know that the more there is cooperation, the more there will be tensions. How to reduce these tensions and ensure employee acceptance is the key question an organization should ask itself.

This theme is continued in the following three articles:

Al-Bazzaz and Grinyer carried out a survey of Corporate Planning in 48 large U.K. companies. They found that the more planners took responsibilities and made contributions, the more problems occurred. Most problems were perceived as structural, with issues such as centralization vs decentralization, formal vs informal, systematic vs judgmental decision making, often causing organizations to implement structural changes. However, rather than trying to find the ideal organization, they believe the aim should be to increase employees' involvement, which will reduce the difficulties. To do this, the planning system needs to be flexible and responsive, and to cater for the human and environmental realities.

Wilson emphasizes this, stressing that whilst proper techniques are important as a foundation, overall it is the 'management style' which matters. His premise is that management is an art, not a science, and too little emphasis is given to leadership.

Berschin maintains that to implement plans successfully requires the motivation and the full involvement of both line and staff personnel in the development and execution stages. In order to adapt planning to the two main organization types — autocratic centralized and democratic decentralized — plans need to be prepared by both head office and divisional staff and contributions should be made by employees at all management levels. Everyone needs to be identified with the goals, and personally motivated towards them. He stresses the difficulty of encouraging new thinking, and of ensuring new ideas are accepted and implemented.

(5) Realism and Culture

To succeed, plans need to be realistic. Much of the concern about involvement and the human factor arises because plans are often seen as unrealistic. This can perhaps be explained in relation to the market place, i.e. the commercial realities and the need to link the internal organization to the external environment.

Three of the success stories — SAS, Singapore Airlines and Rank Xerox — emphasize the necessity to meet market needs and to fit the organization and its services on products with those needs. Shipper and White's article also stresses the need to recognize changes in the environment and to direct the organization's internal processes to meet the external needs.

In effect the realism and the implementability of the plan will depend on the cultural 'fit' between all the internal and external factors.

(6) Resources

Inadequate resourcing, failure to take into account the time factor, lack of skills, inappropriate technology and too little top management support and involvement were all seen as contributing to failure in implementation. It is refreshing to find a situation where these have not been so much of a problem as to prevent success. The last article describes the rise of Singapore Airlines. This organization has been enormously successful and has not only invested heavily in resources, especially people and communications, but has done this in a visionary and enlightened way.

Throughout, the contributors emphasize the need for 'communication'. It is, however, an overused and commonly misunderstood word, and the writers show that 'communication' is a tool which helps management to deal with people. It is not merely an 'information flow', but a way of behaving, a whole culture, and the feeling has to be genuine to be beneficial. *The people who have to implement the plans should be seen not as targets or resources, but as accomplices whose involvement as 'an accessory before the fact' is critical.*

To repeat a concept from Carnall's article:

> Empathy means an understanding of how people think and feel and not an assumption of knowing what other people think and feel. The skill of empathy is a struggle to understand. Individuals respond to that struggle.

PART ONE

Managing Strategic Change

Successfully Implementing Strategic Decisions

Larry D. Alexander, Assistant Professor of Business Strategy, Virginia Tech, Virginia, U.S.A.

Ninety-three company presidents completed a questionnaire evaluating the implementation of one strategic decision each in their respective firms. Ten strategy implementation problems were experienced during implementation by over 50 per cent of the sample group. Firms experiencing high success in implementation, according to an index of implementation success, were compared with the low-success firms to determine which problems were rated at significantly different levels. In 11 instances, the mean rating for the high-success implementation firms was significantly lower in terms of problem intensity. Follow-up interviews with 21 presidents (plus 25 governmental agency heads later on) identified five factors which help promote successful implementation.

Introduction

Although strategy implementation is viewed as an integral part of the strategic management process, little has been written or researched on it. The overwhelming majority of the literature so far has been on the long-range planning process itself or the actual content of the strategy being formulated. We have so far been giving lip service to the other side of the coin, namely strategy implementation. Consequently, it is not surprising that after a comprehensive strategy or single strategic decision has been formulated, significant difficulties are often encountered during the subsequent implementation process.

This study surveyed 93 private sector firms through a questionnaire to determine which implementation problems occurred most frequently as they tried to put strategic decisions into effect. Later on, in-depth telephone interviews with chief executive officers of 21 of these firms were conducted to comprehend these problems more fully. These interviews, combined later on with another 25 interviews with governmental agency heads in another study of implementation in the public sector by this researcher, help to identify factors which promote successful implementation.

Review of the Literature

The available literature on strategy implementation was reviewed in order to identify potential strategy implementation problems. Most of the 22 potential problems were identified from such helpful works as Alexander,[1] Andrews,[2] Galbraith and Nathanson,[3] Hobbs and Heany,[4] Kotter and Schlesinger,[5] Le Breton,[6] McCarthy et al.,[7] Quinn,[8] Steiner and Miner,[9] and Thompson and Strickland.[10] In addition, several in-depth case studies on strategy implementation by Pressman and Wildavsky,[11] Murphy,[12] Quinn[13] and Alexander[14] also helped to identify more potential problems. Finally, a few of the 22 implementation problems were suggested by chief executive officers in earlier interviews conducted by this writer.

Companies Surveyed

The 93 firms participating in this survey were strategic business units of medium and large sized firms. Some 72 firms (77 per cent) were listed in the Fortune 500 list of leading industrials. If Fortune's second 500 list of industrials is included along with Fortune's top 50 listings for utilities, retailing and services, then 89 firms (96 per cent) responding were included on one Fortune list or another.

The firms' SBUs (strategic business units) sampled differed with respect to their size, industry and geographical location within the United States. For example, 26 (28 per cent) of the SBUs had less than 400 employees, 23 (25 per cent) had 400–999 employees, 29 (31 per cent) had 1000–4999 employees, 13 (14 per cent) had over 5000 employees, and 2 (2 per cent) were unidentified. While most of the corporations operated within a number of different businesses, this study was focused on implementing strategic decisions within individual SBUs.

The author is Assistant Professor of Business Strategy at Virginia Polytechnic Institute and State University, Blacksburg, VA 24061, U.S.A.

The Strategic Decisions Evaluated

In the questionnaire, each responding company president (or division general manager) was asked to select one recent strategic decision that had been implemented in his SBU. He was asked to select one in which he had a great deal of personal knowledge about its subsequent implementation. Table 1 shows the types of strategic decisions that were evaluated. The main part of the questionnaire then asked the participants to evaluate the extent to which some 22 possible implementation problems actually were a problem in its subsequent implementation using a five-point Likert-type response scale. Finally, questions were asked to evaluate the overall success of the strategy implementation effort itself.

Most Frequently Occurring Problems

The 10 most commonly occurring strategy implementation problems are shown in Table 2

in descending order according to mean ratings. Two adjacent pairs of numbers on the five-point Likert response scale are combined for display purposes only as follows: minor and moderate problems (points 2 and 3), and substantial and major problems (points 4 and 5). The 10 listed items are the only ones rated as problems by over half of the sample group.

The first seven listed implementation problems occurred to at least 60 per cent of the firms. They are:

(1) implementation took more time than originally allocated by 76 per cent;

(2) major problems surface during implementation that had not been identified beforehand by 74 per cent;

(3) coordination of implementation activities (e.g. by task force, committees, superiors) was not effective enough by 66 per cent;

(4) competing activities and crises distracted

Table 1. Types of strategic decisions implemented

Type of strategic decision	No.	%
Introducing a new product or service	29	31
Opening and starting up a new plant or facility	17	18
Expanding operations to enter a new market	15	16
Discontinuing a product or withdrawing from a market	11	12
Acquiring or merging with another firm	10	11
Changing the strategy in functional departments	6	7
Other	5	5
	93	100

Table 2. Ten most frequent strategy implementation problems

Potential strategy implementation problem	Mean	Frequency of any degree of problem =	Frequency of minor/ moderate problems +	Frequency of substantial/ major problems
Implementation took more time than originally allocated	2·71	71 (76%)	45 (48%)	26 (28%)
Major problems surfaced during implementation that had not been identified beforehand	2·63	69 (74%)	45 (48%)	24 (26%)
Coordination of implementation activities was not effective enough	2·34	62 (66%)	45 (48%)	17 (18%)
Competing activities and crises distracted attention from implementing this decision	2·29	60 (64%)	41 (44%)	19 (20%)
Capabilities of employees involved were not sufficient	2·28	59 (63%)	40 (43%)	19 (20%)
Training and instruction given to lower level employees were not adequate	2·14	58 (62%)	47 (50%)	11 (12%)
Uncontrollable factors in the external environment had an adverse impact on implementation	2·28	56 (60%)	40 (43%)	16 (17%)
Leadership and direction provided by departmental managers were not adequate enough	2·23	55 (59%)	39 (42%)	16 (17%)
Key implementation tasks and activities were not defined in enough detail	2·09	52 (56%)	36 (39%)	16 (17%)
Information systems used to monitor implementation were not adequate	1·94	52 (56%)	43 (46%)	9 (10%)

attention from implementing this strategic decision by 64 per cent;

(5) capabilities (skills and abilities) of employees involved with the implementation were not sufficient by 63 per cent;

(6) training and instruction given to lower level employees were not adequate by 62 per cent; and

(7) uncontrollable factors in the external environment (e.g. competitive, economic, governmental) had an adverse impact on implementation by 60 per cent.

Three additional implementation problems listed in Table 2 occurred to somewhat fewer firms but still experienced by over 50 per cent of the sample firms.

Three-quarters (76 per cent) of the sampled firms found that their implementation efforts took more time than originally allocated. A number of explanations were given by CEOs in the follow-up telephone interviews. As one executive put it, 'In retrospect, we were overly optimistic in thinking how much time it would take to implement a new strategic decision. We thought that everything would work fine which it never does.' From the interviews, this problems seems to occur because top management:

(1) understates how long various implementation tasks will take to complete,

(2) downplays the likelihood of potential problems that may or may not occur, and

(3) is blind to other problems occurring altogether.

Obviously, when all three of these occur during implementation, it can greatly lengthen the time it will take to implement the decision effectively.

Solutions to the problem of taking too much time are numerous. More time should initially be allocated from the start to handle unexpected problems and, in general, the unknown. More manpower initially can be put on important strategic decisions, and particularly later on when unexpected problems emerge. In addition, rewards and penalties can also be used to bring about the desired results.

This latter suggestion is exactly how one CEO handled a strategic decision that had been dragging on and on. As he put it,

Even though we wanted to withdraw from this particular line of fashion clothes, we kept coming up with new ideas. For every two items we'd drop from this line, we'd introduce one new one. Thus, we kept getting seduced back into this line even though I knew we had to discontinue it. After two years, I finally solved the problem by telling my staff that if you or your subordinates present me with any

new sketch for this clothing line, that person will lose his job.

Major problems (and obstacles) surfaced during implementation that had not been identified beforehand were experienced by almost as many firms, specifically 74 per cent. These can be internally oriented problems, brought on by the firm trying something new, insufficient advance planning, and strategy formulators not getting actively involved in implementation to name a few. Or they can be caused by externally oriented factors such as the uncertainty involved with a new product or new market, uncontrollable events in the external environment, or legal/political complications introduced by new legislation or regulations among others.

Consider what happened to one domestic oil equipment firm that was implementing its strategic decision to construct oil wells in an Arab country. All sorts of problems surfaced that had not been identified beforehand as potential problems. Certain employees could not go into that country to work on the project because of their particular race or nationality. Bringing explosives into that country to blast rock in preparation for building the oil well foundation was delayed because the host government was suspicious that they could be used against the government itself. Neither of these problems had been identified beforehand by the firm or its Arab partner, who led them to believe it really knew the ropes and how to operate in the host country. In addition, another oil firm already in that country for many years tried to put up administrative road blocks by using its contacts in various governmental agencies of the Arab country.

Clearly, some of these problems could have been identified and resolved had the firm selected a better Arab partner. In addition, some of these potential problems overlooked by its Arab partner could have been identified had the firm talked with other U.S. firms already doing business there. However, it is safe to say that some of these problems could probably never be anticipated beforehand.

The presence of competing activities and crises that distracted attention from implementing the strategic decision was yet another frequently occurring problem. Some 64 per cent of the firms experienced this implementation problem. One aerospace components firm was starting to implement one strategic decision when along came one order from an airline firm that amounted to 25 per cent of its total sales in a typical year. Obviously, considerable time and attention had to be given to this major order for about 3 months which clearly had priority over the other strategic decision. Actually, the firm decided to forget trying to implement the new strategic decision for a while and put it on hold. Given the size of the customer order, this seemed the best way to handle these competing events.

Another firm was trying to implement one strategic decision when the market for its coal-related products collapsed in 1977. Because of this unexpected crisis, pressure was put on managers at all levels to do everything possible to increase sales and profits rather than to implement this new management resource planning system. Still another firm was diverted from implementing a new overall strategy for the division and had to help a very major customer design and manufacture one of its products which was encountering major production problems. This was done to insure that this delinquent customer would get enough revenues from the sale of its products to, in turn, pay money owed to this firm. Thus, it appears that the number and type of competing activities and crises that can occur are almost limitless.

One of three things typically occurs when competing events exist. Time and attention are taken away from implementing the new strategic decision. They are taken away from other existing programs which suffer. Or often, some time and attention are taken away from the new and existing programs.

Some 60 per cent of the firms experienced uncontrollable factors in the external environment that had an adverse impact on implementation. Some of these problems are truly surprise events. Examples of these include:

(1) a hurricane tearing off a roof of a new plant which damaged equipment;

(2) the Professional Airline Traffic Controllers strike and the 25 per cent reduction in flights which reduced the demand for a firm's new jet-pull-out tractor; and

(3) a surprising upturn in an industry's sales when a firm was trying to move three plants into one new modern facility.

In this latter example, this firm competing in the abrasives industry had planned to make this move during a time of slackened demand. All economic forecasts for 1978/1979 suggested a softness in the economy; consequently, the firm thought this would be an excellent time to consolidate operations. Unfortunately, after the move got started, that year turned out to be the best year ever for the industry which caused added problems trying to satisfy high customer demand while moving operations.

While most uncontrollable problems in the external environment cannot be anticipated, contingency plans can be developed for some of them. Then, if that problem does occur, at least the firm will be in a better position to take corrective action to minimize its impact on the firm.

Two somewhat lower rated items, which are:

(1) advocates and supporters of the strategic decision left (the division or company) during implementation (experienced by only 27 per cent of the firms) and

(2) the key people who developed and made the strategic decision, did not play an active enough role in its subsequent implementation (40 per cent),

illustrate how two problems can combine to make things even worse. One company president put it this way,

> Our company was acquired by another parent firm with no background in this business. A new group vice president was installed to straighten out the mess here. He and I developed a strategy to break even in about 15 months with proper equipment, but then 6 months later, this group vice president was replaced for reasons beyond my knowledge. His replacement was not familiar with our operations, wants us now to go in about a 180 degree different direction, and only looks at bottom line results.

In another firm, a company president appointed a key subordinate to be the project manager, directly overseeing the implementation of the strategic decision. Half way through its implementation, that subordinate got so frustrated with the whole thing that he took a job elsewhere which really ground things to a halt. While the loss of a key person implementing a strategic decision can cause problems and lengthen the implementation time, the loss of the key architect of the decision can potentially stop the implementation forever.

High Versus Low Implementation Success

The sample of 93 firms was then divided into high ($n = 33$), medium ($n = 29$), and low ($n = 31$) success depending on the relative degree of success in implementing the strategic decision. This was based on an implementation success index made up of an average of three questions rated on a five-point scale ranging from 'low extent' to 'high extent'. These questions sought to determine the extent to which the actual implementation effort:

(1) achieved the initial goals and objectives of the strategic decision;

(2) achieved the financial results (sales, income, and/or profits) that were expected; and

(3) was carried out within the various resources (money, manpower, time, etc.) initially budgeted for it.

Analysis of variance and Student t-tests were calculated for each of the 22 potential implementation problems to determine whether there were first significant overall differences and then specific significant differences between the high-success and low-success groups. In 21 instances, the high-success group in implementing their respective strategic decisions had lower mean scores than the low-success group for the respective problem.

Seven of the same 10 problems shown in Table 2 along with five new problems were found to be significantly different with the analysis of variance comparing high-, medium- and low-success groups. Then, in 11 instances (marked by asterisks) as shown in Figure 1, the Student t-test showed that the mean score for high-success implementing firms (as shown by the solid line) was significantly less than that for the low-success group of firms (as shown by the dashed line). The five implemen-

tation problems that had t-test significance at the 0·005 level or above are:

(1) key implementation tasks and activities were not defined in enough detail;

(2) problems requiring top management involvement were not communicated to them fast enough;

(3) changes in roles and responsibilities of key employees were not clearly defined;

(4) key formulators of the strategic decision did not play an active enough role in implementation; and

(5) major problems surfaced during implementation that had not been identified beforehand.

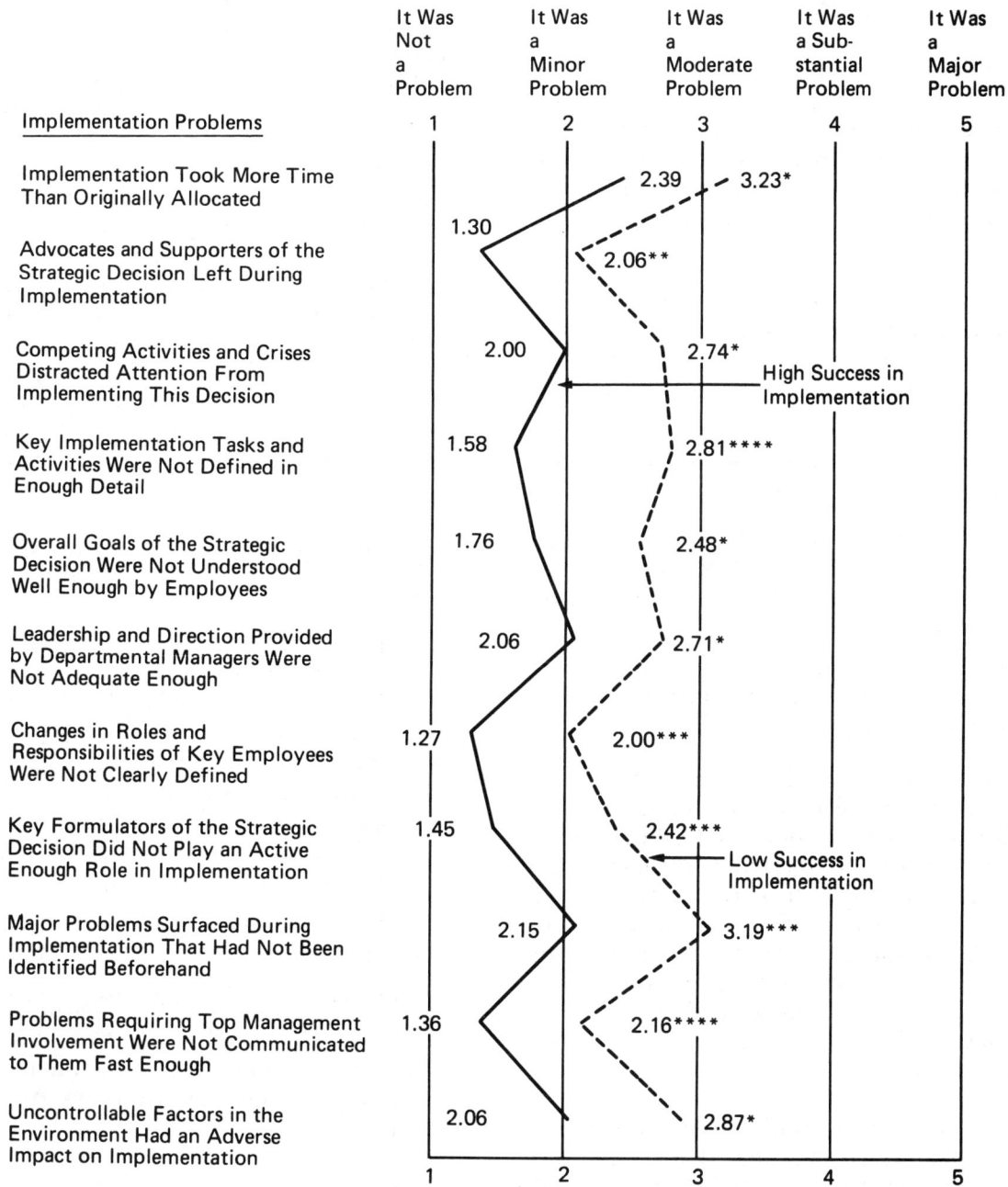

*p = 0.05, **p = 0.01, ***p = 0.005, ****p = 0.001

Figure 1. Mean ratings and Student t-tests for high- vs low-success implementation efforts

Thus, Figure 1 clearly suggests that the presence of more higher rated implementation problems has a negative effect on implementation success. Low-success firms experienced an average of 12·8 problems rated at any intensity level. In addition, 5·0 of these same 12·8 implementation items were rated as substantial or major problems by low-success firms. Conversely, high-success implementation firms experienced an average of only 9·2 problems, of which only 1·5 of them were rated at the substantial or major level.

Promoting Successful Strategy Implementation

In the followup telephone interviews with CEOs, one major purpose was to understand better various implementation problems that did hinder the implementation effort. However, another reason for these interviews was to get these executives to draw on their extensive experience and speculate on the things that help to promote successful strategy implementation. Although these generalizations are not statistically valid, they were mentioned most frequently by 21 CEOs plus 25 additional interviews with agency heads from federal and state governments in a comparison study.

Communication, Communication, Communication
This seemingly simple suggestion was mentioned more frequently by CEOs than any other single item. The reason it is repeated three times is to reflect exactly what was said by a number of these company presidents. They felt that top management must first of all clearly communicate with all employees what the new strategic decision is all about. Hopefully, it involves two-way communication that permits and solicits questions from affected employees about the formulated strategy, issues to be considered, or potential problems that might occur. In addition, communication includes clearly explaining what new responsibilities, tasks, and duties need to be performed by the affected employees. It also includes the why behind changed job activities, and more fundamentally the reasons why the new strategic decision was made in the first place. Finally, CEOs mentioned that two-way communication is needed throughout the implementation process to monitor what is actually happening, analyze how to deal with emerging problems, and in deciding what modifications might be needed in the program to make it work.

Start with a Good Concept or Idea
The need to start with a formulated strategy that involves a good idea or concept was mentioned next most often in helping promote successful implementation. In a nut shell, what this idea suggests is that no amount of time and effort spent on implementation can rescue a strategic decision that is not well formulated to begin with. More than being thoroughly planned out, the idea must be fundamentally sound. Thus, this suggests that strategy implementation can fail for one of two reasons. One is caused by a failure to do the things required during implementation to insure that a well-formulated strategy is successful. The other cause of failure is due to a poorly conceived formulated plan that no amount of implementation effort can help rescue.

Obtain Employee Commitment and Involvement
This third suggestion builds on the first two and interrelates with them. CEOs suggested that one way to accomplish this is to involve affected employees and managers right from the start in the strategy formulation process. On the contrary, when a strategic decision has been developed in a vacuum by a few people, top management should not be surprised that it is resisted during implementation by the affected employees. Top management should not be surprised if the formulated plan has major flaws in it because key employees and affected groups did not participate in its formulation. In fact, just the opposite may be true. Top management ought to be surprised if a formulated strategy, developed pretty much without key employee involvement, is implemented successfully.

Involvement and commitment should also be developed and maintained throughout the implementation process. If middle and lower level managers and key subordinates are permitted to be involved with the detailed implementation planning, their commitment typically will tend to increase. The workability of the specific action plan should also be improved simply by getting the affected employees involved—and committed—early on as well as throughout the implementation process.

Provide Sufficient Resources
CEOs mentioned at least four different kinds of resources. The obvious one is money, which, considering the sizeable scope of many strategic decisions, is a bottom line requirement. Conversely, failure to provide adequate funding may contribute to limited success or outright failure. Manpower is another key resource which can have either a positive or a negative effect on implementation. Technical expertise (or knowledge), as related to the new strategic decision, is still another resource mentioned by some CEOs. The idea suggested here is that firms need to have in-house expertise or hire a few new employees who possess it in order to implement strategic decisions involving new endeavors. A final resource mentioned is time. Sufficient time to accomplish the implementation, adequate time and attention given by top management to the new effort, and hopefully not too many other competing programs demanding the time of affected employees who will implement this one.

Develop an Implementation Plan

This final suggestion is a plea to develop many of the specifics to be done during implementation. In essence, this details who is to do what and when it is to be accomplished. A few CEOs mentioned that this plan must strike the right balance. If the implementation plan is too vague, it is of little practical use. Conversely, if the plan is too detailed, it may tend to force various functional departments to follow it precisely, even when it clearly needs to be modified.

Several CEOs also mentioned that a part of that plan should be to identify likely implementation problems. Instead of being blindly optimistic that nothing will go wrong while implementing a strategic decision, do just the opposite. Try to identify the most likely problems that might occur and then develop contingency responses for those eventualities.

Summary and Conclusions

A number of strategy implementation problems do seem to occur on a regular basis. In fact, 10 of the 22 potential problems rated occurred to at least 50 per cent of the sampled firms. While problems do occur frequently, the vast majority of firms experience them as minor or moderate problems. However, when a firm encounters several implementation problems, rated at the substantial or major level, it can have a very adverse impact on the implementation process.

Surprisingly, some of the traditional strategy implementation factors mentioned in the literature were not judged as frequently to be problems. Rated among the least frequent of the 22 implementation problems were:

☆ rewards and incentives utilized to get employee conformance to program were not sufficient (cited as a problem by only 18 per cent of the respondents);

☆ support and backing by top management in this SBU and at the corporate level were not adequate (21 per cent);

☆ financial resources made available were not sufficient (27 per cent);

☆ organizational structural changes made were not effective (33 per cent); and

☆ changes in roles and responsibilities of key employees were not clearly defined (38 per cent).

It may be that firms do such a good job in these areas than problems are prevented. Or it may suggest that other implementation problems identified in this study are more important than what the literature has somewhat led us to believe.

High-success firms experience implementation problems to a significantly less extent than do low-success implementation firms. In fact, some 11 problems were experienced to a significantly less extent by high-success firms when compared with low-success firms. In addition, high-success firms experienced problems rated at the substantial or major problem intensity level three times less frequently than did low-success firms. In addition, high-success firms also encountered fewer total problems during implementation.

Successful implementation in part involves preventing various implementation problems from occurring in the first place. It also involves taking quick action of resolve and address problems that do occur. Obviously, the faster corrective action is initiated during implementation, the more likely it can be resolved before it impacts adversely on the firm.

Successful implementation also involves doing the things that help promote success rather than just preventing problems from occurring. Although the five suggestions presented here are not statistically significant, they do help reinforce the importance of satisfying basic managerial tasks to help bring about success.

References

(1) L. Alexander, *Strategy Implementation Annotated Bibliography*, Harvard's HBS Case Services, Case No. 9–380–797 (1980), plus 1983 Supplement.

(2) K. Andrews, *The Concept of Corporate Strategy*, Dow Jones-Irwin, Homewood, IL (1971).

(3) J. Galbraith and D. Nathanson, *Strategy Implementation: The Role of Structure and Process*, West Publishing Co., St Paul, MN (1978).

(4) J. Hobbs and D. Heany, Coupling strategy to operating plans, *Harvard Business Review*, pp. 119–126, May–June (1977).

(5) J. Kotter and L. Schlesinger, Choosing strategies for change, *Harvard Business Review*, pp. 106–114, March–April (1979).

(6) P. Le Breton, *General Administration: Planning and Implementation*, Holt, Rinehart and Winston, New York (1965).

(7) D. McCarthy, R. Minichiello and J. Curran, *Business Policy and Strategy: Concepts and Readings*, Richard D. Irwin, Homewood, IL (1979).

(8) J. Quinn, *Strategies for Change: Logical Incrementalism*, Richard D. Irwin, Homewood, IL (1980).

(9) G. Steiner and J. Miner, *Management Policy and Strategy: Text, Readings, and Cases*, Macmillan, New York (1977).

(10) A. Thompson and A. Strickland, *Strategy Formulation and Implementation: Tasks of the General Manager*, Business Publications, Dallas (1981).

(11) J. Pressman and A. Wildavsky, *Implementation*, University of California Press, Berkeley, CA (1973).

(12) J. Murphy, Title I of ESEA: The politics of implementing federal education reform, *Harvard Educational Review*, pp. 35–63, February (1971).

(13) J. Quinn, General Motors' downsizing decision. In D. Harvey's *Business Policy and Strategic Management*, pp. 669–695. Charles E. Merrill, Columbus. OH (1982).

(14) L. Alexander, Pacific power and light: Implementation of an innovative home weatherization program. In A. Thompson and A. Strickland's *Strategic Management: Concepts and Cases*, pp. 880–905, Business Publications, Dallas (1984).

Strategy in Action—Techniques for Implementing Strategy

Richard Reed and M. Ronald Buckley

With a few notable exceptions, the literature on strategy implementation has viewed the subject from a problem-solving perspective. This article takes the alternative view that strategy implementation should be based on problem avoidance. Arguably, strategies are formulated to provide an optimal risk–benefit profile which is congruent with longer term goals. Consequently, strategic intent and the requirements for attaining the strategic benefits must be communicated to those managers whose actions provide the vehicle for commuting envisaged potential into actual achievement. Through identification and control of the necessary managerial actions many problems of implementation can be avoided. The authors suggest that a multi-faceted approach which combines the use of goal-setting and critical success factors with performance appraisal can facilitate the strategy implementation process.

A few years ago, a large diversified engineering concern targeted one of its European business units for growth and, because of poor strategy implementation, turned what was a logical strategic move into a near disaster. The European strategic business unit (SBU) was managed autonomously from the parent company. It manufactured large valves for use in the oil and petrochemical industries. These valves were highly specialized and, in the words of the SBU manager, the business unit was a 'bespoke producer of valves'. This precise focus meant that they had remained profitable by dominating a market niche and avoiding direct competition with the large U.S. companies who control the field.

In implementing the strategy for growth, product-line extensions and related diversifications were made which brought the SBU into the arena of direct competition. The net result was a product proliferation that achieved sales growth but had a negative impact on profits as competition increased and prices were depressed. Increased organizational inefficiency, created through the poorly managed

diversification activities, also had a negative effect on the loyalty of long-standing customers.

What went wrong? The corporate intent of the growth strategy was inadequately communicated to the SBU. Goals remained unclear. It was assumed that the incumbent managers possessed the necessary skills. Managerial performance was assessed solely on sales volume. There was no detailed action plan. The list of implementation *faux pas* continues. The answer to the rhetorical question of 'what went wrong' is complex and is, in part, what prompted some of the ideas expressed in this paper.

The Implementation Problem

There are remarkably few works which address the issue of directional control of strategy in implementation. Two of the most noteworthy are by Salter and by Stonich.[1,2] Salter takes a relatively broad spectrum approach and considers the impact of time-frames, risk and divisional relationships while Stonich concentrates on the specifics of portfolio balancing. Stonich suggests that systems of reward and control may be adapted to reflect the needs of high, medium or low growth SBUs by varying the emphasis on such measures as return on assets, cash flow and market share. The success with which individual managers achieve their goals depends primarily upon earlier inputs.[3] Consequently, success may be viewed as depending upon the strategy implementation process. Implicit within both the work of Salter and Stonich is the notion that strategic success, and therefore overall corporate success, reflect the directional emphasis communicated by senior executives during actual strategy implementation.

We adopt the view that strategy formulation is founded in logic. The final selection of a strategy is based on an optimization of firm–environment fit and results in perceived strategic benefits being balanced against inherent risks. Thus, the eventual pay-off from a chosen strategy is derived from a

Richard Reed is Assistant Professor of Management at Washington State University and Ronald Buckley is Assistant Professor of Management at the University of Oklahoma.

maximization of its benefits and a minimization of the risks.

We also adopt the view that implementation is itself a period of high risk. It typically involves dealing with changes in the external environment and making changes internally to organizational structures, budgeting, control systems, job requirements and many other organizational features. There is no all-encompassing model of the implementation process that offers complete guidance through the maze of interrelated problems that emerge from the variously adjacent areas of study. The literature and research in this area is so extensive that it will be considered separately so that some of the idiosyncrasies may be explored. The literature on externalities is even more comprehensive and beyond the scope of this paper. Instead, we concentrate on what is to date the missing link in implementation—problem avoidance.

Existing Approaches to Implementation

Strategy implementation is a topic that is receiving increasing amounts of attention. However, the literature has generally reflected an aspect-oriented approach to the subject emphasizing topics like strategy-structure fit, resource allocation and strategy success and executive style. Organizational Theory, Management Information Systems, Budgetary Control and others[4] all offer partial problem-solving solutions. As with other areas of strategic management, general rules are elusive.

Strategy-structure
Since the early 1960s, through the work of such notables as Chandler[5] and Leavitt[6] there has been a general confirmation that performance depends on an optimal strategy-structure fit. This has been refined into the postulation that there must be a congruence between all facets of the organization if a formulated strategy is to be carried through to success.[7] The supportive research for this notion is extensive.[8-10] Initially, structure was thought to be the dependent variable in the strategy-structure equation. More recently, support has been generated for the alternative hypothesis that strategy may be formulated around the existing structure.[11] The appeal of this notion is immediate in so far as the risks of implementation can be substantially reduced simply by operating a no-change organization policy.

Ultimately the strategy-structure argument is barren because what really matters is success and this can only be expected with any degree of certainty when there is a strategy-structure fit that is designed to cope with the operating environment.[12] According to Ansoff, the future organizational structure will need to be multi-faceted.[13] Managers will be responsible for Strategic Business Areas, Resource Areas and Business Units if companies are to cope with the ever increasing environmental complexity. Thus, optimal fit will depend on total flexibility. Extension of this idea would suggest that future strategies should be implemented on a contingency basis. That is, they must be totally flexible and consequently in a constant implementation-modification state.

Budgeting
Not only is the budgeting process a means of resource allocation, it is also a means of information dissemination. It is a practical flow of information between organizational levels on what the future direction of the organization will be. Through the allocation or redistribution of resources it also intimates changes in emphasis across the organization. As Bower points out, the whole activity can be politically fraught.[14] Bearing in mind the status attached to size of budgets and the power struggles that occur at budget setting time, it is possible for the planning intent of any resource redistribution to be ignored.[15]

As a tool for implementing planned strategies the budgeting system has limitations. The main measures used are dollar-based although some physical activity measures may also be evident, e.g. output levels or efficiency levels in production.[16] More often than not it is also used as a means of manager performance appraisal through the examination of their ability to meet targets, variance, and so on. Such bias renders the budgeting process ineffective in communicating the importance of any of the more subtle benefits or risks of a strategy.

Management Style
Another wisely discussed aspect of strategy implementation is the matching of management style with organizational units. Khandwalla[17] considered management style in relation to characteristics of risk-taking, technocracy, 'organicity', participation and coercion. Thus, style is seen to be related to the operating environment, and, by inference, so is managerial ability. Skills ideal for one situation may be wholly inappropriate in another situation. For example, the entrepreneurial risk-taker may be an ideal candidate for a strategy involving growth, but may be wholly inappropriate for retrenchment.[18,19] There is a general assumption that managerial abilities are fixed and immovable quantities. Evidence of 'specialists' in corporate turnaround who move away from company to company to use their particular talents supports this notion. Further evidence can be found in the entrepreneurs who are unable to grow with their companies. They either leave to start again (as in the case of both Apple and Lotus) or stay and allow a regression to occur through an inability to delegate and control.

Support for the notion that a strategy–management style fit is equated with corporate performance can also be found in Khandwalla's work.[17] If, as this suggests, corporate performance is dependent upon style, then managers should be replaced as a necessary part of any strategy implementation if their style or skills are deemed inappropriate. The alternative to replacement is the use of retraining programmes. Monetary costs, emotional costs and time restrictions (among other costs) may be seen as prohibitive for either or both of these.

Goals and Controls

Goal-setting is one of the most important and least evolved areas of the implementation process. Translating strategies into concrete organizational goals is a difficult process and this, in part, explains the norm of problem-solving in implementation rather than problem avoidance. Inadequate goal specification and misaligned targets force firms into problem-solving. Wernham[20] suggests that the existence and communication of superordinate organizational goals have a positive effect on strategy implementation. However, Wernham sees internal inconsistencies in intermediate (functional) goals as having a negative and demotivating effect.

Research has demonstrated that effectiveness in achieving goals is enhanced when control levels are high.[21,22] However, it has also been shown that the greater the volatility of the operating environment the looser those controls are.[23] Uncertainty and change are the hallmarks of a volatile environment the same as they are for strategy implementation. Arguably, tighter controls for promotion of greater effectiveness in general business operation should have a parallel within the implementation process. More control means more information which can be used to control, but during implementation the management information systems and instruments of control are at their weakest due to the revisions and changes that normally take place.

Problem Avoidance in Implementation

The discrete subject approach to the research of strategy implementation has spawned an abundance of partial solutions. Business problems are not all unique but because of individual company strengths and weaknesses and, of course, the impact of temporally related environmental influences, they effectively become so. Thus, company–problem–strategy interrelationships appear virtually limitless in number. To accommodate this, research on implementation has adopted a reactive problem-solving perspective which is, arguably, a true reflection of the approach found in practice.

The individual organizational and environmental contingencies that preclude the establishing of rules for strategy formulation and selection also prevent the establishing of general rules for implementation.

However, where it can be argued that proactive strategies are superior to reactive strategies, it can also be argued that a proactive approach to implementation is better than a reactive approach.

By definition, reaction to a problem in implementation means that the problem has already occurred. Whatever it may be, its solution will mean backtracking, changing direction and taking corrective action. Not only do these responses inevitably incur time and monetary penalties, but they may also incur opportunity costs. Logically, a proactive approach which seeks to avoid these penalties and costs is superior. Because implementation can be directed and controlled within the company, the sentiment of proactivity in implementation is less nebulous than its counterpart for strategy formulation and selection. Consequently, it becomes realistically attainable and its impact—problem avoidance—becomes more meaningful.

A prime requisite of problem avoidance in implementation is the communication of strategic intent beyond the rarified levels where strategy is formulated. In the mustering of resources for the actual implementation itself, it is relatively easy for focus to shift and the original intent to become obscured as more and more individuals, at various levels in the organization, are necessarily involved in the process. Making strategic intent clear and meaningful requires translation of the strategy's potential benefits into specific managerial requirements and actions. This effectively bypasses problems which thwart the progression from potential benefit to actual achievement.

Strategic Benefits and Managerial Requirements

An examination of the strategic benefits and implementation concept quickly shows that issue simplification is required if anything more than a total contingency approach is to be developed.

Lists of potential benefits that may be derived from individual strategies are abundant. Every author in the policy and strategy field produces an exclusive list of favourite benefits. Additionally the benefits ascribed to one strategy may equally well be cited against another. In the absence of any clear guidelines as to which benefits are most consequential for which strategies, a Pareto model was adopted and the benefits quoted most often in the policy texts were selected. Paraphrasing the descriptions to gain uniformity produces eight benefits which appear as being universally recognized (see Table 1).

Whereas lists of benefits are voluminous in the literature and through their repetition are identifiable in terms of their weightiness, strategy-associated risks are not. In essence, the majority of risk is derived from the non-achievement of expected outcomes and failure to gain anticipated returns from committed resources.

Table 1. Summary of strategy benefits

Benefits	Strategy
(1) Synergistic gains in functional and non-functional areas	(1) Acquisition, diversification, market development, vertical integration
(2) Increased resource utilization	(2) Acquisition, diversification, market development, rationalization, vertical integration
(3) Increased earnings ability (long-term)	(3) Acquisition, diversification, market development, rationalization, vertical integration
(4) Reduced earnings cyclicality	(4) Diversification, market development
(5) Reduction of risk	(5) Acquisition, diversification, end-gaming, market development
(6) Risk avoidance	(6) Diversification, divestment, end-gaming
(7) Portfolio balancing	(7) Diversification, divestment, end-gaming, rationalization
(8) Cash flow maximization (short-term)	(8) Divestment, end-gaming, rationalization

Rarely, if ever, are the payoffs from strategies automatic.[24] Synergies, increased short-term earnings, risk avoidance and all other potential benefits are likely to remain potential unless actively pursued during implementation. The managerial requirements and actions which are the necessary catalyst for transferring potential into actual gain are outlined in Table 2. As shown by the table axes, determinants of the actions are strategies and potential benefits.

Controls and Feedback
In the discussions thus far, we have inferred contrast between the traditional problem-solving approach to strategy implementation and the proposed problem-avoidance approach. We have argued that problem avoidance occurs through the communication of strategic intent by concentration on anticipated benefits and risks. For the majority of benefits shown in Table 2, necessary control criteria are related to inputs rather than outputs. While some aspects of rationalization or portfolio balancing can be measured and effectively rewarded by outputs (e.g. return on assets), the majority of strategic benefits demand that the more nebulous inputs (e.g. communication and co-ordination) be addressed. Yet, all too often, measures of strategy success or failure are based on a limited number of output variables—sales, profit, and so forth.

Drucker argues that profits are the outputs of an entire organization, not the output of individual managers.[3] In addition, there exist a number of contextual variables which can (and do) have an effect upon organizational profitability. For example, in an economic downturn, profitability

may decrease due to a general economic slump and not as a direct consequence of any managerial actions. On the other hand, in a high-growth industry where customer demand is high, increases in profit may result with minimal managerial effort. Further, profits may increase due to an unanticipated fortuitous event. For example, the bankruptcy of a competitor may result in more demand for a product or service—witness Pan Am, TWA and BA benefiting from increased demand for trans-Atlantic travel after the collapse of Laker.[25] These are examples of situations which are beyond the control of individuals in organizations or even organizations themselves and which have an important impact upon ultimate success. However, it remains that in the majority of circumstances profits are primarily due to previous managerial performance and there are a number of important areas in which control and direction can be exercised.

As Merchant points out, planning and control are important organizational activities because they serve as a guard against individuals pursuing activities which will be detrimental to the organization or alternatively failing to do something that they should do.[26] This is highly suggestive of the need for the frequent and clear communication of strategic intent. Yet, research has shown that many managers are not intimately aware of the strategy which is being followed by their organization.[27] Thus, it would be incorrect to assume that strategic awareness exists, even at relatively high levels in an organization.[28] As Latham has stated, 'the attainment of a strategic plan will not occur through osmosis'.[29] The strategic plan needs to be communicated to all the individuals whose performance is vital to its successful implementation.

Numerous techniques can be used to communicate strategic plans throughout the organization. The problem is that many of the available techniques (e.g. company seminars, meetings or retreats) must be force-fit upon the organization. Instead, we suggest that communication be accomplished through already existing organizational mechanisms. This will result in maximum communication with minimal changes in the operating procedure.

Utilizing Existing Organizational Procedures

Performance Appraisal
A straightforward way to accomplish communication is through the performance appraisal and control systems which exist in almost all organizations. Evaluation and reward could be related to performance, and performance could be judged, as it pertains to the successful implementation of the selected strategy. This would be the ideal situation. The situation which is encountered in most organizations is measurably different to this. Much of the

Table 2. Managerial requirements associated with benefits/risks

Benefit/risk — Strategy	Synergistic gain	Increased resource utilization	Increased earnings ability (long-term)	Reduced earnings cyclicality	Reduction of risk	Risk avoidance	Portfolio balancing	Cash flow maximization (short-term)
Acquisition	Integration of all areas of activity by communication and co-ordination	Continued search for synergistic gains and economies of scale and scope	Search for competitive advantage and market share growth opportunities		Operational emphasis aimed at containment of competition and utilization of scale economies			
Diversification	Co-ordination and communication for cost reduction and idea generation	Entrepreneurship in products or services and opportunity searching in all functional areas	Entrepreneur-ship in markets and/or technologies (related or unrelated)	Organizing functional activities for growth in new/alternative product markets	Search for threats and proactive response to avert such	Forecasting accuracy and realism in new product/service development	Concentration on sales growth or cash flow as appropriate	
Divestment						Objectivity in interpretation of forecasts and assessment of potential	Objectivity in assessment of risk versus opportunity	Objectivity in short-term gain versus long-term income
End-gaming					Strict cost control and freeing of assets with low utilization rates	Achieving accuracy in forecasts of market decline rates	Maximization of long-term cash flow	Maximum pruning of costs and divestment where possible
Market development	Co-ordination between functional areas to support marketing drive	Identification of existing but unrealized market opportunities	Search for future high potential market opportunities	Market development activities—temporal emphasis	Proactive marketing aimed at containment of competition			
Rationalization		Balancing efficiency and effectiveness in operations	Identification of resources with low and/or reducing returns				Objectivity in pruning product ranges and emphasis on cash flow in 'harvest' situations	Cost control on all products and divestment of marginal ones
Vertical integration	Co-ordination and communication to improve quality, reduce costs, waste, etc.	Continued search for cost effectiveness and scale economies	Search for market control opportunities and minimization of competition effects					

evaluation and reward theory that is available for utilization at higher managerial levels is geared to organizational output rather than to individual input. Typically, these outputs form the basis of a pay plan. As with other areas in which performance suboptimization occurs, a pay plan which considers only output criteria can develop dysfunctional side effects relative to strategic aims and the long-term goals of the organization.

Lawler reported that a relationship existed between the specificity of reward linked to productivity or profit and such side effects as low co-operation.[30] Salter links cash, stock options and other forms of manager compensation with performance and suggests that the strategy time horizons should be reflected in selected measures in the performance appraisal system.[1] Stonich has suggested differing balances of return on assets, cash flow, strategic funds programmes and market share increases as weighed factor performance measures for reflecting growth needs of SBUs.[2] But, outside of portfolio balancing, this has limited application in implementation.

Most importantly, in and of themselves output criteria contain minimal performance-related information. For example, a report on profit compares expenditures with revenues. This may be an overall indication of the success or non-success of a selected strategy and, as has been alluded to, it may be the result of certain contextual variables which are out of the realm of control of individual managers, or even the organization. Although output measures may be quite easy to utilize, they are fraught with a number of problems which would inhibit their use in the performance appraisal process or the process by which a selected business strategy is communicated to the people in an organization.

Goal-setting

In spite of the fact that we have ruled out using some of the major performance appraisal information which is currently collected in organizations (that which is related to output variables), we believe that there are still some components of the performance appraisal process which may be instrumental in both the implementation and communication of corporate and horizontal strategies. Specifically, we believe that the process of goal-setting, when carried out in a fashion which identifies factors that are vital to successful strategy implementation, becomes a pivotal issue in both the communication and implementation of the strategy.

Because performance appraisal as practised at higher managerial levels concentrates on short-term, measurable output (e.g. profit), managers see their performance in these terms and not in terms of its relationship to the critical success factors which are associated with strategy implementation. This results in an incongruous situation where performance becomes suboptimal. As such, it probably explains why Lorange and Murphy found that corporate planners perceived practical inconsistencies between strategic aims and inplace management incentive schemes.[31] One way to remedy this difficulty is to facilitate more interaction between the human resources and the strategic planning functions.

Goals can be identified and established in such a way that their content and intent can be clarified for those who must achieve them. This is, though, where a troublesome problem concerning the goal-setting process comes more into focus. Translating organizational strategies into specific and concrete goals is a difficult process. While, in theory, this is a necessary condition for strategy implementation, there exists relatively little guidance pertaining to an effective way to accomplish it.

Critical Success Factors

Boynton and Zmud have suggested the development of critical success factors (CSFs) as being a means which, when successfully completed, will ensure competitive performance for an organization.[32] [Further details on the method of establishing CSFs can be obtained from Leidecker and Bruno, *Long Range Planning*, **17** (1), 23–42 (1984).[33]] Before the development of critical success factors can take place, a framework of key activities —as related to corporate and horizontal strategies— needs to be constructed. This has been confirmed in practice within the U.S. aircraft construction industry. The starting point for this is the communication and comprehension of the intent of selected strategies which, in turn, is derived from an understanding of the related benefits and risks.

There is no such thing as an optimal fixed number of critical success factors. They vary with the strategy and the environment in which an organization exists. They may be wholly internal to the company or they may interface with the environment. For example, in a televised interview Rod Canion, Compaq's CEO, identified two such factors as being critical to the ongoing and continuing success of 'his' company which, over the 5 years since its inception, has managed to capture 20 per cent of the small computer market.[34] The first factor concerns the maintenance and support of Compaq's dealer network (i.e. the interface with the environment). Compaq's computers carry a price tag of less than $10,000 and, like all computers in this price range, they require the normal amounts of service and support. But, to undertake this activity in-house would reduce Compaq's customer service levels, and the company's overall profitability, to the same level as other computer companies that elected to drop their dealer networks in favour of initially increased sales margins. The second factor identified by Canion as being critical to Compaq's success is wholly internal to the company and concerns the speed and flexibility of technological response. As soon as new technology is available, the company adapts it to the needs of its customers. Both these (critical success) factors have major implications for the way Compaq is achieving growth through the implementation of its market development type strategy. Arguably, without the identification of these CSFs, Compaq would have languished as just another computer company.

Essentially, CSFs constitute *intermediate* goals, the completion of which will lead to the superordinate goal—successful strategy implementation and achievement of the strategy's benefits. When these strategy-driven CSFs are identified, pure managerial talent and expertise becomes necessary in order to develop and carry through a satisfactory action plan to tie down the detail of implementation.

Carlyle and Ellison produced a series of questions which were intended to determine the 'criticality' of job dimensions.[35] These questions can be adapted for the present discussion. They are:

(1) What percentage of time is spent performing the factor? A high percentage of time does not necessarily imply that the factor is critical but a low percentage of time should raise doubts about the critical nature of the factor.
(2) If the factor were performed inadequately, would there be a significant impact on the mission or the profitability of the organization?
(3) Is there a consequence which is significantly involved? Could inadequate performance of the factor contribute to loss of time, money or assets?
(4) Are there any legislative or regulatory requirements which mandate that the performance of a factor is critical? Would inadequate perfor-

mance mean that the organization fails to meet statutory or regulatory practices or is engaged in prohibited practices?

Summary
Thus far, a number of separate but interrelated techniques have been suggested for utilization in strategy implementation. The first, performance appraisal, is known, understood and used in many organizations. The second, goal-setting, is known and understood but less widely utilized. The third, critical success factors have, in one form or another, been discussed in the literature since the 1960s but have only recently started to make a noticeable impact inside and outside the literature base. Figure 1 illustrates their interrelationships and how they fit into the scheme of strategy implementation. More particularly, the figure shows how they should reflect the often poorly communicated intentions that are implicit within selected strategies.

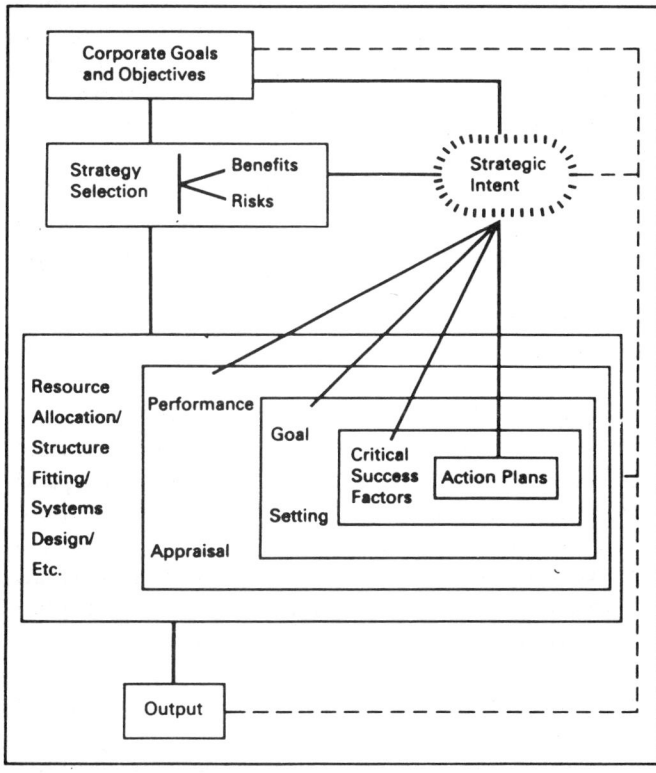

Figure 1. Performance appraisal, goal-setting and critical success factors in implementation

There are a number of additional components which need to be improved or built into the organizational scheme in order to successfully integrate the aforementioned functions. The importance of thorough job analysis becomes paramount when using critical success factors because it is a specification of all of the tasks which are required for successful job performance. From these tasks, using the procedure outlined earlier, in conjunction with those suggestions made by Leidecker and Bruno,[33] the criticality of the factors can be estimated.

In addition, a series of feedback mechanisms should be built into the strategy implementation phase and carried through during the entire process of evaluating the success of a strategy. Feedback yields a number of important pieces of information for: (i) providing a series of interim measures to assess the effectiveness of the strategy implementation process, (ii) providing direction for corrective changes in implementation and, (iii) providing an indication of the suitability of a manager and his/her style for the particular strategy. With such measures, it is also possible to make more effective decisions concerning the most appropriate strategy–manager–appraisal fit which will be optimal for the organization.

Conclusions

In some recent empirical research, P. C. Nutt found that an 'interventionist' approach to strategy implementation was most successful.[36] The interventionist manager justifies the strategy and creates an environment which is conducive to an understanding of the strategy implementation. One of the most oft-mentioned reasons for ineffective performance is that management has not adequately communicated what is to be done in an organization. It would be foolish to think that employees are omniscient and will absorb the direction of the organization without being informed about what that direction is or should be. The lesson here is that if employees are to be entrusted with the implementation of a strategy, they should also be entrusted with a sharing of the planning and development of the strategy implementation.

It would be misleading to state that the techniques and tools considered here will guarantee sweeping, successful strategy implementation. However, they do provide a means of avoiding many of the problems that can beset implementation attempts. The following checklist is provided to help executives improve the chances of problem avoidance and thereby improve the chances for success:

(1) Identify *strategic intent* by matching *strategy benefits* with the organization's needs.
(2) Interpret strategic intent into the *specific managerial actions*, at all necessary organizational levels, that are needed to attain the benefits.
(3) Collate and translate all actions into *comprehensive action plans*.
(4) Produce a framework of *key activities* and identify the *critical success factors*.
(5) Use *goal-setting* to translate the CSF key activities into *targets* for individual managers—note: these are likely to be inputs rather than outputs.
(6) Link *reward and appraisal* systems to individual manager goals.
(7) Use an *interventionist approach* to *communicate* an environment of participant involvement aimed at *problem avoidance*.

(8) Finally, *monitor* the implementation process to ensure adherence to plans and/or to *modify* plans as situations change.

Acknowledgement—The authors wish to acknowledge and thank Ian Wilson (SRI International) whose numerous suggestions greatly improved this paper.

References

(1) S. Salter, Tailor incentive compensation to strategy, *Harvard Business Review,* **51**(2), 94–102 (1973).

(2) P. J. Stonich, Using rewards in implementing strategy, *Strategic Management Journal,* **2**, 345–352 (1981).

(3) P. F. Drucker, What results should you expect? A user's guide to MBO, *Public Administration Review,* **36**, 12–19 (1976).

(4) For example, on the problems of conflict in implementation see W. D. Guth and I. C. MacMillan, Strategy implementation versus middle management self interest, *Strategic Management Journal,* **7**, 313–328 (1986).

(5) A. D. Chandler, *Strategy and Structure,* MIT Press, Cambridge, MA (1963).

(6) H. Leavitt, Applied Organizational Change, in J. March (Ed.), *The Handbook of Organizations,* Rand McNally, Chicago, IL (1965).

(7) J. R. Galbraith and D. A. Nathanson, *Strategy Implementation: The Role of Structure and Process,* West, St. Paul, MN (1978).

(8) J. Child and R. Mansfield, Technology size and organization structure, *Sociology,* **6**, 369–393 (1972).

(9) J. Lorsch and J. Morse, *Organizations and Their Members,* Harper & Row, New York (1974).

(10) P. Khandwalla, Mass output orientation of operations technology and organization structure, *Administrative Science Quarterly,* **19**, 74–97.

(11) D. J. Hall and M. A. Sais, Strategy follows structure, *Strategic Management Journal,* **1**, 149–163 (1980).

(12) R. T. Lenz, Environment, strategy, organization structure and performance: patterns in one industry, *Strategic Management Journal* **1**, 209–226.

(13) H. I. Ansoff, *Implanting Strategic Management,* Prentice Hall International, Englewood Cliffs, NJ (1984).

(14) J. L. Bower, *Managing the Resource Allocation Process: A Study of Corporate Planning and Investment,* Harvard University, Cambridge, MA (1970).

(15) N. Newman, *Constructive Control,* Prentice Hall, Englewood Cliffs, NJ (1975).

(16) P. Lorange, *Corporate Planning: An Executive Viewpoint,* Prentice Hall, Englewood Cliffs, NJ (1980).

(17) P. N. Khandwalla, Some top management styles, their context and performance, *Organization and Administrative Sciences,* **7**(4), 21–52 (1976).

(18) M. Gerstein and H. Reisman, Strategic selection: matching executives to business conditions, *Sloan Management Review,* **24**, 33–47, Winter (1983).

(19) A. Gupta and V. Govindarajan, Business unit strategy, managerial characteristics and business unit effectiveness at strategy implementation, *Academy of Management Journal,* **27**, 25–41 (1984).

(20) R. Wernham, Bridging the awful gap between strategy and action, *Long Range Planning,* **17**, 34–42 (1984).

(21) J. T. McMahon and G. W. Perrit, Toward a contingency theory of organizational control, *Academy of Management Journal,* **16**, 624–635 (1973).

(22) J. Woodward, *Industrial Organization,* Oxford University Press, New York (1970).

(23) P. Lawrence and J. Lorsch, *Organization Environment,* Harvard Business School, Boston, MA (1967).

(24) R. Reed and G. A. Luffman, Diversification: the growing confusion, *Strategic Management Journal,* **7**, 29–35 (1986).

(25) The demise of Laker increased demand for the remaining airlines crossing the Atlantic and price-hikes followed. However, the outcome of legal actions brought in the United States against Pan Am, TWA and BA, by Freddie Laker, suggests that the collapse of Laker Airways was more than a 'fortuitous event'. Under the Sherman Anti-Trust act, it was found that a conspiracy had occurred and appropriate damages were levied. Despite BA having the level of damages modified under the British Protection of Trading Interests Act, trans-Atlantic passengers who travelled after the bankruptcy of Laker received refunds from the price increases that resulted from the 'reduced competition'.

(26) K. A. Merchant, *Control in Business Organizations,* Pitman, Boston, MA (1984).

(27) D. C. Hambrick, Strategic awareness within top management teams, *Strategic Management Journal,* **2**, 263–279 (1981).

(28) D. C. Hambrick and P. A. Mason, Upper echelons: the organization as a reflection of its top managers, *Academy of Management Review,* **9**, 193–206 (1984).

(29) G. P. Latham, The appraisal system as a strategic control, in C. Frombrun, N. M. Tichy and M. A. Devonna (Eds), *Strategic Human Resource Management,* Wiley, New York (1984).

(30) E. Lawler, Reward systems, in J. R. Hockman and J. L. Suttle (Eds), *Improving Life at Work,* McGraw-Hill, Santa Monica, CA (1977).

(31) P. Lorange and D. Murphy, Bring human resources into strategic planning: systems design considerations, in C. Frombrun, N. M. Tichy, and M. A. Devonna (Eds), *Strategic Human Resource Management,* Wiley, New York (1984).

(32) A. C. Boynton and R. W. Zmud, An assessment of critical success factors, *Sloan Management Review,* **25**, 17–27, Winter (1984).

(33) J. K. Leidecker and A. V. Bruno, Identifying and using critical success factors, *Long Range Planning,* **17**(1), 23–42 (1984).

(34) R. Canion, Inside business, CNN (Cable News Network), Turner Broadcasting, Atlanta, GA, 4 October (1987).

(35) J. J. Carlyle and T. F. Ellison, Developing performance standards, in H. J. Bernardin and R. W. Beatty (Eds), *Performance Appraisal,* Kent Co., Boston, MA (1984).

(36) P. C. Nutt, Identifying and appraising how managers install strategy, *Strategic Management Journal,* **8**, 1–14 (1987).

Bridging the Awful Gap Between Strategy and Action

Roy Wernham, British Telecom, London, U.K.

This article describes the lessons learned from a study carried out within British Telecommunications as part of the author's doctoral research programme. It was found that strategy was formulated and implemented, with direct action taken and resources committed, by Divisional managers at all three organizational levels in BT so that implementation did not always follow the lines intended by the HQ strategic planners. Implementation was found to be an interactive rather than a rational/sequential process. Marked variations in practice were observed and explanations for these are offered. The relative success of the strategies differed widely, both overall and within the divisional field units. The manner of implementation and factors managers perceived to help and hinder it were studied. Success or failure was felt to hinge on getting a few basics right: resources, organizational 'fit', historical performance and the expectations it generated (track record), information and support, market acceptance, technical competence, consistent goals and top management support.

Introduction

There has been much recent interest in the problems of implementing strategy in academic circles as well as among practising managers.[1] The essential reason for this interest is the widely shared experience that all too often plans don't work as their authors intended. This article describes a programme of research by the author into the problems of implementation in a (then) large Nationalized Industry, British Telecommunications (BT).[2]

Planning in BT

BT was formed from the telecommunications part of the former Post Office (PO) Corporation in 1981. The PO began corporate planning in 1971; an early PO Board paper on the subject indicated that its purpose was 'to provide a stable and coherent basis for planning throughout the Business'. This

was seen to be particularly desirable in telecommunications, a capital intensive industry with long lead times. Business Plans have been made annually almost every year since. The planning team suspected that often past Plans might not have proved to be the blueprints for action that their authors had intended; a backward look comparison of the 10 and 5-year forecasts, and strategic outlines in the 1971 and 1975 Plans, with what had happened confirmed the doubts. Had external events intervened or were the plans themselves deficient? What happens during implementation? Questions like these led to the research. It was quickly apparent that the PO experience was not unusual.[3,4] Taylor's note[3] that 'No plan survives contact with reality' was particularly arresting. The research aimed to explore the nature of this 'reality' and how it affects implementation.

Planning in the Nationalized Industries was greatly encouraged by successive Governments throughout the 1970s, partly as an aid to Government understanding of their investment plans in the context of longer term strategies.[5] Moreover, such plans provided Government with an additional mechanism to influence or control development of the Industries.[6] While there has been some study of the economic and legislative aspects of Nationalized Enterprises, little is known about the way in which they are managed.[7-9] There are grounds for suspecting that their special relationship with the political scene brings with it some unique problems.[10,11] While there have been some empirical studies of strategy formulation, little field research has so far been undertaken on implementation.[12-14]

Traditional Model of Strategy and its Implementation

The term strategy comes from the Greek 'strategos' meaning the art of the general. There is no clear

Dr. Wernham is Deputy Corporate Planner for British Telecommunications plc, 2–12 Gresham Street, London EC2V 7AG.

consensus in the academic literature on how it should be defined. What is perhaps the dominant school of thought has been followed here in regarding it broadly as the allocation of resources to achieve certain aims or objectives.

The usual textbook view of strategic management is of a highly rational, analytical process with broad policies being laid down at top levels and translated into progressively more detailed sub-plans as they descend in straight line fashion through a homogeneous and subservient organization. Strategy formulation and implementation is generally shown as a rational/sequential process (Figure 1). An analysis of the environment and of the organization's current position, a WOTS UP (Weaknesses, Opportunity, Threats and Strengths Underlying Planning) analysis,[15] leads to clear, preferably quantified goals. Alternative ways of reaching these goals are considered and the most promising selected. It is then implemented and progress is measured and controlled.

This tidy and straightforward view of the process rests on a number of important assumptions including:

☆ The process is indeed a chain reaction of the kind just outlined.

☆ The organization's environment is stable or if it is changing, does so in discrete, tidy steps.

☆ The organization is homogeneous, a unity rather than a coalition.

☆ Top management's goals and values are shared or at least accepted throughout the organization and they have the power to impose their will if need be.

☆ The chosen alternative is capable of being implemented.

☆ Sufficient resources will be allocated to enable the plan to be carried forward as defined.

The Traditional View revisited

In recent times, a number of these assumptions have been challenged by both theory and research which suggests that:

☆ Many organizations must cope with turbulent environments where change is fast; the problems are novel and hard to deal with.[16]

☆ In these circumstances, it may not be appropriate to have closely specified, quantified goals which may not remain stable long enough to be achieved, something broader and fuzzier may be better.[17]

☆ The organization may not be homogeneous but a coalition of subdivisions, all to a degree doing their own thing—particularly true of Divisional firms as compared with the Functional organizations in which the traditional model took root.[18]

☆ The process may be interactive rather than a chain as Figure 2 seeks to show.

There are, then doubts about how far the traditional model represents the way in which the real world works, and whether it is oversimplified for presentational or teaching purposes to the extent that it seriously distorts the reality. What does happen then managers try to put plans into action? What problems tend to occur and what helps them achieve their goals? The author set out on a programme of research to try and address these

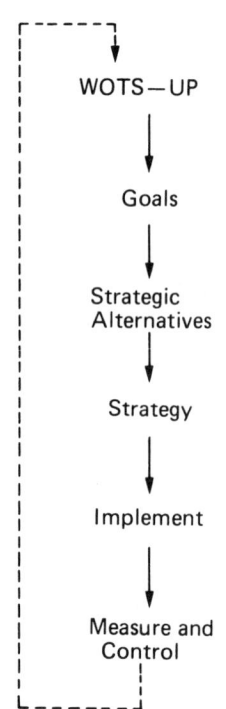

Figure 1. The traditional model of strategic managment

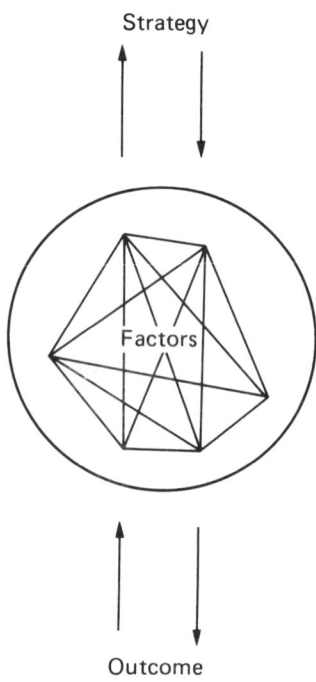

Figure 2. An alternative view

questions. The methods used and findings will now be discussed.

Aims and Method, of the Research

The overall aim was to identify the factors influencing the implementation of strategy within BT and assess their relative importance. Attention focused on three representative topics which were used as 'tracers' and were followed through the BT organization much as a geologist might 'label' a subterranean water course with fluorescein to trace its path.

The three tracers were:

☆ MAC (Measurement and Analysis Centres)—a system to generate and trace the progress of tests calls placed through the telephone network to measure the quality of service being provided and identify faults.

☆ Radiopaging—a service whereby a person who is out of the office but is carrying a pocket 'bleeper' can be alerted through a radio signal that he is required.

☆ SRT (Special Range Telephone)—a new range of decorative or fashionable telephones for customers who wish to have a telephone that has a distinctive appearance.

National HQ Managers, Regional Chairmen/ Directors (RDs) and Area General Managers (GMs) from England and Wales, were interviewed; they are referred to collectively as Unit Managers (UMs). During the study, tape-recorded interviews were obtained with some 64 UMs and analysed exhaustively. The interviews covered general material as well as the three selected tracers, each of which represented one aspect of BT's overall customer service strategy, being followed through the organization to see what happened to it. The fieldwork took place during the passage through Parliament of the Telecommunications' Act 1981 which established BT as a separate Corporation from the Post Office and opened the way to competition in areas where BT had previously enjoyed a monopoly.

Discussion of Results

Strategic Management Process

This study questions much of the traditional model of strategic management finding rather a process of interactions between coalitions of semi-autonomous units, with common cultural ties and identity. Each level of the organization, including HQ, tried to put its own stamp on events. Areas and Regions frequently did not accept HQ initiatives passively but would try to adapt or even reject them.

Political manoeuvring was readily apparent with different players manipulating the power bases they had, often to obtain extra resources. The attempts could take a number of forms. There could be a straight request with no duress. Junior managers in the higher level Unit, might be lobbied so as to seek their help in pressing a case. Favours might be offered or the target manager(s) invited to lunch. Some UMs attempted to use their own co-operation as a bargaining counter in a way that could embarrass the higher level Unit unless their wishes were met. Sometimes a number of lower level UMs would co-ordinate their actions or approaches to the higher level Unit where it was a matter of common concern. A delicate balancing act could be observed between UMs who were at some times dependent upon one another, and at other times rivals for available resources. As some of those interviewed put it:

> 'I have used every method in the book, or out of the book, dirty or otherwise, in order to get more than my share because I think the (unit) needs it . . . I have gone as far as cultivating *(X)* because I think he's got the ear of *(Y)* so you get at the power base . . . I've invited *X* (here), I've listened to him . . . that sort of thing brings dividends.'

> 'We fetched the (junior managers) over from (HQ) to get them on our side who would then persuade (their boss).'

> 'At a meeting (with a senior HQ manager) I made absolutely clear that unless we had (more resources) . . . we would (not co-operate). It was sheer blackmail by me.'

HQ managers appeared to try and restrict the options open to the field Units, to define the strategy to be adopted quite narrowly and themselves take on parts of the work. These efforts often failed:

> 'I said to (my junior managers), I don't care how you get hold of them, just get some and they did. I'm not sure how they did it—I never asked— . . . There were very strict controls put on (these items) so our more enterprising managers broke the rules and quite rightly so.'

Paradoxically, most field UMs perceived themselves to have a good deal of room for manoeuvre in general.

> 'You meet these people from (HQ). They waffle and then they go home and to hell with it. They don't really control what goes on here. They might think they do but they don't really.'

The basic message here is that the view found in many management texts of a powerful HQ able to impose its will on compliant field units exaggerates both the power of the HQ and the compliance of the field. Both have their own resources of power, eg to give or withhold money or co-operation, and mobilize these resources to achieve particular ends. The astute planner will use this process by appreciating what are the goals of the parties and the bargaining resources they possess (including himself) and ensuring that he is able to offer others something they want.

A related feature that emerged was:

Contacts between UMs. Frequency of reported contacts between UMs varied enormously and showed a strong inverse relationship with distance. UMs of Units located in the large conurbations had very frequent contacts, apparently because the BT administrative boundaries did not correspond with the natural boundaries of the communities being served. Action by one Unit could have market or personnel implications for adjacent Units or for others even further afield due to what was described shared community of interest.

As one local UM described the relationship with his colleagues in a large conurbation:

> 'We telephone one another pretty frequently. We meet both formally and informally. I guess there is not much of import that goes on within (this city) that we don't all know . . . and warn others before it hits them . . . Very tight. You can't run it any other way . . . It is very tight knit . . . We meet, even if its a social thing—but work gets done even at a social thing—once a fortnight. Physically we are in the same room.'

This had important repercussions at the next higher level (Region). Where a strong community of interest existed—mainly in the largest conurbations—there were frequent contacts between local UMs and with Regions undertaking some of the functions exercises elsewhere at the lower level, for example, promotional activities.

> 'I can't do anything on my own. We represent only a part of (conurbation). Any approach has to be co-ordinated and done through the Regional office.'

The Regional role was not always welcome:

> 'You need to be watchful. It isn't them and us but you do need to watch the fortunes of the Area *vis-a-vis* the Region.'

Where there was less community of interest, UMs contacted one another much less frequently and perceived much greater autonomy, but usually contacted UMs in their own Region more than those in other Regions.

> 'We are independent operators . . . I like to think we are a little like feudal barons . . . There is no question that every day or so we ring other Unit managers up, we don't.'

> 'I don't find it necessary to talk to other Unit managers though I'm not too proud to seek advice if I need it.'

In some exceptional cases, contacts between neighbouring UMs in different Regions were frequent; in each case, a strong community of interest existed across the Regional boundary. Thus the local Units (geographical Divisions) were far from being homogeneous, those in the largest conurbations having substantially different characteristics from those elsewhere.

Interview Findings for Individual Tracers

Findings on the individual tracers may be summarized thus:

MAC was widely welcomed by UMs and seen as important because it would provide a much needed facility to give a better measure of the standard of service being provided and thereby enable service to be improved. It was given high priority. It was put into the larger centres first to maximize the short-term benefits from it. Detailed implementing action was undertaken at all levels, with HQ in particular providing advice and technical services and having a major say in how the programme was constructed, i.e. the order in which field Units received their equipment.

Radiopaging was put into eight major centres first and had been heavily delayed, in part by development of the integrated national system, chosen in preference to the discrete local services with which a competitor had achieved modest success. BT Radiopaging was perceived as a technically valid response to the market need and fitted in well with the existing organization; few wholly new or different procedures were required. However delays had been experienced and were said to have been inadequately communicated to field Units. As a new and potentially useful service for business customers, it was well regarded but was accorded a lower priority than MAC by most, but not all, UMs. Much promotional material was produced centrally and some specific action, e.g., advertising, was undertaken at all three levels.

SRT was regarded as a residential service and was seen by some UMs as a rapid response to the challenge of competition from private retailers of decorator or fashion phones—although its origins lay well before that. It was felt to have public relations value in demonstrating to both staff and customers alike that BT intended to compete effectively in the residential telephone terminal market. Past shortages of materials of SRTs and other products had produced a mistrust, a lack of confidence among field UMs and their staff. The Range, was, with a few exceptions seen as a valid response to the requirements of the market. The administrative arrangements placed unusual demands on those in the field trying to sell SRTs; they were only partially successful, being disregarded by many UMs. The HQ Unit took direct action by selling SRTs at exhibitions and by placing national press advertisements with responses to be made to HQ rather than to local Units.

Tracer Strategy Adaptations
While the *aims* declared by the various Units for each of the tracers showed little variation, their *strategies* varied somewhat from each other and

from those put forward by the HQ UMs. For MAC, little variance from the HQ strategy was observed and there were no major inconsistencies between it and what the field Units were doing. For Radiopaging and SRT however, there was much less agreement and several inconsistencies in approach.

HQ/Regional/Area Differences. Answers by HQ, Regional and Area UMs were compared for each of the major dimensions on which data was collected. UMs were generally agreed on aims and the factors that had helped implementation. There was wide agreement among field UMs about the problems there had been but striking disagreement between them and the HQ UMs. There was also much disagreement on the strategy being followed and how well implementation had gone overall—suggesting that each level formed its own partisan view of such matters. HQ UMs were about as likely to *agree* with the field UMs as were field UMs to agree with each other. They were far more likely to *disagree* with field UMs than were field UMs to disagree with one another. It appeared then that feedback of information to HQ was defective at least in respect of the bad news, points of disagreement between the field and HQ (Figure 3).

Problems of Implementation

A number of general problems emerged from the research which were observed to a greater or lesser extent in respect of all three tracers. These are listed in Figure 4 and are presented broadly in order of the frequency with which they were mentioned by respondents.

Resources. The resources either of men, money or materials were often not available where and when they were required. There were two aspects to this:

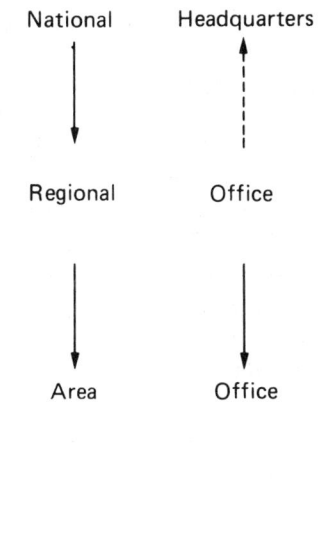

——— Good Communication

- - - - Poorer Communication

Figure 3. Transfers of information between levels

Problems

Resources—Money, Men, Materials

Other Priorities

Organizational Validity

History, Confidence

Delay

Lack of Information/Timing Ads

Market Validity

Technical Validity

Conflicting Goals

Figure 4. Problems of implementation

the absolute volume of resources might be inadequate for all that was expected to be achieved; the relative volume of resources was inadequate owing to other competing uses being given higher priority.

> 'It's been made very clear to me that you can do whatever you like so long as you don't ask for any money.'

> 'It's more a question of priorities than actual staff shortages. At the end of the day manpower problems are a matter of priorities. We always have resource problems.'

Certain aims were widely perceived by UMs as much more important than others and plans which were felt to contribute to their achievement were given higher priority—and hence resources—than were others.

Organizational Validity. Organizational validity[12] is an indicator of how well a plan 'fits into' the existing organization and procedures. To the extent that people were required to adapt widely their existing patterns of behaviour, problems were likely to occur. Following an existing procedure or a slight adaptation to it is much easier to absorb and creates less resistance than wholesale change.

> 'The rules for stocking them are too involved. My simple mind says beat the system. So we have a few hidden away.'

> 'There were a series of silly rules governing product B which seemed to hamstring the whole thing.'

History. A word that frequently came up in the interviews was 'confidence'. Confidence that others would deliver what they promised. Confidence was based on the track record of present plans or other plans that the implementers felt were related. Just as nothing 'succeeds like success', it seems that nothing 'fails like failure'. Reputation is a very hard parameter to measure but is important for all that.

> 'You have a human problem. When supply has been bad, they are a little careful before they flog it too

wholeheartedly in case they personally look silly to their customer. That is a hurdle that has to be got over. Well it has been got over with product A, the arithmetic seems to have been done correctly at the moment. You see, I'm doing it too, saying 'at the moment'. Next year I might be telling you a different story.'

Delay. This is effectively a subset of the last point. Overoptimism, especially in estimates of timing, had been a hallmark of all three tracers in the research. It had moreover, contributed to a loss of confidence among the field staff who, having seen one schedule fail, were less inclined to believe the next.

> 'One thing you do need to realize is the time it takes to introduce an idea and make it effective, it depends on what it is but it's a lot longer than people think . . . it's 2 years before it's really moving in my experience.'

> 'The thing goes back. It was going to be December, then May, now June. It drives me crackers.'

Lack of Information/Support. Back up materials whether publicity information, software or just plain know-how were important elements in acting upon plans. Lack of adequate support quickly eroded confidence and led to available effort being transferred elsewhere as confidence flagged.

> 'Information doesn't come down the line freely. Business men ask me what products we have coming along. I haven't a clue.'

> 'We have no means of finding out when out of stock items will be available again, which is awkward because that is always the next question, the customer asks . . . and you are made to look stupid when you say you don't know.'

Market Validity. This concept refers to the extent to which the product or service is viewed by those at the front line of the organization as meeting the market need as they see it. Did it do what they felt that customers wanted to do? Where it did, the chances of successful implementation were greater, perhaps because the market reacted more favourably or perhaps those implementing it scented success and put more effort into it. These trends are likely anyway to be mutually reinforcing.

> 'I tried to sell product C to a builder but it developed that the initial area of coverage was not wide enough for him.'

> 'Strangely enough, range A don't sell all that well here . . . While (we) are doing well in general terms, range A no.'

Technical Validity. Technical validity indicates how far the product or service matches up to its specification and the hardware performs the functions claimed for it. Once again this is in essence a test of credibility and a matter which will either add to, or subtract from, the confidence of the staff concerned with its introduction and their motivation to achieve.

> 'I get the feeling they are cheap and nasty.'

> 'People can't have model A and model B on the same installation. They can (here). It's a popular combination. We modify the wiring.'

Conflicting Goals. Internal inconsistencies within the goals of the strategy being pursued were found to have a demotivating effect and to cause confusion among those concerned with implementation. There may well be intrinsic conflicts to be resolved, e.g. between secure storage and handling of stocks and giving customers maximum exposure to the product to achieve higher sales.

Where there are, it is as well that they should be made explicit and the means for their resolution clearly defined if confusion at grass roots level is to be avoided.

> 'Monitoring existing services versus provision of new is a long standing problem. The facile way out is to say they are equally important but it is not always possible.'

> 'There is a conflict between our tradition of providing a uniform service, anywhere in the country, at a standard price, regardless of cost, moving away from that to meeting competition where you have got to balance your tariffs in relation to the cost of providing the service.'

Factors Making Implementation More Effective

In an attempt to look at the reverse side of the 'problems' coin, the research pinpointed certain factors that were found to be helpful in making implementation more effective, things that were felt to have gone well. There were positive features to be applied as well as traps to be avoided (Figure 5).

Some of the main factors assisting implementation that emerged were:

Superordinate Goal. The existence of a superordinate or higher organizational goal, with which the strategy could be clearly identified and which it was seen to be contributing directly towards, was found to be of great value. It was then much more apparent to implementing staff that the strategy was

Superordinate Goal

Resources

Technical Validity

Market Validity

Information and Support

Staff Enthusiasm/Confidence

Top Management Backing

Figure 5. Factors assisting implementation

making a real and direct contribution to the overall effectiveness of the organization rather than appearing simply as an end in itself or as a largely optional extra having dubious value for the enterprise.

'We are not satisfied with the performance of the network and saw this as a way of improving it.'

Resources. The assumption that resources are available, resources in the widest sense presents problems that are not trivial. It was found that people were often asked to do tasks and then denied the money, manpower, expertise or consumable materials which they felt they would need to accomplish it. The provision of adequate resources (though not transferable to other projects) was a powerful aid to success.

'It is one of those things we did when we said we would . . . The bits all came and reasonably on time. I might not like the priorities but they are more difficult to dodge if I've got the bits.'

Technical Validity. It seems that nothing succeeds like success. Producing a product or service that lives up to the claims made for it in the sense of the technical performance of the hardware seemed to breed a confidence in those who implemented it that inspired a genuine enthusiasm and laid the groundwork for further success. Difficulties that were perceived as teething troubles were a different category; the existence of a sound concept, adequately engineered appeared to be the key.

'The main thing is (project *X*) is basically a good tool anyway. The concept is naturally right.'

'The most impressive thing about it is that it works.'

Market Validity. Production of a service or product that meets a genuine need is a powerful factor for success. The value of a product like the national Radiopaging service to customers was quickly evident through word of mouth recommendations and the ease with which sales were made. There was little doubt about customer acceptance or that the enthusiasms of staff and customers alike were genuine and perhaps mutually reinforcing.

'We have got several hundred customers lined up—spontaneous demand.'

'We are onto a winner with Radiopaging. We can't fail. Customers will be falling over themselves to have them.'

Information and Support. Really a part of the total resources question is provision of adequate and reliable information and supporting materials such as sales brochures and literature. Provision of reliable information e.g. on date of introduction helped to breed confidence in the product and in the competence of the team producing it—just as failure in this direction eroded confidence. It appears that the team that is seen to do its homework and does not hide potential problems is more credible than that which gets things wrong or paints a falsely optimistic picture.

'There has been a lot of assistance from Regional and national HQs to draw it together.'

'Headquarters have spent quite a bit of effort in time and money on that sort of promotion which gives the awareness that we capitalize on.'

Staff Enthusiasm/Confidence. A powerful factor was the confidence and enthusiasm of the implementing staff stemming from such things as their faith in the product and service being produced and their perception of the competence of the team producing it. All the other factors mentioned had a bearing on this. With it, implementation has every prospect of success, without it, an uphill struggle is certain.

'The (Unit) now loves (*X*) and has taken it in as part of its own business and that is a very good sign.'

'The local supervisor is very, very keen on it. They guard it you know. Even I am not allowed to go into the wrong room in case I press the wrong knob and undo all the hard work they have put in.'

Top Management Backing. According to the textbook view, see Steiner[15] for example, top management backing is essential for success. While it was mentioned by respondents as a factor that had contributed to successful implementation in this research, it did not emerge as being so important as the other factors listed above. It helps but it probably will not pull a bad scheme from the fire.

'Y was very keen on this, has been all through, so I don't think there has been any lack of urgency there.'

Conclusions

The traditional textbook strategic management view, that a strategy is successively defined in greater detail as it progresses in a logical 'cascade' from higher to lower levels within a homogeneous organization needs to be qualified. Each organizational level appears to take action to put its own stamp on the strategy, so that strategy formulation and implementation are part of a continuous interactive process, rather than successive steps in a linear sequence and are therefore much less 'top down' than many texts would have us believe. Unit Managers at all levels perceived considerable scope to formulate their own strategies.

The view of the world as seen by managers in different parts of the organization looks very different—much as the view from the penthouse suite of a tall building differs from that at ground level overlooking the dustbins—despite the existence of shared patterns of judgment. For example, HQ UMs' views of how successful implementation had been did not square well with those of field UMs. (Success of implementation was measured by objective criteria where measures existed, e.g. number of units sold, or by subjective criteria where they do not, e.g. reputation among users).

A number of factors were found which consistently caused problems in implementation and contributed to delay. The principal factors were:

☆ Lack of resources in the widest sense. This included money, materials and men but extended beyond simple numbers to include the existence of adequate knowledge, men with the right skills and support functions.

☆ Historical performance of current and past plans ('track record') and the expectations of success or failure that have been created.

☆ Lack of fit between: the actual hardware performance and specification; market performance and need; organizational demands imposed by both new and existing practices.

☆ Deficiencies in the transfer of information between Units at different levels.

☆ Requirements to achieve conflicting goals.

Certain factors were found to assist implementation. The main ones were:

☆ Adequate provision of resources.

☆ Matching: hardware performance to expectation; market performance to need; organizational procedures to current practices.

☆ Senior management support: success was associated with enthusiasm on the part of senior managers though the connection was less strong than might have been expected.

☆ Direct contribution to a major and widely acknowledged organizational aim.

☆ Staff confidence in the strategy being pursued which was in turn a function of information, training and historical experience.

A fact that stood out very clearly, and came as something of a surprise in view of the literature on resistance to change, was that change was by no means always resisted. Indeed it was often warmly welcomed by organizational members who saw real benefits flowing from it. As one manager put it:

'X has met 100% acceptance in the field and really has been the answer to the maiden's prayer there.'

Application

Perhaps the most obvious conclusion, but one that all too often goes unrecognized, is that strategy cannot be formulated on a blank sheet of paper as if no constraints exist or there is no past to come to terms with. The real world is complex and the manager who ignores its complexity will suffer from problems of implementation. Important components of this complex reality, many of them 'obvious' yet frequently neglected, include:

☆ *Resources* in the broadest sense. It is a necessary but not sufficient condition that these must be adequate. This means ensuring that the necessary manpower is available, with the mix of skills and knowledge needed to do the job, that they have the tools and materials and organizational support to do the job and the necessary funds are there (and cannot be siphoned off for use on something else!).

☆ Organizations find it easier to go on doing the kind of things they have done before, the better a new strategy *fits* the old, with differences minimized rather than exaggerated, the better its chances of success. Old habits and procedures that are ingrained die hard and change slowly and with difficulty. Often much can be done by adapting an existing framework thereby achieving a smoother, faster, transition with less disruption and fewer hiccups than the ostrich-like policy of attempting to start from a clean sheet and pretending that the past does not exist to colour attitudes and work habits.

☆ Faced with *conflicting goals*, managers select those which best suit their circumstances of the moment at the expense of the others. A requirement to achieve several conflicting goals presents a reluctant manager with an ideal opportunity to choose the things he wants to do and duck what he does not want to do. A coherent set of goals, even if they cannot all be specified in detail, give greater consistency.

☆ The attitudes of senior staff are important, but so too are those at lower levels. *Resistance to change is not inevitable*, attitudes depend on how people perceive changes affecting them in their job. There is evidence that change is welcomed and not resisted if it is perceived to be for the 'better'. The textbooks stress the need for top management support. This piece of research suggests that it is indeed helpful but will not compensate for a bad plan. Where staff felt that a change was 'good', it was widely welcomed. Only 'bad' change was resisted. The attitude of top management was largely irrelevant. The moral here is to seek out and stress the advantages of a proposed change so that it is perceived as beneficial and welcomed rather than try to rely on force majeure which can be resisted successfully on occasion by those lower down in the organization.

☆ *Confidence* is elusive and hard to define but a vitally important factor. Past experience conditions attitudes to future developments and people's expectations. Whether as individuals or organizations, we are all prisoners of our past. Today's overpromise is tomorrow's albatross. The need to develop a reputation for competence and being able to deliver what is promised is essential.

☆ The *technology* and the *marketing* arrangements must be fit for the purpose to which they are applied (and strategic planners are both producers and marketeers). This is related to the previous point. A product that does reliably what it is supposed to do or marketing arrangements that meet the real needs of customers give all concerned a confidence that shows. No amount of window dressing can compensate for a faulty product. The right product is the starting point—and that goes for planners too.

Acknowledgement—This paper is based on part of the author's Ph.D. thesis at City University Business School. The views expressed are those of the author and do not necessarily represent those of British Telecommunications, British Telecommunications plc, or the City University. The author gratefully acknowledges the assistance of British Telecommunications who funded the research, and also of Mr. A. J. B. Scholefield and the referees for helpful suggestions.

References

(1) SSRC, *Central–Local Government Relationships,* Social Science Research Council, London (1979).

(2) R. Wernham, *A Study of Strategy Implementation in a Major UK Nationalised Industry,* unpublished PhD thesis, City University Business School (1982).

(3) B. Taylor, New dimensions in corporate planning, *Long Range Planning,* 9 (6), 80–106 (1976).

(4) J. M. Hobbs and D. F. Heany, Coupling strategy to operating plans, *Harvard Business Review,* pp. 119–127, May–June (1977).

(5) Cmnd 7131, *The Nationalised Industries,* (HMSO, London) (1978).

(6) D. J. Harris and B. C. L. Davies, Corporate planning as a control system in UK nationalised industries, *Long Range Planning,* 14 (1), 15–22 (1981).

(7) Y. Aharoni, Performance evaluation of state owned enterprises, *Management Science,* 27 (11), 1340–1347 (1981).

(8) A. Y. Lewin, Research on state-owned enterprises introduction, *Management Science,* 27 (11), 1324–1325 (1981).

(9) J. Zif, Managerial strategic behaviour in state-owned enterprises—Business and political orientations, *Management Science,* 27 (11), 1326–1339 (1981).

(10) J. G. Smith, Strategy—The key to planning in the public corporation, *Long Range Planning,* 14 (6), 24–31 (1981).

(11) J. L. Bower, Effective public management, *Harvard Business Review,* pp. 131–140, March–April (1977).

(12) R. L. Schultz and D. P. Slevin, Implementing operations research/management science, American Elsevier, New York (1975).

(13) C. W. Hofer, Research on strategic planning, *Journal of Economics and Business,* pp. 261–285, Spring–Summer (1976).

(14) E. Bardach, *The Implementation Game,* MIT Press, Cambridge, Mass. (1977).

(15) G. A. Steiner, *Top Management Planning,* Macmillan, New York (1969).

(16) H. I. Ansoff, *Strategic Management,* Macmillan, London (1979).

(17) J. B. Quinn, Strategic goals: process and politics, *The McKinsey Quarterly,* pp. 35–53, Winter (1979).

(18) R. M. Cyert and J. G. March, *A Behavioural Theory of the Firm,* Prentice-Hall, Englewood Cliffs, N.J. (1963).

Managing Strategic Change: An Integrated Approach

Colin A. Carnall

This paper sets out to identify and discuss an integrated approach to the management of strategic changes. Managing effectiveness, dealing with organizational cultures and managing organizational politics are discussed, focusing upon how to do so in order to encourage risk-taking, creativity and learning and to build self-esteem and performance. Such an approach allows the achievement of major changes in ways which lead to employees developing a fuller understanding of the nature of the business, its problems and its future.

Introduction

Implementing organizational change effectively. This is one of the managerial challenges facing all of us. In both the private sector and the public sector, in manufacturing, banking, health care and education, this challenge is presented, often in very stark circumstances. We are concerned about value for money, the development and marketing of new products and services, flexibility, whether of design and manufacture (through computer-aided design, robots, flexible manufacturing systems), or in organizational structure and managerial style. We are increasingly concerned about product/service performance and quality. Customers and clients are ever more vocal and critical. Often they can 'vote with their feet'. If the automobile I buy tomorrow performs poorly and unreliably I am unlikely to buy that make again. In education we talk of 'parent involvement', of 'parent power'. The central focus of management is switching from internal concerns and the development of professional disciplines in isolation. For example, engineering designers, who might once have sought optimum technical solution alone, are paying real attention to design as a synthesis of technical, commercial, product and aesthetic considerations.

All organizations face challenges like these. A food-processing firm faces social changes such as new attitudes to diet, commodity market pressures, as supply problems mount, competitive pressures and the problems of bringing up to date what had been a company which had always been paternalistically managed. Banks face de-regulation, technological change and an increasingly international competition. Health and education face pressures for greater accountability, both for the use of resources, and for the quality of the services they provide. Can the professional autonomy of doctors and teachers remain unchanged? An engineering company (manufacturing packaging machinery) develops marketing and new products and leads a drive for quality as a means of re-building its position in world markets.

Analysed simply we could divide the concern over the management of major changes into two main questions. 'What changes should we implement?' and 'How may we implement them successfully?' To develop answers to these questions requires specific skills. To diagnose the need for change. To audit performance. To develop a vision of improvement. To describe or define new strategy. Achieving change also requires the skill to get things done, to achieve action. It is often disturbing and disruptive. By definition change upsets the 'status quo'. Leadership is central because to achieve effective organizational change requires us to elevate analysis over consensus. Easy options are in short supply! Implementing major organizational change demands the combination of action and analysis into a new managerial synthesis.

In this paper we propose to discuss this new managerial synthesis necessary for effective change. We propose to develop two main themes as follows:

(1) What are the managerial skills required for effective organizational change? We will examine a number of key managerial skills.

(2) Change is disruptive and disturbing. How do people experience change and how may they be

The author is Director of the MBA Programme at Henley—The Management College. He previously worked in the mechanical engineering industry.

helped to cope with the pressures of major changes?

All organizations deploy these managerial and coping skills to lesser or greater extents. Our purpose is to identify these two sets of skills so that managers can more effectively identify strengths and weaknesses and, thereby, further develop their capacities to achieve effective organizational change.

Managerial Skills For Effective Organizational Change

To manage change effectively involves the ability to create a new synthesis of people, resources, ideas, opportunities and demands. The Manager needs skills rather like those of an orchestral conductor. Vision is essential and creativity paramount. Yet the capacity to create systematic plans to provide for the logistics of resources, support, training and people is central to any change programme. People must be influenced, departmental boundaries crossed or even 'swallowed up'. New ideas must be accepted and new ways of working embraced. New standards of performance and quality need to be achieved. The politics of the organization are crucial. Support must be mobilized, coalitions built, opposition handled and bargains struck. The programme must be maintained, teams built and supported. People need help to cope with the stress, anxiety and uncertainties of change. Continuity and tradition must be overturned, in part, as the old is replaced by the new. Yet, continuity and tradition provides people with stability, support and meaning and should not needlessly be destroyed. The effective management of organizational change demands attention to all of these somewhat conflicting issues and challenges. So in a period of change *synthesis* is the key. In this section we shall deal with three skill areas, as follows: (i) managing transitions; (ii) dealing with organizational cultures and (iii) the politics of organizational change.

(i) *Managing Transitions*
Company A manufactures a range of engines. It is a wholly owned subsidiary of a U.S.-based multinational corporation. It supplies engines to a small number of end-user companies, each of which incorporates them into its own products. By 1980 the company was experiencing severe external and internal pressures (Figure 1).

This is a familiar enough pattern. A cycle of decline creating major challenge for management to find ways of achieving a transition to effectiveness. *The first and most important challenge was to develop an open attitude toward change.* The company had experienced little or no change in 30 years. Employees were accustomed to stability and managers possessed little or no skill in the management of change. New management at Group level, recognizing this company as declining economically, brought in a

External Pressures	Internal Pressures
Recession High Interest Rate Falling Orders	● Inadequate Organizational Structures
High Energy and Material Costs	● Lack of Confidence and Fear of Change, Including the Fear of Redundancy
New Products/Materials Technology being Adopted in Engine Design and Manufacture.	● Accustomed to Slow Change (or Paralysis)
Increased Competition both from Abroad and Because Some End Users were Beginning to Switch to Build Their Own Engines	● Limited Managerial Competence in Managing Change
	● Lack of Experience with New Technology
Changes at Group as a Consequence of a Change in Ownership	● Low Productivity and Quality
	● Ageing Plant with Attendant Maintenance Problems.
	● Low Morale, High Absenteeism, Industrial Disputes.
	● Cash Flow Problems

Figure 1. Internal and external pressures in an engine manufacturer

new top management team comprised of a Managing Director, Engineering Director and Finance Director. The new team moved quickly. The strategy adopted is shown schematically below (Figure 2).

The first step was to test the reality the company faced and to draw people into that process of testing. Employees at all levels needed to understand the problems the company was facing. Beyond this it was essential that people be given the chance to seek out and develop solutions. Thus on the one hand, openness in negotiations and communications with employees meant that the problems were better understood. On the other hand, through involvement of employees and by bringing in new skills (particularly marketing), new ways of doing things were sought. Employees were drawn into solving problems such as quality, absenteeism, factory layout and so on. Project groups from design, marketing and the production departments became involved in seeking new products. People were given the opportunity to try out new ideas, to experiment, to seek solutions. This then started a process of attitude change. Recognizing the problems and becoming involved on processes aimed at developing solutions lead to a more open approach to the idea of change. Seen as unavoidable, employees began to recognize the possibility that constructive, albeit not painless, action was feasible. In these ways management and employees were facing the challenge identified in Figure 3 (based upon Argyris and Schon[1]).

Significant change involves learning. If reality is tested openly, and if open or constructive attitudes to change prevail, then we are most likely to achieve significant changes. Change is possible without open reality testing but only where people excluded

Testing Reality	New Attitudes and Structures	Achievements
● Threat to Closure and Redundancy		● New Technology Introduced in Manufacturing Technology and in Materials
● Encouraging Understanding of the Problems	● Developing New Attitudes to Work and to Change	
● Developing New Ideas for the Future — New Products		
● Search for New Markets and Business (Including Subcontracting)	● Training for New Technology and to Deal with Change	● Quality Control System Introduced
● Open Negotiation and Communication	● Re-organization and Contraction	● New Products
● Full Involvement of Employees and Unions	● Investment in New Technology	● Labour Flexibility

Figure 2. A strategy for change

from this testing process are not fully engaged in the changes to be implemented. If they are not involved in testing reality they can neither understand the need for change nor feel committed to the changes, let alone learn from them. One word of caution. Public or extensive testing of reality in a declining situation merely creates anxiety unless a constructive attitude to change prevails, particularly within management. Thus to argue that effective communication is enough, without giving people the opportunity and support to seek solutions to problems will merely sustain the spiral of decline. In this company the reality-testing process lead to new attitudes which themselves both facilitated, and were in turn, sustained by training programmes for new technology, improved maintenance, quality control, by the emergence of new investment and new equipment, and by reorganization (including the formation of a marketing department and the introduction of quality control systems). The spiral of decline was being reversed.

Managing this transition to effectiveness, then, demanded learning and change.

(a) Learning is produced by *exploring dilemmas or contradictions* (e.g. improved quality was essential and end–user's had to be convinced that they should continue to use company A's product *but* ageing plant, managerial problems and low morale made this difficult to achieve).

(b) Learning is based *upon personal experience and experimentation*. People will only learn if they understand the problems and are brought into the process of seeking solutions.

(c) Learning can be encouraged in a climate which *encourages risk-taking*, doing things, trying out new ideas.

(d) Learning requires the *expression of deeply held beliefs* and will *involve conflict*. Only then can ideas emerge and be properly assessed before

Testing Reality: (Problem Solving)

		Restricted (Within the Management Team)	Extensive (Involvement of Those Affected)
Attitudes to Change	Negative	Little Learning or Change	Anxiety Creating Behaviour
	Positive	Learning and Change can Occur only if *not* Dependent on Other People	Learning and Change Possible

Figure 3. Learning from changing? Implementing strategic change

being incorporated into new systems, products, strategies, etc.

(e) *Learning can be helped by recognizing the value of people and ideas.* Developing learning styles which encourage individuals rather than close off discussion and creativity.[1]

Company A had, by 1983, reduced staffing, improved the organization structure, introduced a quality control system, for the first time, achieved labour flexibility and developed new products. The leadership challenge faced successfully in this case was that of achieving change in the ways described whilst maintaining the business through very difficult times. 'Selling' the solutions to Group and 'buying' time were central to this and part of the politics of change, a matter we turn to next.

(ii) *Dealing with Organizational Cultures: a Major Financial Institution*
Company B is a large financial institution with hundreds of branches in major towns and cities in its home country. It operates internationally. In recent years it has been very successful with growth of profitability and turnover. Yet it faces major challenges. De-regulation, new technology, competition and growing complexity of the services it provides, both to private and corporate customers, are amongst the challenges it faces. The company is involved in a major programme of branch rationalization. Some branches are being closed, others remodelled to provide either private or corporate services, others are being expanded as key branches. Early on in this programme of change it became clear that the company's property management department needed attention. Its property management performance was poor and outmoded. Its capacity to plan and carry through the branch rationalization programme seemed doubtful.

Property management was the responsibility of a central department employing 250 professional staff, mainly architects and surveyors, managed by a general manager. The general manager was drawn from the senior management team on a 2-year posting. All general managers at that time had finance backgrounds. Indeed the culture of company B powerfully sustained the belief that the *only* important work was finance. All other work, whether property, computing or marketing, was secondary. Career paths for non-finance people were limited, departments being managed by people with finance backgrounds. The extent to which non-finance staff were undervalued may be seen by noting that in the property management department no one could remember anyone having any training and development since the day of their appointment. The morale of the property management department was low and the level of interdepartmental conflict (between the surveyors group and the architects group) was very high.

The company is organized into 12 regions, each managed by a Regional Director. Property management at regional level was unco-ordinated. Regional Directors took many of the decisions without being properly accountable, formally. Refurbishment decisions were under Regional Directors' control yet the costs of refurbishment were a charge on a head office account, not on the region's books. Moreover the lack of co-operation between architects and surveyors diffused any professional input into property decisions taken at regional level.

The Organizational Culture. Company B typifies the *role culture** under significant external and internal pressures. Often stereotyped as bureaucracy this culture is characterized by stability, prescription, rules and standards. Functional departments are clearly specified. This can be a very efficient culture in stable environments. Role cultures emphasize high levels of commitment by individuals either to a department, or in a professional role culture, to a particular profession. In this culture position power is a predominant form of power. But in this case the stability of the 1960s and 1970s had been replaced by the turbulence of the 1980s. Now property management expertise was essential if the branch rationalization programme was to proceed.

To detail the organizational change quickly a property management professional was brought in to take charge and develop a modern property management strategy. This was only the second time in the history of company B that a non-finance manager had been appointed to this level and the first time such an appointment had been made from outside. Under his control property management was decentralized to regional teams, managed by regional managers. Small teams, closer to the region, would be more likely to develop improved working relationships. Training and development was put in place for the professional staff. A career path was now opening up for them. All of this was moving property management toward a *task culture.* Here influence is based on expertise, the expertise needed to carry out the task. Teams of people work together to achieve objectives and tasks. This culture places demands upon people but also provides for the merging of individual and organizational objectives. It is an adaptable culture in which the needs of the task predominate rather than systems and procedures. In this case architects and surveyors now work together more closely. Regional teams are managed by architects or surveyors. For professional purposes there is a professional development role played by a deputy general manager in the, now, small head-office property management function. Arguably company B has moved toward a culture more appropriate to the challenges it faces.

---

*The terms role culture, task culture and power culture are taken from Charles Handy.[2]

Organizational issues which must be faced if more adaptable organizational cultures are to be achieved are as follows:

(a) *Management autonomy,* particularly with regard to reward systems. To what extent should local management have the ability to make decisions about gradings and salary dependent on market conditions and personal performance.

(b) *Interchangeability,* movement across specialist/ professional boundaries by internal promotions, fixed-term secondments, or short training periods would help develop broader knowledge and experience. To what extent should promotion depend upon diversity of experience? Moves of this sort can sustain task forces or project teams. It can also reinforce individual autonomy, creativity and knowledge.

(c) *Openness or public testing* of issues and problems would also be aided by interchangeability.

(d) Recent developments in management information systems seem likely to bring about systems which managers can interrogate! This will aid *communication* partly through the *access* so provided, partly by the promise of simplification of procedures and paperwork such developments promise.

(e) Functional and professional advice can be provided to a more local level utilizing task-team approaches such as that described briefly in the case with professional development, planning and control being centrally organized. The focus should be on *business needs* rather than on professional demands.

Other organizational cultures have been identified. The *power culture* is worth a moment's thought. Frequently found in small, growing companies, including property and finance. These organizations are highly dependent on one or more strong leaders. Control is exercised from the centre and decisions are made very largely on the outcome of a balance of influence rather than on rational grounds (which the uncertainties of our changing world will rarely allow in any event). An organization with this culture can react well to change but the quality of top people is crucial. Individuals who are power-oriented, risk-taking and politically skilled will do well in this culture wherein accountability is personal and direct.

Managing in Different Cultures. One final thought on culture. We have discussed the links between organizational culture, the tasks to be performed and the rate of environmental change. But culture is a broader part of our affairs. At home and abroad we often find ourselves working with people from different occupational, local and national cultures. Effective management thus demands the capacity to deal with cross-cultural issues and influences. The important skill here is that of *empathy.* Managing change involves the need to influence people.

Empathy, sensitivity to cultural differences, and the struggle to understand them and to communicate in an intelligible fashion, is essential.

The property management professional brought this skill to bear in his work with the professional staff involved in the change process described. Whilst these boundaries cannot easily be crossed, people respond to the attempt, and change programmes are all the more feasible and relevant for a leavening of cultural sensitivity. This skill will be discussed further in the section on coping with change.

(iii) *The Politics of Organizational Change*
To understand how organizations are managed, experienced and changed we need to understand the politics of organizations. In turn this involves the examination of political process, activity and skill. Why is the use of power and politics a necessary part of managing change? Partly this is because of the need for innovation.

> Innovative accomplishments stretch beyond the established definition of a 'job' to bring new learning or capacity to the organisation. They involve change, a disruption of existing activities, a redirection of organisational energies . . .[3]

Of course this is right. But the impetus to the use of power runs deeper. Any significant organizational change demands that existing ways of thinking about and talking about what we do can be overturned. Dominant views must be usurped. Experience tells us that the first attempt to articulate an alternative view, a novel concept, will fall on barren ground, very often. More likely it will meet opposition and even outright rejection. To overcome such opposition or rejection neither logic, evidence nor participation of all concerned, appears to be enough. New ideas can seem unorthodox and even risky. A manager seeking support for new ideas must be sensitive to political processes. Our discussion of the role of political skills in the management of change follows the framework set out in Figure 4.

Resources. Managers, and others, utilize a variety of resources as they engage in the politics of organization. They may have *formal authority,* or may be perceived as such, by virtue of their position. Moreover, they may have *direct control over resources.* The use of a resource control to negate change programmes is widely practised. If a change programme needs engineering resources, and if the Engineering Manager can withhold those resources, perhaps by claiming that other priorities must prevail, then change can be delayed. *Control of information, agenda and access* are all important political resources. It is commonplace to say 'Information is power'. The power to control the organization internally, power regarding the development of future policy. This point was made by Henry Kissinger when he discussed the new role

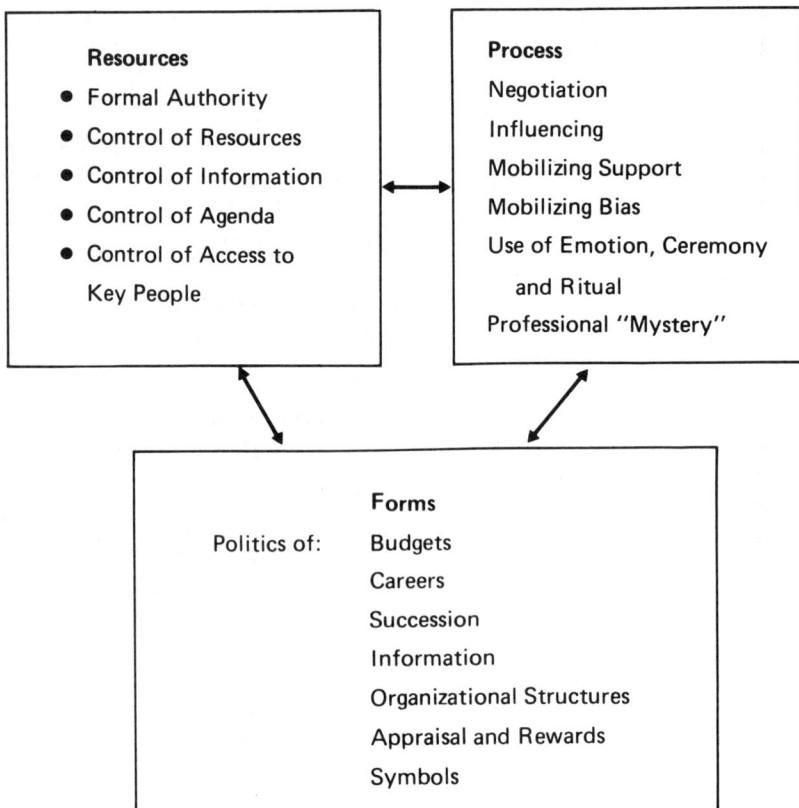

Resources
- Formal Authority
- Control of Resources
- Control of Information
- Control of Agenda
- Control of Access to
  Key People

Process
Negotiation
Influencing
Mobilizing Support
Mobilizing Bias
Use of Emotion, Ceremony
    and Ritual
Professional "Mystery"

Politics of: **Forms**
Budgets
Careers
Succession
Information
Organizational Structures
Appraisal and Rewards
Symbols

Figure 4. Politics and organization

Nixon and he had agreed for the National Security Council at the beginning of Nixon's first term.

> A President should not leave the presentation of his options to one of the Cabinet departments or agencies. Since the views of the departments are often in conflict, to place one in charge of presenting the options will be perceived by the others as giving it an unfair advantage. Moreover, the strong inclination of all departments is to narrow the scope for Presidential decision, not to expand it. They are organized to develop a preferred policy, not a range of choices. If forced to present options, the typical department will present two absurd alternatives as straw men bracketing its preferred option—which usually appears in the middle position. A totally ignorant decision-maker could easily satisfy his departments by blindly choosing Option 2 of any three choices which they submit to him. Every department, finally, dreads being overruled by the President: all have, therefore, a high incentive to obscure their differences. Options tend to disappear in an empty consensus that at the end of the day permits each agency or department maximum latitude to pursue its original preference. It takes a strong, dedicated and fair Presidential staff to ensure that the President has before him genuine and not bogus choices.[4]

Recognizing the narrowness of view which often emerges from specialist, departmental and sometimes from professional concerns, Kissinger here demonstrates the crucial importance of *controlling the presentation of options* to a President. Without doing so the President may be at the mercy of departments. Departments may preclude policy debate by the nature and range of the options presented to the President. They may also structure a policy debate by purposely obscuring differences over policy in the pursuit of consensus.

Processes and Forms of Politics. The forms politics of organizational change may take are varied. Fairly obviously, budgets, career development, succession planning information, structures, appraisal and reward systems have political dimensions. Decisions in such areas will carry a political element. We might say that this is undesirable but we should not close our minds to the possibility that the reality is different from what some would say is the ideal. To understand decisions within a budgeting context, we must consider political issues. In much the same way, to understand how changes are implemented, we need to recognize the resources, processes and forms of politics.

The politics of organizational change comprise various processes and take various forms. We identify these in Figure 4 mainly to identify the linkages between resources for power, and the processes and forms of organizational politics. These create issues and opportunities whenever changes are underway. Organizational politics is inevitable during periods of change and provides an impetus to initiative, creativity and change, if constructively managed. For many the word politics has a perjurative element to it. Managing change should be about satisfaction, concern for people, participation and the like. Everyday experience tells us that this is not enough, however. If the politics of change be accepted how may it be managed constructively? In essence this involves *managing in order to encourage risk-taking and positive attitudes to change.* Politics balanced by concern for the practical isues to be faced. Politics unconstrained leads to negative attitudes to change, low risk-taking and high levels of anxiety. The test of constructive organizational politics, then, becomes the guidelines identified above for the management of the transition to effectiveness.

Coping with Major Organizational Changes

Thus far we have considered some of the managerial skills associated with the effective management of change. We now proceed to consider the impact of change upon the people directly affected, which will often include many middle and senior managers. We are concerned here with the people who must take on new tasks, develop new skills, be transferred, regraded or re-trained. Once changes emerge people must learn to cope as individuals. We will describe a simple model of how people experience change and then consider how they can cope with the pressures created by change. Understanding this can allow senior managers to provide practical support to people undergoing change and may better enable them to avoid creating constraints on people which make their personal task of coping all the harder.

Often the problems of implementing change are discussed as 'resistance to change'. In fact the change situation is both more complex than this phrase suggests and capable of a more constructive interpretation. Managers often encourage 'resistance to change' by dealing with people as if that is the response they expect. Here we are concerned to consider the practical and positive steps which can be taken *to support people as they cope with change.*

The Coping Cycle
Change creates uncertainty, anxiety and stress. Moreover, changes which have a big impact on the work people do will affect their self-esteem. So much is well-established.[5-7] Linked to this impact on self-esteem will be a performance effect. In fact in periods of change performance is affected in three ways, as follows:

(i) The new systems, processes, methods etc., will have to be learned. This takes time and there is a *learning curve effect.*

(ii) There is also a *progress effect.* As the new system, etc. is installed and commissioned snags are ironed out and modifications introduced to achieve performance improvement. New systems do not work perfectly first time round!

(iii) Finally there is the *effect of self-esteem.* Significant organizational changes create a decline in self-esteem for many of those directly affected. This will effect performance. Whilst the links of satisfaction and self-esteem with performance are complex and not fully understood there seems to be some association of these factors.

In practice performance will decline once major changes are underway as a result of a combination of these factors. *Our view is that the main driving force to re-building performance quickly will be re-building self-esteem.* This can be helped by action on the learning curve and progress fronts. In the model we propose five stages. These are capable of more detailed analysis but for our purposes this simplified form seems workable (Figure 5). The model originates in

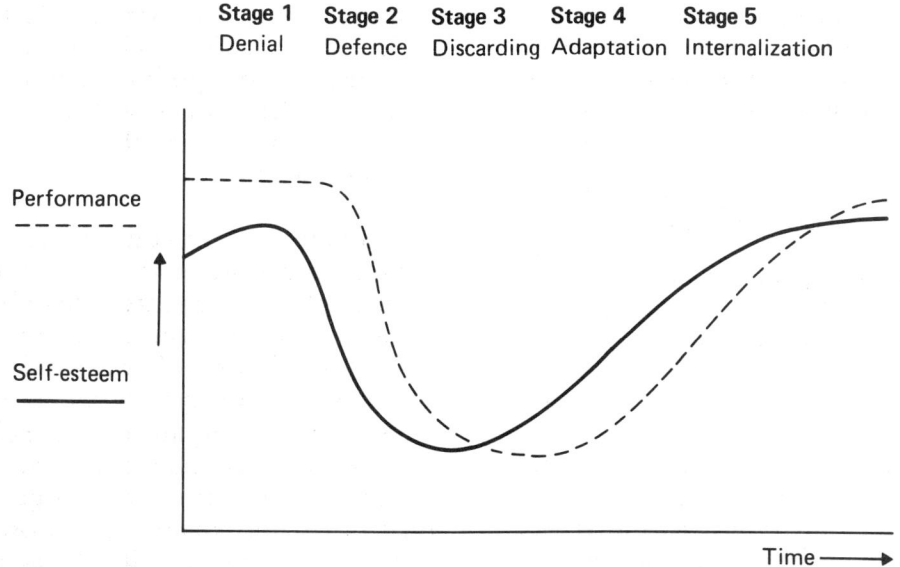

Stage 1 Stage 2 Stage 3   Stage 4   Stage 5
Denial   Defence Discarding Adaptation   Internalization

Performance

Self-esteem

Time ⟶

Note: Absolute levels unimportant, only relative levels are meaningful. Problems of measurement are significant but do not obscure the assessment of relative levels of performance or self-esteem.

Figure 5. The coping cycle

the literature on coping with bereavement and on work dealing with coping with personal life changes.[8]

Stage 1: Denial. 'We have always done things this way?' 'Why change, we are making a profit aren't we?' 'Don't change a winning team'. These are some of the ways denial can find expression. Faced with the possibility of change people will often find value in their present circumstances; often in work situations which they have complained of previously. This apparent paradox should not surprise us. People are impelled by contradictory motivations. Coal miners threatened with the closure of a pit will defend their pit and jobs with some vigour, yet still believe fervently that working conditions are arduous and even dangerous.

If major organizational changes come suddenly and dramatically then a kind of paralysis can often occur. People seem overwhelmed, unable to plan or even understand what is going on. Often there is a longish period of gestation as ideas are discussed and concrete changes planned. If these changes are not particularly new or dramatic then this paralysis may be felt just as intensely. However, the tendency to deny new ideas, at least at first, does seem to be a fairly general reaction. The advantages of the present situation are emphasized and attachments to the job, the work-group and the existing skills are recognized.

Thus it is that self-esteem can increase, particularly if the presence of an external threat leads to increased group coherence. If self-esteem does increase we would guess that performance would not improve, either because the discussion of impending change can absorb energy, or because often there are systems in place which may hold back performance improvement, e.g. payment systems. If the change is dramatic, novel and traumatic, say involving a sudden job change or redundancy, then this stage can involve an immediate decline in performance. Generally, however, there is a warning period and performance will not decline immediately. *One way individuals respond at this stage is to 'minimize' the impact of the change.* This allows people time to face up to a few realities.

Stage 2: Defence. However, in time reality obtrudes. The early discussion of changes leads to concrete plans and programmes of change. Now the realities of change become clearer and people must begin to face new tasks, working for a new boss, or with a different group of people, perhaps in a different department or a new location. Thus they become aware that they must come to terms with the way they work, and perhaps with changes in life more generally, if, for example, relocation, involving a house move, is required. This can lead to feelings of depression and frustration because it can be difficult to work out how to deal with these changes. This stage is often characterized by defensive behaviour.

People may attempt to defend their own job, their own territory. Often this will be articulated as ritualistic behaviour. The author can remember the introduction of computer-aided learning in Business Schools many years ago. Many embraced these developments enthusiastically. Many simply rejected them; 'my subject is unsuitable'. One colleague provided an impressive show of activity on the computer, finally concluding that after much effort he had failed to make computer-aided learning work for that subject. Years later computer-aided learning in that subject is commonplace. Was this a ritual? Again this defensive behaviour seems to have the effect of *creating time and 'space' to allow people to come to terms with the changes.*

Stage 3: Discarding. There now emerges a process of discarding. The previous stages have focused powerfully upon the past. Now people begin to let go of the past and look forward to the future. We do not know how this happens. We know that support can be helpful, as can providing people with the opportunity to experiment with new systems without the pressure of formal training programmes and so on. Now it is possible for optimistic feelings to emerge. It may well be that the discarding process is impelled by an awakening sense that the present anxieties are just too much to bear, or that perhaps the future is not as forbidding as it first seemed. Now we may observe behaviour which appears to identify the individual with the changes involved. They will start to talk openly and constructively about the new system. They will ask questions about it. In a sense they will say 'Well here it is, we are committed to it, here's how I see it'. People may begin to solve problems, take the initiative and even demonstrate some leadership. Thus it is that self-esteem improves.

Discarding is initially a process of perception. People come to see that the change is both inevitable and/or necessary. It becomes apparent to them. Adaptation starts with recognition. Here we see human courage amidst difficult circumstances as the individual accepts new 'realities'. This can be exciting for individuals and groups. Taking the risks of publicly facing a new reality there is a sense in which they re-establish their own identity; the identity which may have seemed threatened by the changes being introduced. Thus it is that self-esteem begins to flow back like the returning tide.

The crisis of change creates great tensions within those involved; this much we have seen. This creates a plethora of reasons for people to feel upset and disoriented. The new job we have been assigned appears to be of lesser status, valued skills seem unnecessary, the new work appears to be frustrating. The new system or machine appears to be unusual, even frightening, although with practice it becomes commonplace. The crucial point is that this process needs time. Discarding involves experimenting and risk. Time is needed for individuals to recreate their own sense of identity and self-esteem as they 'grow' into the new situation.

Stage 4: Adaptation. Now a process of mutual adaptation emerges. Rarely do new systems, procedures, structures or machines work effectively first time. Individuals begin to test the new situation and themselves. Trying out new behaviour, working to different standards, working out ways of coping with the changes. Thus the individual learns. Other individuals also adapt. Fellow workers, supervisors and managers all learn as the new system is tried out. Finally, technical and operational problems are identified and modifications made to deal with them: thus progress is made.

Significant amounts of energy are involved here. Often the process of trial and error, of effort and set-back, and the slow building of performance, can be a source of real frustration. In these circumstances people can evince anger. This is not resistance to change. Rather it is the natural consequence of trying to make a new system work, experiencing partial, or complete, failure, which may or may not be under the control of the individuals concerned. *This anger is not evidence of attempts to oppose but rather articulates the feelings of those trying to make the new system work.* Whilst managers should ensure the right training and support is available we argue they should generally remain in the background allowing the people directly involved to make it work. By doing so that people will develop the skills, understanding and attachments needed for the system to be run effectively in the longer term.

Stage 5: Internalization. Now the people involved have created a new system, process and organization. New relationships between people and processes have been tried, modified and accepted. These now become incorporated into understandings of the new work situation. This is a cognitive process through which people make sense of what has happened. *Now the new behaviour becomes part of 'normal' behaviour.*

It seems that people experience change in these ways, initially as disturbance, perhaps even as a shock, then coming to accept its reality, testing it out and engaging in a process of mutual adaptation and finally, coming to terms with it. Self-esteem and performance varies, initially declining, and then growing again. The variation of performance flows from mutually reinforcing individual and operational causes, as we have seen. The 'engine' for re-building performance is the self-esteem of the people involved. Note here that we talk of relative levels (notional performance might be improved ten-fold as a consequence of new technology) the problems we have discussed may mean that in the early stages following the introduction of the new technology only 60 per cent of notional performance is achieved. Whilst this means 40 per cent of notional performance is being lost it does represent a

six-fold improvement! Finally we do not suggest that people go through these stages neatly, nor that all go through them at the same time, or at the same rate. Some may not go beyond the denial of change. The important point is that people do seem to experience significant changes in these ways and that this leads on to a number of practical ways in which the problems of coping can be handled.

Coping with the process of change places demands on the individuals involved. Various issues need to be faced either by the individuals or by managers. Note however that these issues are of concern to all effected by an organizational change, including managers. We will set down a simple framework for Coping with Change: listing issues to be faced, based upon ideas from various workers in the field[1,3,5,7] and the author's own experience. These issues are identified in Figure 6. Time and space will allow no further discussion of this figure except to say that it can provide the basis of short workshops for people involved in change. Several managers known to the author arrange 2-hour workshops in groups of 10–12 people in which people are asked to discuss and then report back on the issues. They feel to be important in a period of change. This can be a powerful method facilitating a more knowledge-able and constructive approach to a major change and can lead to useful ideas. The author also remembers talking these ideas over with a senior manager in a diversified group who had introduced computerized photocomposition within a news-paper company in the early 1970s. They had

(A) Know Yourself

(1) Would I Have Chosen For This to Have Happened?
   Do I Accept It?
   Can I Benefit?
   What is the Worst that can Happen?
   Have I Experienced Similar Changes?
   How Did I Cope?

(2) Can I Take Initiative?

(3) Do I Know What I Want?
   What I Don't Want?

(4) Can I Cope With Stress?
   Avoid Conflict
   Time Management
   Don't Blame Yourself

(5) Do I Take Stock of my Situation?

(B) Know Your Situation

(1) Can I Describe the Changes?
(2) Do I Know How I am Expected to Behave?
(3) Can I Try Out the New Situation in Advance?

Figure 6. Coping with changes: issues to be faced

allowed the typesetters to try out the VDUs in a test-room but not in a training environment. Providing support, they avoided any sense of formal training and were surprised to find that, allowed to learn at their own pace, the typesetters embraced the technology enthusiastically and quickly.

Re-building Self-esteem
The ground covered in this section is summarized in Figure 7, below.

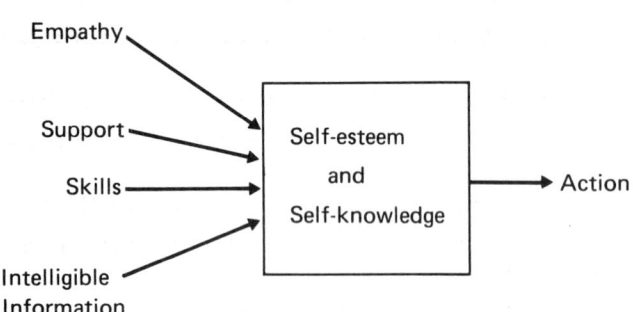

Figure 7. Re-building self-esteem

Simplifying, somewhat, we suggest that individuals have four main categories of need if they are to re-build their self-esteem amidst a programme of organizational change. They need *intelligible information*. They will probably need to develop *new skills* if only the skills of dealing with new people as colleagues or supervisors. They will need *support* to help them deal with the problems. Encouragement to try out new systems is important. Provision of short workshops planned to achieve part or all of the work discussed in the preceding section can help. Technical support to solve problems is often needed. Access to people who can help is useful. Control over the rate of personal learning should be possible. All of these things can help. First and foremost *empathy*, understanding, is a key issue. Kirkpatrick[7] rightly sees this as one of the key skills for managing change. Pierre Casse[9] defines empathy as follows:

Empathy is the ability to see and understand how other people construct reality, or more specifically how they perceive, discover and invent the inner and outer worlds. We all use empathy. All the time. We constantly guess what people think and feel. The problem is that in most cases we guess wrongly. We assume that what is going on in somebody else's mind is somewhat identical to our own psychic processes. We tend to forget that we are different. Sometimes, drastically different. To practice empathy is to recognize and take full advantage of those differences.[9]

We see the skill of empathy as the struggle to understand. We can never fully see a situation as others see it. But we can struggle to try and individuals will respond to that struggle. They will also respond to someone, who clearly does not try. Making information intelligible to its recipient requires this skill. We need to try to see things as the recipient will in order to communicate. Often we do not try. We pass on the information we have. Usually we do so without attempting to make it intelligible, if we pass it on at all!

Conclusion

In this paper we have discussed ways and means of introducing major changes effectively. Here we wish to stress one crucial point. Effective organizations are those which introduce change quickly and in which people, employees and managers, learn about the business as this process proceeds. Achieving change without learning is possible, but sometimes not without struggle, if powerful groups oppose. Introducing change in ways which do not encourage learning is likely to entrench negative attitudes to change, in the future. Only if people and organizations change, by learning from the experience of change, can effectiveness be achieved and sustained. We have attempted to draw together a range of ideas and practical steps to help people manage change effectively.

All these ideas and steps need to be integrated for effectiveness. Only if we manage transitions effec-

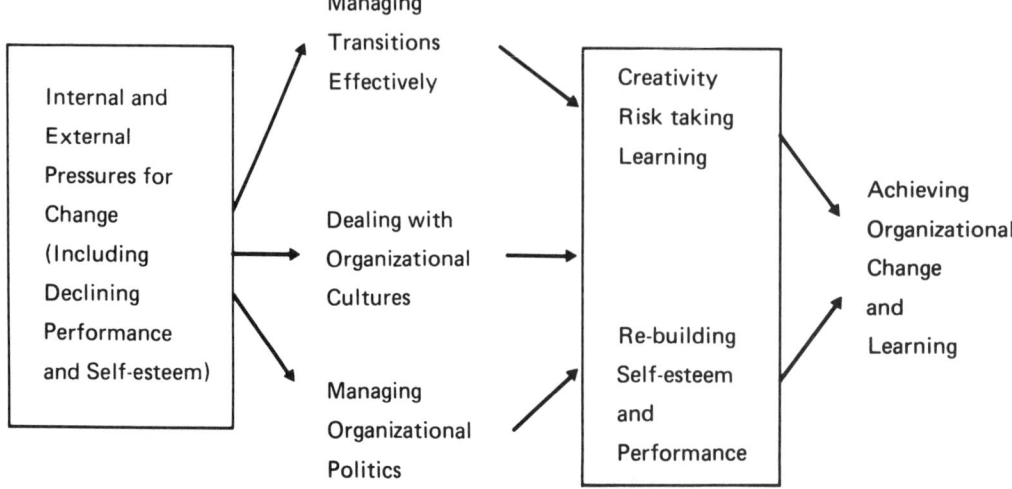

Figure 8. Managing major changes

tively can learning and change occur. This also acts as a constructive constraint on the politics of change which can so easily appear to get out of control. Moreover, managing change effectively reduces anxiety and helps those who find change stressful to cope with as individuals. This is turn leads to a more positive attitude to change. Thus it is that we come full circle. If these ideas are synthesized in a managerial approach to organizational change than there seems to be a better prospect of success and effectiveness. Difficult and demanding in practice we offer these ideas as the basis of how managers are able to see changes through. We summarize the ideas presented here in Figure 8, presented below.

The key point is that only by synthesizing the management of transitions, dealing with organizational cultures and handling organizational politics constructively, can we create the environment in which creativity, risk-taking, learning and the re-building of self-esteem and performance can be achieved. If we can sustain such a synthesis, then learning and change can follow. More important, because people have learned about the business through the process of changing, the organization will probably become more effective. By creating the conditions for extensive problem-solving and positive attitudes to change, future effectiveness is created. All of this is hard work. What we have described goes far beyond 'being nice to people'. This is the challenge we face in this changing world.

References

(1) C. Argyris and D. Schon, *Theory in Practice: Increasing Professional Effectiveness*, Jossey-Bass (1974).

(2) C. Handy, *Understanding Organisations*, 3rd Edn, Penguin (1985).

(3) R. Kanter, *The Change Masters*, George Allen & Unwin (1983).

(4) H. Kissinger, *The White House Years*, Weidenfeld & Nicolson (1979).

(5) G. Cooper, *Psychology and Management*, Macmillan (1981).

(6) M. Ket de Vries and D. Miller, *The Neurotic Organisation*, Jossey-Bass (1984).

(7) D. L. Kirkpatrick, *How to Manage Change Effectively*, Jossey-Bass (1985).

(8) J. Adams, J. Hayes and B. Hopson, *Transition—Understanding and Managing Personal Change*, Martin Robertson (1976).

(9) P. Casse, Training for the Cross-Cultural Mind, Society for Intercultural Education, Training and Research, Washington (1979).

Linking Organizational Effectiveness and Environmental Change

*Frank Shipper, Assistant Professor of Management
and Charles S. White, Teaching Fellow, College of Business Administration,
Arizona State University*

Advisors on strategic planning often give two separate pieces of advice to managers: first, managers must interact with rather than react to the external environment. That is, they should be proactive, not reactive. Second, the organizational effectiveness must be improved. However, seldom is any linkage established between these two pieces of advice. The first premise is primarily an external view, and the second is an internal view. If these two views are not linked, the results may range from slightly below optimum to bankruptcy. The purpose of this article is to show how these two views can be linked.

Although no disagreement exists on the fact that the basic desire of strategic planning is to improve organizational effectiveness, no agreement exists on how to portray effectiveness.[1] The clearer a manager can picture improvements in effectiveness to himself and his subordinates the higher the probability that significant change will occur. A frequently used portrayal is the goal attainment model. In addition, a resource allocation model and an organizational efficiency model have also been suggested. Although each model can be appropriate, each one focuses on a different area of the organizational function as shown in Table 1.

The resource allocation model focuses on obtaining raw materials such as financial support, employee recruitment and new product development. The efficiency model focuses on the manufacturing

process of turning raw materials into finished products. The goal attainment model focuses on such measurable items as market share, increased profits and sales. Since the measurement of effectiveness is a reflection of the model selected, the choice of the appropriate model is quite important. Otherwise a manager can obtain an abstract collection of results instead of a coherent set of outcomes.

To further complicate the selection of the appropriate model of effectiveness, the external environment has multiple facets. Three major facets are (1) the degree of market competitiveness, (2) the rate of technological innovation, and (3) the variability of economic fluctuations that affect the industry. These three environmental conditions, however, can be used as primary indicators as to which effectiveness model is appropriate. In this article, the primary focus of each effectiveness model is examined. The indicators of the three environmental factors are detailed, and the appropriate match between the organizational effectiveness model and the environmental conditions is delineated.

Internal Effectiveness

The modeling and subsequent measurement of the internal effectiveness of organizations has frequently been characterized as a set of input–throughput–output processes as shown at the bottom of Table 1. This portrayal emphasizes the need to consider the interrelated and interacting nature of the organizational activities. Although courses of action directed at a specific process may be desirable for their ease of implementation, the spurious side effects may incur more costs than the

The research on which this paper is based was partially funded by Grant in Aid from Arizona State University.
Frank Shipper is Assistant Professor of Management and Charles S. White is Teaching Fellow, both at the Department of Management, College of Business Administration, Arizona State University, Tempe, Arizona 85281, U.S.A.

Table 1. Organizational focus of three effectiveness models

Areas of responsibility	Resource acquisition model	Efficiency model	Goal attainment model
Management	Management selection	Management development	Managerial promotability
Finance and accounting	Financial arrangements	Return on investment	Increased profits
Production	R & D procurement	Productivity	Volume
Marketing	New product development	Inventory turnover	Market standing
Personnel	Employee recruitment	Employee training	Retention
	⇑	⇑	⇑
Primary focus	Resource acquisition	Production process	Results
	⇓	⇓	⇓
Materials flow	Inputs —————————	— Throughput —————————	— Output

Source: Developed by authors.

benefits from the action. For example, *Life*, *Look* and *Saturday Evening Post* all fell into a pattern of repeated special offers in order to increase circulation. However, the inflow of revenues from both advertisers and subscribers was not sufficient to offset the additional expenditures. Consequently, the additional sales were achieved at a net loss to the companies. Therefore, when diagnosing organizational problems and prescribing actions, the input–throughput–output model helps to highlight the need for actions that are rational, logical and congruent within the entire organizational framework.

Inputs in this context refer to an organization's required resources. They include raw material, capital, people, ideas and anything else a strategic planner may wish to acquire. *Throughput* refers to the ongoing conversion process a firm employs and serves as the link between the firm's raw materials and outputs. Finally, *outputs* refer to the results the organization achieves. The acceptance of the organization's outputs by its customers is one way the organization is linked to its external environment. Through this acceptance, the firm obtains the ability to rejuvenate its resources and continue operations into the future.

Each of these functions is a necessary part of any enterprise. For an individual firm to attempt to approach its potential for effectiveness, it must ensure that all three functions are in a healthy state, and that they are linked together in a coherent manner. What needs to be recognized is that either under-attention or over-attention to a particular area can cause problems. Before prescribing a scheme for accenting the need for appropriate attention in each of the three areas, each one will be examined in depth.

Inputs
The resource allocation models have defined organizational effectiveness as the ability to compete successfully for acquisition of scarce and valued inputs. This is analogous to a living organism that competes for food. Without the

ability to acquire resources, an organization can live only as long as it has reserves. This criterion emphasizes survival.

The over-emphasis on this approach can be illustrated by some of the regulatory agencies of the government. For example, the Federal Aviation Agency (FAA), as one part of the airline industry, for years held many board meetings and lower level meetings, and wrote countless regulations specifying the inputs of each airline such as the route and fare structures of the airlines. When the regulatory power was abolished, prices fell and the route structure was expanded by many airlines in order to better meet the needs of both customers and the airlines. Without regulation, the industry could better focus on outputs rather than inputs and throughputs.

The under-emphasis can be illustrated as a partial contributor to the demise of the Penn Central Railroad. Unbelievably, the Penn Central showed an accounting statement profit the year before it went bankrupt. Part of the reason was that the firm was not replenishing its resources, but was living off its reserves. One of its reserves was the track, which was not properly maintained. Therefore, schedules could not be met, cargo damage was high, and derailment was frequent.

In summary, two major problems can occur when resource allocation is used as a sole measure of effectiveness. First, when over-emphasis occurs, empire-building is likely. However, the efficiency of the conversion processes may be low, and the outputs may be unacceptable to the customers. Second, when under-emphasis occurs, the firm may grind to a halt. The resulting shortages and restrictions can hold the firm captive.

Throughput
A firm's throughput or conversion processes delineate the production technology applicable to the firm and establish the upper bounds for potential effectiveness using the efficiency criteria. The efficiency model when used to measure effective-

ness in the conversion process is portrayed by the value added to the input as it is transformed into output. The core technology of a firm involved in the transformation is both the physical conversion process, and also the supporting human processes. For example, one firm that is a leader in heavy equipment has devoted considerable resources to improving the human processes without major changes to the technical processes. This firm has found that the potential for improvement is so rewarding that all information regarding the improvements is treated as proprietary. Both internal and external consultants are restricted from writing about the improvements. Thus, both the physical and human technology combine to provide the potential for efficiently turning inputs into outputs.

An over-emphasis on the processes can lead to activities designed to buffer the technology from the firm's environment. Some of the barriers erected are patent protection, government subsidies, union work rules and import quotas. Since these buffers appear to lead to internal deterioration over time, competition will arise. For example, one contributor to the decline of the railroads was the practice of featherbedding. The frozen human processes did not allow the railroads to optimize the efficiency of the organization. Consequently, the trucking industry attracted the cargo, which it could handle quicker and cheaper for the customers.

An under-emphasis on throughput can lead to processes that are out-of-date and noncompetitive. For example, the shipbuilding industry has concentrated on acquiring contracts that were restricted by governmental regulations to U.S. shipyards. The internal processes have become a nightmare. Due to such inefficiencies, one yard had to shut down just to inventory and locate the resources available on site. Still other yards have continued to build ships based on the principle that the entire keel must be laid first. Consequently, overseas shipyards have become more productive due to the utilization of modular construction techniques. The result has been that American firms turned to buffers to protect their out-of-date technology such as subsidies and additional regulation to protect them from competition.

Outputs
The outputs of an organization are often depicted by goal-attainment models. In this model organizational effectiveness is defined by the degree to which the organization meets its goals. The functions of goals are first, to establish direction to the internal processes, and second, to provide the means whereby the organizational resources can be replenished. When goals are over-emphasized, a manager can be caught in the pitfall known as 'the ends justify the means'. Because of this outlook, governmental protective agencies, restraining

legislation, and unions have come into existence asserting that the means are just as important.

When goals are under-emphasized, resources are frequently allocated to spurious processes which progress in a helter-skelter fashion. The conglomerates of the 1960s were victims of an under-emphasis on a broad range of goals and an over-emphasis on one goal. Through the merger of accounting statements and the pooling of interests, they showed an increase in earnings year after year. The stockmarket reacted in turn by either maintaining or increasing the price-earnings ratio. Hence a pyramid was built; the first in could sell out at a substantial profit, but the last in needed to wait for additional companies to be brought into the scheme. Internally, processes were confused and confounded. Synergy was often praised, but seldom found on the operational level. The outcome has been that many conglomerates experienced financial difficulties when they ceased to be able to expand and profits either leveled off or decreased. When the operating units were examined, no rational arrangement to this structure could be found. Some conglomerates were forced by financial pressures to sell off and sometimes simply to close down unprofitable operations. Few have been able to return to the equity money markets to obtain the low risk and low cost resources once available.

Thus it is obvious from the preceding examples that either an over-emphasis or an under-emphasis on any one of the internal processes—input, throughput or output—can be detrimental to an organization. it should also be equally obvious that internally the three processes should be considered as an overall set of processes which must be merged together as if one.

The External Environmental Conditions

Although agreement exists that the external environment has multiple facets, no agreement exists on the number. Lawrence and Lorsch have suggested two, whereas more recently Hofer and Schendel have suggested five.[2] This article will examine three facets—degree of competitiveness, rate of technological innovation, and variability of economic fluctuations—as portrayed in Figure 1. The point is not how many there are, but whether managers can recognize indicators in the external environment that would suggest future threats to the organization. In addition, can these threats be recognized early enough for managers to take appropriate action? Therefore, the three facets will be examined in detail.

Degree of Competitiveness
The degree of competitiveness is intended to characterize the amount of interactive competition

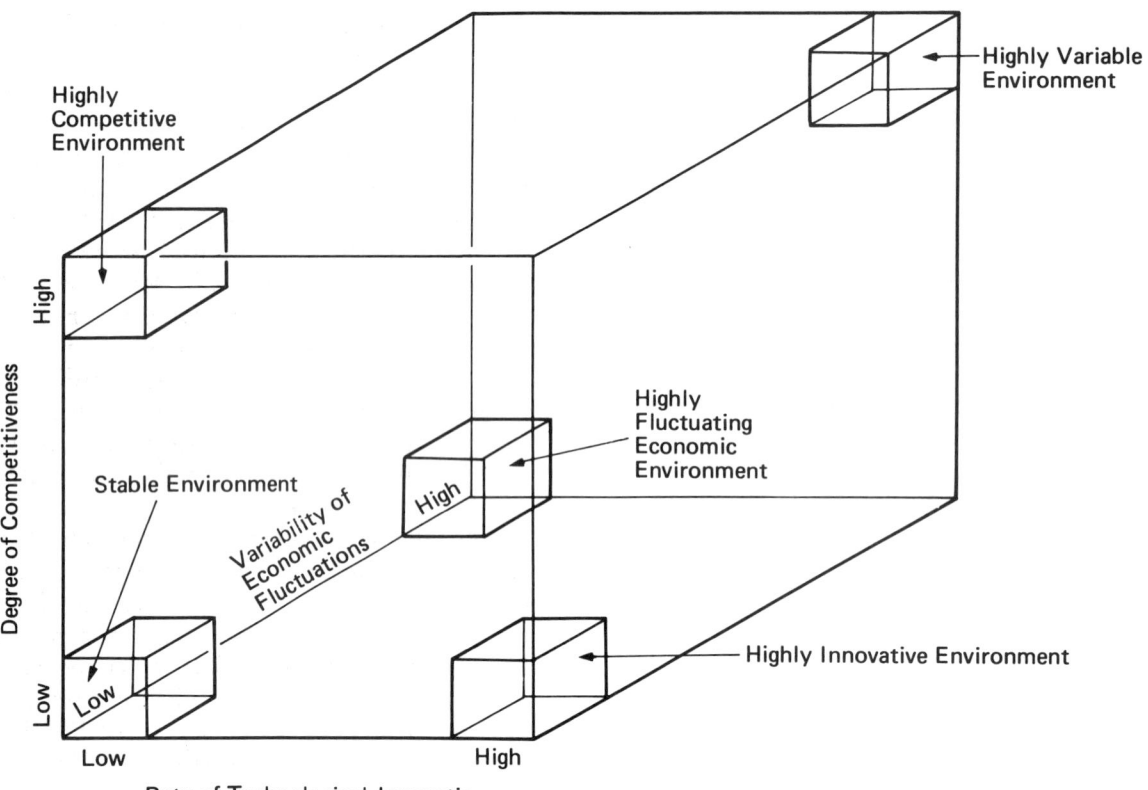

Figure 1. The 3-D environment cube

in the marketplace. Recently, the competition for the marketplace has become a two-stage process. The first stage is societal acceptance. Societal acceptance has been qualified both by government regulations and public reaction. For example, government regulations have caused the manufacturers of children's pajamas to reformulate the material at least twice. The first change was to make them fire retardant and the second, to alleviate the possibility of a carcinogenic effect of the original fire retardant agent. Public reaction can take many forms such as consumer boycotts of coffee due to price increases, and rumors about the contents of certain fast food products. One toy manufacturer even withdrew a product, the Evel Knievel doll, to prevent adverse public reaction due to the notoriety gained by the product's real life model.

The second stage is product competitiveness in the market place. This stage can straddle geographic boundaries, as in the auto industry where foreign imports have increased their market share. It can jump traditional industry lines such as the competition between glass, steel, aluminium and plastic for a share of the container market. The primary concerns, if one firm tries to increase its sales, are the degree of friction among competitors and the amount of encroachment that must occur among other competitors' respective market share.

The major determining factor of the degree of competitiveness is the product/market life cycle. During the initial and growth stages, competitiveness will be low. The basic focus will be to establish primary demand. In subsequent stages—shakeout,

maturity and decline—the degree of competitiveness will heighten.

As competition increases, pricing variability increases with undercutting occurring periodically such as in the laundry soap industry. At any given time at least one or more major brands will have a broadside on the package in a vivid color declaring an amount off the regular price. Another form of product differentiation used in a saturated market is advertising illusion. The use of the dangling modifier such as 'whiter than white', 'cleaner than clean', becomes commonplace.

Another sign is the use of target marketing. When the market is mature, the demographics of the users are well known. Each competitor will have an advertising pitch. The various advertisements will be used in different focused magazines. The selection of the media will be carefully determined to focus on a particular segment of the market. Even the packaging will be designed as much for display purposes as for its function. For example, in the beer industry both the container and the advertising per unit cost more than the contents. In any given month one will find different advertisements for the same product in magazines aimed at black, female or male readership. In this type of environment the creative, innovative and flashy campaign is the hallmark of the competitive edge.

Rate of Technological Innovation
Previously this environmental condition has been characterized as either high or low technology. However, the degree of technology is not as

important as the rate of change. For example, both the slide rule industry, a relatively low technology industry, and the watch industry, a relatively high technology industry, were shaken by the introduction of electronics. The old competitors in the slide rule industry were left out of the transition from a mechanical device to an electronic device. The old line watchmakers were able to make the transition from a mechanical device run by springs and balance wheels to the electro-mechanical model run by batteries and balance wheels or a tuning fork, but few made the transition to the electronic watch with digital readout and quartz crystals.

One of the key indicators in this area is learning curve pricing. In learning curve pricing the product is sold below cost during the early stages realizing that as demand is built economics of scale and the learning process will reduce cost in latter stages. Companies in the electronics industry will use this method in order to gain market acceptance of their product and experience in producing the high technology item. They realize that with short life cycles for their products, the company who gets there first with the most will be able to ride the growth curve through the shakeout stage and hopefully enter the mature stage as the industry leader.

Companies in this type of environment will launch a two-prong strategy. First they will invest heavily in research and development with willingness to do both applied and basic research. Government contracts are frequently a favorite vehicle for financing both the basic and some of the applied research in the electronics industry. Through this means they seek to become a recognized product technological leader. The second prong will be aimed at production technology. In order to design to a predetermined level of cost acceptance by consumers, care will be taken to use interchangeable and standardized parts where possible. Emphasis will be placed on designing a continuous production process with a high degree of automation if the product has a high sales volume. For example, with the electronic watch the number of parts required has been greatly reduced from the mechanical watch. In addition, assembly has been automated since fewer intricate assembly operations are required. Thus, in this type of environment each competitor seeks to establish a distinctive competence either with the product technology or the production technology or both.

Variability of Economic Fluctuations
During the last 10 years the variability in economic fluctuations not only for the economy as a whole, but also for industries, has increased. In the copper industry, major mines in the United States have had to be opened and closed based on the fluctuations of the price of copper. The fluctuation has been as much as a 27 per cent decrease in 11 months. Such changes have caused the operations of many mines

to go from profitability to an inability to justify continued operations.

The 'boom and bust' of the housing industry is well known. In each downturn, companies that have financially over-extended themselves go under. However, even for other industries the cost of capital has become a major concern. The stock market, with its historically lower price/earnings ratio, has become less attractive as a primary money market. The variability in prime interest rates also has increased recently. This has spilled over and affected the cost of capital in all the money markets; thus timing has become an important issue, as well as the ability to refinance if the rates drop.

Another variability not often considered is the lead time to develop both sources of raw materials and skilled employees. During a recent boom, raw materials for certain industries became so scarce that buyers were reduced to a barter system. For example, buyers in the chemical industry could not obtain petroleum feedstock except by arranging a trade with the petroleum supplier. The petroleum buyer could not obtain drilling pipe because of a shortage in the steel industry. However, the chemical industry buyer could trade a scarce raw material to the steel industry buyer, who in turn traded steel well casings to the petroleum industry buyer, who in turn supplied the chemical buyer with petroleum feedstock. Although this incident may be unusual, the underlying problem is widespread. Because of the recent set of minibooms and recessions, channels for supplying raw materials and highly skilled individuals simply do not develop. The associated uncertainty discourages the industries involved from making the large and long-term investments required for appropriate development and return. Therefore, in an economic upturn, scarcity of underdeveloped resources quickly develops and demand-pull inflation occurs which rapidly deflates the economic impetus.

Thus, it is clear from these illustrations that the external environment can change rapidly due to either the degree of competitiveness in the marketplaces, the rate of technological innovation either within or across industries, or the variability in economic fluctuations. Also, equally clear is that one condition does not automatically preclude either of the other two. Therefore, the wise strategic planner should consider each before formulating plans and programs.

The Balancing Act

The strategic planner of an organization is in a double bind between the demands of organizational effectiveness and the rapidity of change in the environment. Organizations in the past have had the luxury of a relatively stable environment, which allowed long lead times to institute change.

However, the environment has become more demanding in all areas for almost every industry. Thus, the strategic planner must do a delicate balancing act allocating limited resources to various internal areas to meet the greatest demands from the environment.

In order to perform the appropriate balancing act, the strategic planner must pinpoint the firm's location on the cube in Figure 1. The axes of the cube are the rate of technological innovation, degree of competitiveness and the variability of economic fluctuations. This large cube pictorially represents the variability that may be found in any one industrial environment. The five smaller cubes represent special cases which can be found when a given industrial environment is examined. The stable industrial environment is the first one to be examined. Whether a stable environment even exists now is a debatable issue, with many agreeing that it does not.[3] Outsiders who suggest that the steel, clothing, shoe and coal industries are stable may do so from a lack of knowledge about the dynamics of the respective industries. Insiders who suggest they are stable, may do so because of a lack of understanding and foresight. Therefore, a strategic planner should look beyond the current status—to the past in order to map trends which have occurred, and to the future for emerging patterns and new ideas. This analysis will allow the planner to ascertain the axes that have played and might play a part in the dynamic change which will inevitably occur.

Competitive Environment
The second special case for examination is the highly competitive environment. An example of this case is the magazine industry. All the general interest magazines such as *Life*, *Look*, *Saturday Evening Post* and *Colliers* were partially victims of the high competition for leadership. However, more magazines, through more outlets, with more advertising revenue are being sold today than in the past. The special interest magazines have segmented and targeted their market so well that indiscriminate mass mailings are far less common. In addition, some magazines such as *People* and *Us* have recognized the across-industry competition with television. The stories are slanted toward the television viewer. Many of the articles are short enough to be read during a commercial break; the type is large for easy reading in dim light; and the main subjects are television personalities. By taking a complementary approach, these magazines have turned a threat into an advantage.

Even the distribution channels have changed in the magazine business. The corner news-stand is only found in a few large cities and the magazine store has become scarce. Magazines today are sold mainly by grocery stores and by subscription. However, due to the constant escalation of mailing costs the latter has become de-emphasized. Some of the more recent magazines can only be bought through outlets. In the grocery stores they have displaced candy displays in the prime space before the checkout counters. The example of the magazine industry is not one of competition being detrimental to the whole, but only to publications that no longer meet the needs of the consumers. The key to success in this type of environment is to find the opportunities available, establish objectives to reflect these opportunities, and align the internal processes and resources to attain the objectives.

Innovative Environment
The next special case is the innovative environment, which has two facets. The first is the high product technology which was discussed earlier with reference to the electronic industry. The second is the high production technology. Many companies, which are suppliers to national retailers, have managed to stabilize the competitive environment by allowing the retailer to handle the marketing. Since the materials required to produce the products are readily available and the market is assured by contract, economic fluctuations are of minor consideration. Thus, the major concern is with internal processes. An example of a company that has thrived in such a situation is Design and Manufacturing, maker of appliances, and major supplier to Sears and other retailers. Design and Manufacturing has succeeded because it has directed its attention to the details of production. Efficiency of the production process is the corporate religion. To realize this goal it has simplified operations, instituted automation and lengthened production runs whenever and wherever economically feasible. The result is that not only has it thrived, but it has also seen Westinghouse and General Motors, with its Frigidaire brand, leave the appliance industry. The key in an environment where the other dimensions are relatively stable and the product technology is low, is to be the most efficient producer in order to offer the customers a quality product at the lowest price.

Fluctuating Economic Environment
The fourth special case is when the economic environment is highly fluctuating in comparison to other environments. A prime example of this situation today is the oil industry. When the first gas crisis occurred in 1973, many independent retailers who had no sources of supplies went under. If the government had not intervened with allocations, many more also would have ceased operations. In the 1979 crisis, even the big oil companies had to curtail portions of their operations. Those which have felt the shutdown of the Iranian fields the least are those with the least dependence on overseas supplies. The key to this type of environment is to obtain control of resources through backward integration. As the fluctuations in economic markets increase the shortages, the cost of supplies will increase. Those companies whether in oil, paper or other industries

dependent on natural resources have a competitive advantage if they have developed their own source of supply.

The Highly Variable Environment

For some time a number of industries have been working in a highly variable environment. For other industries it is only a matter of time. One industry that has been engulfed by this highly variable scenario already is the computer industry. Contrary to some antitrust lawyers' belief, it is a highly competitive industry. Whereas IBM once had 85 per cent of the total market, its share today has slipped to 55 per cent. International competition has increased from such countries as Japan, Sweden and West Germany.

The economic fluctuations are high, but surprisingly on the down side. The price per unit of processing continues to decline. Companies without the ability to build the basic components have not survived in the computer industry. The rate of technological innovation has remained high. Five-year-old products are out of date. Yet, with all the rapidity of change the industry as a group has continued to grow and prosper in comparison to the economy as a whole.

There is no real secret, but the major companies in this industry have learned to interact successfully with change on all three axes through careful planning. Texas Instruments, which has been praised as the prototype for modern management, has developed and implemented an overall strategic planning model called objectives–strategies–tactics (OST).[4] Roughly, each step of OST corresponds to goal attainment, efficiency and resource acquisition models respectively. TI has defined approximately 12 objectives, 60 strategies and 250 tactical action plans to communicate clearly the on-going organizational operations.

In addition, it has developed and established programs to respond to each of the environmental areas. First, in the competitive environment TI has used learning curve pricing to establish and gain market share during the growth stage of a new product. In latter stages, it has used design to price to ensure that its products remain competitive or undercut competition. In this second phase, the product assembly is rationalized, simplified and reduced to the fewest number of parts in order to gain production efficiency.

In the innovative environment, TI has taken steps to ensure that new ideas are encouraged. One TI program designed to encourage all employees to participate is called IDEA. Any employee can receive up to $25,000 for an idea to develop a new product or process. Over 50 per cent of the ideas funded pay off for the company in an economical sense. No accounting information is available in the

motivational pay-off. However, as an example, the TI digital watch was an outgrowth of this program.

Another program to encourage productive ideas is called People and Asset Effectiveness (P & AE). In this program 83 per cent of the employees are organized into semiautonomous work teams. The team participates in the planning and controlling of their work processes in order to increase productivity.

To effectively deal with the fluctuations in the economic environment, TI followed a two-prong attack. At the operating unit level, TI was one of the first companies to adopt zero-base budgeting. After a manager has obtained approval for the unit's operating budget, managerial responsibility is emphasized through the use of milestones and checkpoints. Corporate interference is low as long as the unit is on course. At the corporate level, financial planning has recognized the inherent risk in the computer-electronics industry. The corporate debt structure is low; the dividend pay-out ratio is also low. Consequently, growth and expansion are financed internally, thus minimizing financial risk.

The point to this final example is that TI, by effectively using strategic planning, has not only accommodated itself to a highly variable environment, but also has grown and prospered far above the average company. A warning should be issued that such a thorough program is not easily implemented. TI took 15 years to reach the present level of operating effectiveness. In addition, feedback and corrections will have to be made as the environment continues to change. But any program in today's dynamic world is only as good as management's willingness to take incremental steps towards a moving idea.

Conclusion

From the preceding discussion it should be clear that the strategic planner is caught between the internal capabilities of the organization and the changes in the external environment. The internal capabilities of a company must be maintained by continuous resource acquisition, increased conversion efficiency and achievement of higher goals. However, the dramatic changes occurring simultaneously in the economic, technological and market-place environments threaten to make any company ineffective in sustaining its current market position. The highly fluctuating environment portrayed creates a predicament where maintaining acceptable results is a race.

The model proposed is designed to aid a strategic planner in mapping the environment the industry is currently involved in,

and directing attention to the internal processes most capable of responding to the external demands. In addition, the model has illustrated that adjustment to one process will require adjustment in other processes. Thus, the strategic planner is caught in a two-way balancing act. The primary determinant of success is the balance between internal processes and the external environment. However, the internal processes must also be balanced if optimum results are to be obtained.

References

(1) P. B. Coulter, Organizational effectiveness in the public sector: the example of municipal fire protection, *Administrative Science Quarterly,* p. 65, March (1979).

(2) P. R. Lawrence and J. W. Lorsch, *Organizations and Environment.* Graduate School of Business Administration, Harvard University, Boston (1967); and C. W. Hofer and D. Schendel, *Strategy Formulation: Analytical Concepts,* West Publishing Company, St. Paul (1978).

(3) R. H. Hayes and S. G. Wheelwright, The dynamics of process–product life cycle, *Harvard Business Review,* p. 127, March–April (1979).

(4) E. R. Gomersall and M. S. Myers, Breakthrough in on-the-job training, *Harvard Business Review,* p. 62, July–August (1966); M. S. Myers, Who are your motivated workers?, *Harvard Business Review,* p. 73, January–February (1964); M. S. Myers, Conditions for manager motivation, *Harvard Business Review,* p. 58, January–February (1966); Texas Instruments shows U.S. business how to survive in the 1980s, *Business Week,* p. 66, September (1978).

Managing Change

Robert M. Worcester

Managing Director, Market & Opinion
Research International, London,
England.

> "Change or Die" must ever face
> the modern operation. External
> events press in, communica-
> tions speed up, processed in-
> formation provides impetus for
> decisions, and constant pres-
> sure from competition forces
> the corporation to improve.
> Nonetheless, change is seldom
> easy, must often be forced on
> unwilling colleagues, and fre-
> quently causes trauma to both
> people and organizations.
> Imposing change successfully
> that is with the enthusiastic
> cooperation of those whose
> lives the change will affect, is
> one of the most demanding of
> management arts, is frequently
> required of managers at all
> levels, and is perhaps the least
> often successfully accom-
> plished. The focus of this article
> is on American experience in
> managing change as studied
> over the past decade by Opinion
> Research Corporation consult-
> ants.

IT COMES AS NO SURPISE TO ANY STUDENT of British business that the past decade, especially the past five years, has seen the greatest rationalization, reorganization, and merger period of British business history. Indeed, the 1960s accounted for nearly sixty per cent of all mergers during the post-war period. While many of these mergers, take-overs, and consolidations have been successful, few have realized the synergy fervently hoped for by their architects. Some, of course, have been notoriously unsuccessful. The one thing that has characterized every one of these activities has been that they have forced change upon the organizations affected. At the same time, events have forced major changes on most companies un-

affected directly by merger. In many companies the advent of regularly pro-cessed management information has been the harbinger of traumatic change; change that some companies found they could not handle.

During this period, many students of management have focussed on the process of change as a key link to corporate success or failure. Among these students are a number of executives of Opinion Research Corporation who in their work with clients are often in the position of counselling change. In an effort to assist themselves and their clients to understand better the change process, a systematic study of writings on the conception of change from sociological, psychological, and anthropological sources was made, management theorists consulted, intensive interviews with management development executives in ten innovative companies were taken, research amongst the graduates of one leading company's comprehensive management training programme was undertaken, and the results were drawn together for a report to clients and reported in this article.

Most organizations are able to adjust to small, routine changes in the 'system'. However, a rethinking of traditional management practice is called for to accomplish large-scale tasks which cut across departmental lines, such as:

- Introducing wholly new products or services
- Handling a major reorganization
- Effecting acquisitions and mergers
- Entering a new market
- Radically improving internal effi-ciency and profitability

At the middle manager level of most companies, however, there is often little conviction that the company is capable of change.

TABLE 1. "HOW WOULD YOU EVALUATE YOUR COMPANY ON RECEPTIVITY TO CHANGE WHEN IT IS NEEDED"?

Middle level managers in ...	Outstanding	Fair	Poor
Metals company	47%	37%	16%
Chemical	44%	43%	13%
Electrical	41%	43%	16%
Electronics	39%	53%	8%
Insurance	38%	55%	7%
Bank	35%	47%	18%
Oil	31%	56%	13%
Retail	29%	51%	20%
Steel	28%	53%	19%
Rubber	23%	60%	17%
Utility	21%	49%	30%
Aerospace	12%	64%	24%

Overall, these results tend to confirm that *managers believe companies reward those who use safe, tested methods rather than those who grapple with new ideas.*

Many managers believe that they must circumvent the 'system' in order to get things accomplished in their companies.

Many managers, in a variety of indus-tries, seriously question whether their company is capable of and really interested in change.

At the root of this belief is the wide-spread conviction, often arising no doubt out of painful experience, that in order to get things done a manager must find ways of short-cutting established processes.

TABLE 2. "TO GET THINGS DONE YOU OFTEN HAVE TO CLOSE YOUR EYES TO ESTABLISHED POLICIES AND PROCEDURES"

Middle level managers in ...	Agree	Disagree	No Opinion
Electronics company	73%	29	0
Metals	68%	30	2
Utility	66%	32	2
Aerospace	65%	35	0
Chemical	63%	37	0
Retail	63%	37	0
Electrical	57%	43	0
Bank	56%	44	0
Rubber	54%	46	0
Insurance	53%	47	0
Steel	43%	57	0
Oil	38%	62	0
Total Companies Average	57%	42	1

This does not mean that these managers advocate scrapping systematic policies and procedures. Over 80 per cent believe that large organizations cannot be run without orderly routines. But the point is that managers typically believe that many established policies and procedures are out of tune with the times or the demand being made on the business. They do not permit a manager sufficient flexibility or initiative in handling problems as they occur, and hence he has to 'get around them'.

Some managers are quite outspoken about the frustrations they feel in dealing with rigid, unbending organizations. Here are examples of managers' comments from four Index studies:

Leading metals producer

"Red tape! It exists. It always seems to have been that way. I call it 'veto management'. If someone vetoes it, it's dead."

" We seem to be afraid to move. In other companies, nothing is impossible. We roll over and play dead. We need more enthusiasm, freer thinking, or something. I don't know if our inability ro run with the ball is because our people are afraid to make mistakes or what."

Large chemical company

"There have been no changes—we go along with the current, gaining some business and losing some but never making decisive steps forward. I guess today when we don't actively progress, we inactively regress."

" Our leaders are the product of the past—one thought, one action, one decision. We are not geared for growth because of our lack of management capability, despite having money. We don't make use of our human resources because we don't trust them."

Basic steel producer

"We should get problems out in the open where they can be solved. Eliminate the 'do nothing' attitude of top management."

" Our new products should be strongly pushed. Company leadership needs to speak out in a loud voice on many problems."

Office equipment firm

"The company often treats management people as children, rather than as responsible adults. Personal initiative is curbed in many instances."

" What I don't like is the lack of concern for achievement. Upper management favours the 'status quo' and wants to be left alone in their own little world."

Yet even employees, including managers with a definite commitment to high standards of excellence and to achieving company goals, often complain that they too are not challenged by their work, not appreciated by their company, and not given sufficient leeway in deciding how to do their work.

**TABLE 3.
PROBLEMS OF DEDICATED MANAGERS**

	Highly Dedicated or Involved Employees and Managers*
Desire these changes ...	
More information on company plans and goals	68%
More credit for individual accomplishments	68%
More say by employees in determining policies that affect them	60%
Critical of the company on ...	
A chance to learn new things	44%
Feeling my ideas are valued	39%
Feeling the company needs me	39%
Feeling that what I do counts for something	35%

*Criteria used are based on responses to questions having to do with a desire to do a better job and to do the work right, the challenge of the work, and the degree of interest it contains.

In ORC research experience, uninvolved employees almost always criticize their company more on these kinds of factors than do highly involved employees. In the study cited above, only 15 per cent of the employees and managers could be classified as highly involved—which is close to the average found in a number of employee studies. If people feel unchallenged in their present assignment, it's not surprising that they are apathetic and uninterested in improving performance or fomenting productive changes.

Also at the middle manager level, many do not feel they have been personally challenged to do anything new or different.

**TABLE 4.
"I WISH MY JOB HAD MORE OF THIS..."**

Use of my capacities	77%
Feeling I'm getting somewhere	76%
Chance for greater responsibilities	71%
Chance to learn new things	61%
Feeling it's really worthwhile to help out	60%

(Managers who feel unchallenged by their work or their boss)

Repeated studies have shown that managers can be motivated to produce change if the right approach is used. Similarly, hourly employees say that supervision does not bring out the best in them. Employees point to secondary benefits, not job challenge, as the outstanding rewards of work.

TABLE 5. I AM SATISFIED WITH...

Getting along with others	54%
Pensions	41%
Job security	35%
Satisfied with ... Making the most of my talents, education, and training	15%
Having my views taken seriously	10%
Having important responsibilities in the company	9%

(Hourly employees)

Top management often deplores the seeming apathy and indifference of employees. Employees see it the other way around—that management has spoon-fed them with fringe benefits but has restricted their responsibility and challenge.

To create more change-mindedness in an organization, the first step is to challenge popular assumptions about what stimulates better performance. Management development executives interviewed in this study stress the need to go beyond present understanding of what motivates people:

●Bring out underlying desire to excel

" Managers need to seek out the factors that make people want to achieve rather than rely on those that merely promote satisfaction with present performance." (Electric Utility).

●Give more responsibility

" It's time we started treating people as adults—give employees real responsibility and leeway in deciding how to get the job done." (Electronics).

●Manipulation no solution

"Human relations, as presently practised in business, is largely manipulative. The many findings of social scientists that get at the deeper human drive to produce are usually ignored." (Retail Trade).

●Focus on work, not therapy

" Managers feel uncomfortable playing amateur psychologist. We need to focus human energy on work problems so that people can get genuine satisfaction from solving them." (Electrical Equipment).

To channel human effort more productively toward corporate goals, managers will have to develop new understanding about the satisfactions people seek from work. The reality most top managements must face is that only a small handful of 'change promoters' will be available at any level of the company. The Index measured the desire for innovation among employees in four different companies on two basic factors:

● Willingness to adopt new ways of doing things
● Taking the initiative in demanding change.

TABLE 6. RESISTERS AND PROMOTERS OF CHANGE

	Most Active Resisters of Change	In Between Indifferent	Most Active Promoters of Change
Scientists and engineers	10%	70%	20%
White-collar	17%	74%	9%
Manual workers	19%	77%	4%

Because most people are somewhere between the two extremes, individual managers by their practices do, in fact, stimulate many employees to be either more changeminded or more resistant to change.

Of course, all the organization's managers cannot be change-minded—many assignments demand 'control-minded' individuals. The basic operating philosophy of the *control-minded* manager . . .

● Implement present policies
● Rely on chain of command
● Shoot for goals just above this year's
● Demand performance to accepted standards
● Resist new ideas until they are proven
● Patch up things when they go wrong
● Focus on day-to-day effort and accomplishment

Control-minded managers are responsible caretakers or stewards of the organization. They serve an important role in the company's success, but are not usually expected to initiate important changes.

The manager whose assignment is innovation has an operating philosophy directly in conflict with that of the control-minded. The *change-minded* manager . . .

● Challenges present policies
● Organizes to meet new needs
● Strives for major advances
● Rejects average performance as inadequate
● Welcomes opportunities to try new ideas
● Seeks fundamental cures for problems
● Explores wide-ranging future possibilities.

Getting these conflicting functions of control and change to operate in tandem is a severe management dilemma.

Balanced growth requires creative conflict 'control-minded' and 'change-minded' managers. Control-minded managers insure stability and *present* profitability; change-minded managers promote growth and insure *future* profitability.

Lt. Col. Urwick[1] stated the paradox this way:

" Any healthy business must have two classes of people:

" The faithful administrators. These are essential. They are the people who maintain the routine, who keep the corporation in order. If it lacks an adequate supply of faithful administrators the corporation will be bankrupt tomorrow because it cannot deliver the goods.

" But a company also needs its lunatics, its eccentrics, its initiators—though it perhaps needs fewer of them. If it does not have them, the corporation will be trying to sell the same goods in five year's time that it is selling today.

And it will go bankrupt.

" A great many of the initiators' ideas are crazy, impractical. Once in every ten times, or whatever the average is, they will produce an idea which is essential. And from these ideas the corporation lives."

Top management's job is to reconcile this perpetual discord. One way is to departmentalize—keep these people apart. However, a better way is to bring the change- and control-minded people together so that out of their inevitable conflict emerges the most productive course of action for change.

There is little doubt, however, that at the present time, conditions promoting change need strengthening in most corporations. Conditions favouring stability are inherent in the very nature of corporations.

Major change inevitably involves going through a period of organizational instability in which success is in doubt. According to behavioural scientists, group acceptance of change involves moving from one state of equilibrium or stability through a period of disruption or instability to a new state of equilibrium—in the case of corporations, hopefully at some higher level of performance[2]. This process is diagrammed in Figure 1.

The important points are:

● Most groups will tend to throw out or reject change unless the forces or reasons for it are more powerful than the resistance that will be massed against it.
● Even where the forces creating change are strong enough to gather a foothold, the group will tend to minimise their impact—to isolate these forces in the same way the body fights disease.
● Once a major change has been absorbed, group behaviour will stabilize around some new norms and subsequent changes will be resisted.

The problem can be attacked from both directions:

From outside the affected group
Increase the forces or pressures creating change.
From inside the affected group
Decrease the resistances to change by making it worthwhile to change.

CREATING CONDITIONS FAVOURABLE TO CHANGE

The people involved must see a compelling reason for change. Innovation-minded people will readily accept the need for change, but the great majority of the apathetic will require some strong selling by management.

Get managers importantly affected by major changes to help early in the planning. Participation in the decisions leading to change increases commitment and

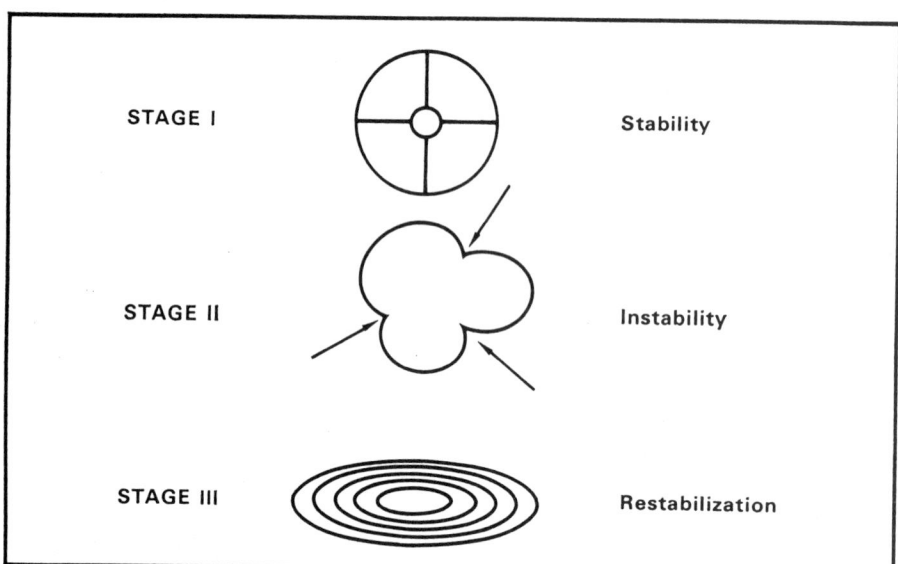

STAGE I   Stability

STAGE II   Instability

STAGE III   Restabilization

FIGURE 1. THE PROCESS OF ORGANIZATIONAL CHANGE.

generates useful ideas for implementing the change.

Avoid sudden and sweeping changes. The most permanent and beneficial results usually occur where change is made in digestible doses without unnecessary upset to the organization.

The company's reward structure can be put to work to promote change. Where people see that they are paid only to 'follow the book', they will not listen when management talks innovation. Enthusiasm for change goes up when management gives visible rewards to innovators.

Disagreement can be used constructively. Little of permanent value emerges without clashing viewpoints. Constructive conflict, not harmony, marks the process of change. Working disagreements through to satisfactory solutions pay off.

Providing a reasonable margin for error frequently helps. People find it difficult to be innovative if it places their jobs in jeopardy. Punishing every mistake or failure leads to reliance on safe, acceptable, proven ways of doing things.

Respect group values and interest in making changes. Small groups within corporations are like small societies, each with its own way of doing things, its status symbols, standards, and system of rewards. Resistance stiffens markedly when change-minded managers flout or ignore group values.

Training in creative problem solving can be effective. Companies that have provided training to managers in advanced problem-solving techniques report considerable success.

One way of generating and implementing major innovation is through management change teams. A powerful lever for large-scale change is a properly organized change team. Such teams, now in action in some companies, differ from the usual management committee in that they include *all* of the following:

A clear-cut mandate from the top to go ahead and make the change—not just recommendations

Representatives from all operations to be affected by the change

High level managers who can both diagnose problems and take action

Line as well as staff members

A budget, time, and other resources to do the job right

Access to all the information needed.

Managements which are tightly manned and have severely restrictive overhead policies often have great difficulty in staffing any planning effort, much less creating change teams with time to carry out their assignments.

Effective team action appears to depend on frank communications among members and willingness to face and resolve conflict. Research in small group effectiveness indicates that a change team can become a unique and powerful device if its members observe these key operating principles.

All decisions are ultimately group decisions worked out through resolving differences of opinion, with the recognition that these usually stem from good causes. Mutual support in carrying out final decisions, without violating management prerogatives, naturally results from this procedure. With adroit management, whole organizations can be shaken out of their lethargy to create dramatic performance improvements. The complete turn-about in performance of an automotive assembly plant is a classic of the change

process[3]. These drastic improvements occurred over a three-year period while the plant was under intense study by an outside observer:

● Direct manpower requirements decreased 14 per cent, with cost savings of $2 million per year

● Grievances changed from most to least among its sister plants

● From slowest to fastest recovery from model changeovers

● From worst to best safety record

● Indirect manpower requirements moved from highest to lowest

● Consistent production of new ideas.

Along with technical changes, the plant appeared to go through the following social or behavioural process in improving performance:

● Acceptance of the Reason: People recognized the likelihood that the plant would close if performance didn't improve.

● Reassurance: Management demonstrated confidence in employees, did not drastically reshape the organization.

● Frank Communications: Management opened up systematic discussions of plant problems with all groups, solicited new ideas informally.

● Joint Problem Solving: Productive work meetings and individual contacts increased, old conflicts were brought out in the open and resolved constructively.

● Mutual Trust Grew: Work relationships and feelings improved as people learned to trust each other in actual work situations.

● Confidence in Their Own Ability Increased: As improvement grew, people developed confidence in themselves and in the methods they were using to work together.

The final test came when the manager who initiated the change left. Performance continued to improve. Better work relations and attitudes had developed solidly within and continued to pay off.

To help managers cope with change, leading companies are broadening managerial horizons, exposing managers to competing viewpoints. Advanced management development programmes now go well beyond company philosophy and policy. In leading companies, the typical management development programme today includes:

● Self-learning through actual experience in group dynamics, creative problem solving.

● Serious challenges by social scientists to pet management theories.

● Seminars by academicians on the social, economic, and political forces shaping society.

● Discussions with civil rights leaders, government officials, union relations experts on current problems.

● Examination of the implications of technological advances for company operations.

Managers say that such comprehensive training does increase their ability to manage change.

Here is how graduates of one comprehensive management development programme evaluated the experience as a help to their fellow graduates in becoming better able to accept and initiate change.

TABLE 7. MANAGEMENT DEVELOPMENT PROGRAMMES AS AN AID TO CHANGE

Helped most of them	60%
Helped some of them	29%
Helped a few of them	8%
Helped none of them	0%
No opinion	3%

Since the majority of these specially-selected managers have been with the company for fifteen years or more, results are based on substantial experience and knowledge of managerial behaviour.

Yet many of the graduates still report resistance to change in the organization.

This ratio is not unhealthy. Some burden of proof must be on innovators to have good ideas and sell them. Eight per cent of the graduates do report reasonable success in introducing new ideas.

The point is not to banish resistance to change, but to bring it into a productive contest with innovation.

SUMMARY

This article has not argued whether or not to change, but how to accomplish change most effectively. Few employees, even managers, see themselves inherently as change agents. Yet many can be enlisted in the change process if they see the reason for change and feel involved.

Sophistication in the management of change is one of the skills that chief executives, managers, and high flyers alike will need in the 70s if they are to cope with the situations that will be forced upon them. ■

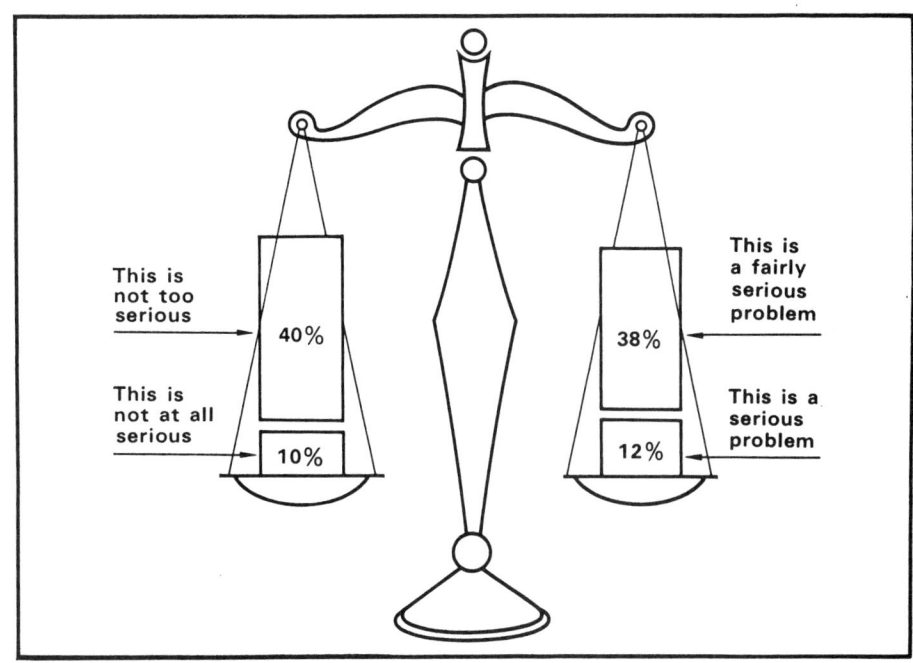

FIGURE 2. "TO WHAT EXTENT DO RIGID ORGANIZATIONAL FACTORS CREATE A PROBLEM FOR YOU IN INTRODUCING NEW IDEAS"?

ACKNOWLEDGEMENT

Much of the material upon which this article is based was developed for a confidential report of the Public Opinion Index, Opinion Research Corporation, entitled "An Approach to Managing Change in the Corporation". The director of the project was Alfred Vogel.

REFERENCES

(1) Lt. Col. Lyndall F. Urwick, *The Value of Eccentricity, Harvard Business School Bulletin,* October 1959.
(2) George Caspar Homans, *The Human Group,* Brace & Co., Harcourt, 1950.
(3) Robert H. Guest, *Organizational Change: The Effect of Successful Leadership,* Dorsey Press, Inc., Richard D. Irwin Inc., Homewood, Illinois, 1962.

BIBLIOGRAPHY

(1) Marvin Bower, *The Will to Manage—corporate success through programmed management,* McGraw-Hill.

(2) H. Van Der Haas, *The enterprise in transition,* London; N.Y.: Sydney, Tavistock Publications Ltd., 408p. 1967.
(3) Paul R. Lawrence, How to deal with resistance to change, *Harvard Business Review,* Vol. 32, No. 3. pp.49-57. 1954.
(4) Harold M. F. Ruch, *Managing Change,* New York (NICB), 1967.
(5) T. Vincent Learson, The Management of change, *Columbia Journal of World Business.* pp.59-64, Jan./Feb. 1968.
(6) E. Ginsberg and E. W. Reilly, *Effecting Change in Large Organisations,* New York, Harper & Row, 1964.
(7) Floyd C. Mann and Franklin W. Neff, *Managing Major Change in Organisations.* Ann Arbor, Michigan, Foundation for Research on Human Behaviour, 1961.
(8) Lyndall F. Urwich, The Value of Eccentricity, *Harvard Business School Bulletin,* Oct. 1959.
(9) F. Herzberg, B. Mausner and B. Snyderman, *The Motivation to Work,* New York, John Wiley & Sons, 1959.
(10) Rensis Likert, *New Patterns of Management,* New York, McGraw-Hill, 1961.
(11) Douglas McGregor, *The Human Side of Enterprise,* New York, McGraw-Hill, 1960.

PART TWO

Putting Plans into Action

Strategic Planning and Participation: A Contradiction in Terms?

H. J. Kloeze, A. Molenkamp and F. J. W. Roelofs

This article deals with the role of strategic planning in organizations. The authors consider it of decisive importance that internal participation should be given more substance, for the particular purpose of reducing demotivation and alienation problems, especially in the field of strategic planning. The authors maintain that strategic planning should be embedded in the organization in such a way as to maintain flexibility and alertness and ensure that it can be controlled and managed. They present a framework for the organisational arrangement of strategic management.

Introduction

Ever stronger emphasis is laid on the importance of strategic planning. There is a marked need for the consequences of decisions to be taken as far as possible in advance. Those in charge are required to make a visible record of the developments anticipated by them; this is no simple matter; the changes which have to be anticipated and responded to are becoming increasingly complex. The pace at which these changes take place is ever increasing. Not only is the organization confronted with technological changes and changing markets and products, it is also faced with political and social developments. The policies of organizations are regarded more and more critically. This implies that decisions are required to be taken according to plan rather than by intuition.

Now the challenge is for strategic planning to be embedded in organizations in such a way as to maintain flexibility and alertness and to ensure controllability and manageability. The present tendency towards decentralization would seem to require re-orientation of the participation issue. Ansoff, in this connection,

notes that 'it is necessary for a responsive policy to be accomplished and for a more direct confrontation with the environment to be achieved. This causes changes in the organization. Especially the larger groups will require splitting up, specific activities being transferred to semi-autonomons bodies (subsidiaries) or more extensive power being granted to divisions.'

Naturally, employees of the organization and especially those participating in the representative consultations, should have sufficient knowledge of theoretical aspects and methods applied, in order to be able to make their contributions to the process of strategic planning. Such information will have to be made available to them as relates to bases, objectives, expectations and marginal terms of the strategic planning in their organization.

The Process of Strategic Planning

Strategic planning is often considered as a rather systematic process of actions in the determination of long-range objectives. Allowing for changing conditions (challenges and threats), it is determined which steps are to be taken and how the related risks can be shaped. The process of strategic planning cannot be interpreted too formally or too rigidly. It represents a permanent search, which is impossible to phase or program completely. The requirement that it should be flexible would also seem to be at variance with approaching the process too rigidly. Especially in matters of strategic importance, it is essential that organization members should be creative. Formalization has a negative effect on inventiveness and renovating urges. There are indications in favour of* a more structured approach to the process of strategic planning; it's— *inter alia*—being argued that this would:

☆ Ensure that attention is paid to strategic issues regularly;

Dr. H. J. Kloeze is a management consultant and currently manager of the Business Economics Department, Thomassen & Drijver-Verblifa N. V., Deventer. Mr. A. Molenkamp is a senior consultant with Klynveld Kraayenhof & Co., Accountants, Amsterdam. Dr. F. J. W. Roelofs is a management consultant currently secretary of the Executives Boards of the United Duth Publishing Companies, Haarlem.

*In this connection, reference is made to the outcome of the conference on 'Strategy Formulation: Different Perspectives', held at St. Maximim on 20,21–22 May, 1976, and organized by the Institut d'Administration d'Entreprise, Aix en Provence.

☆ add to consistency in the field of strategic planning;

☆ make it possible for specialists to develop knowledge and experience in the field of decision making on strategic matters;

☆ enhance synergy between the respective sections of the organization both horizontally and vertically.

However, recently there have also been those who have come out in favour of having the formal planning concept replaced by an informal process. Ansoff[1] in fact propagates the creation of such a system as to make it possible for environmental challenges and threats to be responded to. It is in this framework that he speaks of 'strategic management' instead of 'strategic planning'. We are of the opinion that a rational approach to strategic planning should imply that the daily operational decisions should be taken, also taking into account the strategic bases and objectives, as distinct from the forced occupation with a discontinuous formal planning cycle hardly affecting operations.

Strategic decisions more often than not are taken to be results of most deliberate and well considered decision making processes. Observations from practice[2,3] show that this needs by no means be so. There are various compounding factors, such as the specific management style of top management, the use of subjective interpretations, the lack of sufficient information and the influence of political processes. Moreover, in these optional problems it is often impossible to gain an insight into all alternatives, or for them to be expressed quantitatively. Summarizing, it must be concluded that it is possible for strategic planning to be structured and formalized only up to a certain extent. And, as distinct from what outsiders will assume, it will often not be rational in character. Therefore, when considering the results of the process of strategic planning, it is important for one to know who was involved in it and what was the actual contribution and the effective influence of the various participants.

The Object of Strategic Planning

Further to the process discussed above, it is now important to give a description of the object of strategic planning, since, for participation in strategic planning to be discussed, it is necessary first of all for this object to be further indicated. This indication is made in phases.

Phase 1: environmental analysis, internal strength/weakness analysis and development of long-range strategy.

Phase 2: development of medium-range strategy and preparation of structural plans.

Phase 3: preparation of operational plans (estimate) and determination of procedures.

The object of strategic management planning is different for any of the above-mentioned phases.

The first phase is primarily concerned with obtaining sufficient insight into such important external developments as affect the organization. In this connection one could cite:

☆ general or macro-economic developments, such as demographic, social, technological and political developments;

☆ industrial or divisional developments;

☆ developments in the product markets and in the 'clients' system' of the organization.

For this insight to be obtained, it is of course necessary for much information to be gathered, processed and analysed in this phase, as it should provide a picture of chances, risks and threats as viewed against the developments outside the organization. When taking stock of the internal situation, the chief emphasis is laid on the evaluation of aspects such as the financial economic situation, staff conditions (know-how, experience, age), the present and future product volume, competitive position, technical equipment and the organizational structure. This phase will be concluded by the development of possible strategies, based on chances, risks and threats as well as strong and weak points, for long-range objectives to be met. In the second phase, a selection will be made from these alternatives, followed by a further elaboration. The object in this phase is for plans in the fields of product market developments, investments, social policy, organizational structure, mergers, reductions etc. to be realized.

In practice, it is especially in phases 1 and 2 that experts engaged for this purpose appear to play an important part in how the strategic planning should actually be given shape. In phase 3 (the operational plans and the steps to be taken) these experts play a less prominent role. It is striking that the switch from one phase to another should always be accompanied by processes of decision making. Thus, in phase 1 the competitive and social position of the organization in question will have to be determined. So will its strong and weak points. It is questionable whether the relevant decision making is in fact always as rational as outsiders are made to believe. It is at least obvious that the 'political processes' mentioned earlier may obscure the decision making. A similar situation may arise when deciding on 'strategy' and plans. Something found to be important is the fact that the parties playing a major role in such processes of decision making are as yet restricted to top management, specific experts and 'Supervisory Directors'.

Certainly in phase 3 the process of decision making grows obscure and complex. Ever greater numbers of groups within the organization are required to make their contributions. Practical decisions are taken where you could ask yourself to what extent they are still inspired by the knowledge acquired in earlier phases.

However, we should realize that the purpose of strategic management planning is to direct the primary process within the enterprise. A primary process, which in itself is the outcome of strategic decisions made earlier. And daily procedures are therefore inspired by it. If a strategic plan requires to be adjusted, it should in fact be possible for actions to be reverted to, or there may be too much time lost in between (see Figure 1). The actual effectivity of the process of strategic planning in an organization depends on the extent to which this is successfully carried into effect.

Some Considerations on How Strategic Planning is to be Dealt with Within Organizations

The laying down and formation of the organizational frameworks within which strategic planning is effected are of particular importance to improving the insight into the process. The extent of formalization of strategic planning desired is mainly determined by circumstances. Factors which could play a role in this connection are:

☆ the stage of development the organization has reached;

☆ the way in which decisions are normally taken;

☆ the scope given the organization;

☆ the length of time to which the strategic decisions relate;

☆ the levels of expertise and experience in the field of strategic planning available within the organization.

Organizationally, matters are often arranged such that the procedure starts at top management level. It is there that the objectives are broadly framed, following which the procedure is further elaborated at lower line levels (top-down). A consistent approach from the lower levels is seldom encountered, although such an approach should in fact be possible within specific marginal conditions. Ansoff[4]—the initiator of corporate planning—also originally started from the concept that strategic functioning lay with top management. After all, top management was responsible for the interaction between organization and outsiders. Other sections of the traditional management pyramid (namely middle level staff and 'doers') obviously took no part in this. However, as early as 1974 Ansoff[5] believed that 'strategy is a matter of importance to anyone in the enterprise, that it is actually the men with their slide-rules, those looking through microscopes, those delivering mail etc. who are the largest source of strategic changes. For all the fine things managers might plan and for all the documents they might produce, there would be nothing doing at work if it were not for the former's co-operation.'

Verburg[6] goes into the concrete possibilities there are for the long range planning to be organized. They are:

☆ the creation of a central long range planning division, with individual tasks

☆ the setting up of planning committees whose members are required to make time available—from that taken up by their regular duties—to sit on these committees.

For the planning committees, two variants are being considered. The first variant provides for the committee playing a co-ordinating and advisory role, the second variant transferring the planning function to the committee entirely. The line officials on the committee will then formulate objectives and develop strategies independently. Verburg's conclusion is that it would be wise to aim at a combination of a central planning division and a committee. As a managing body, the

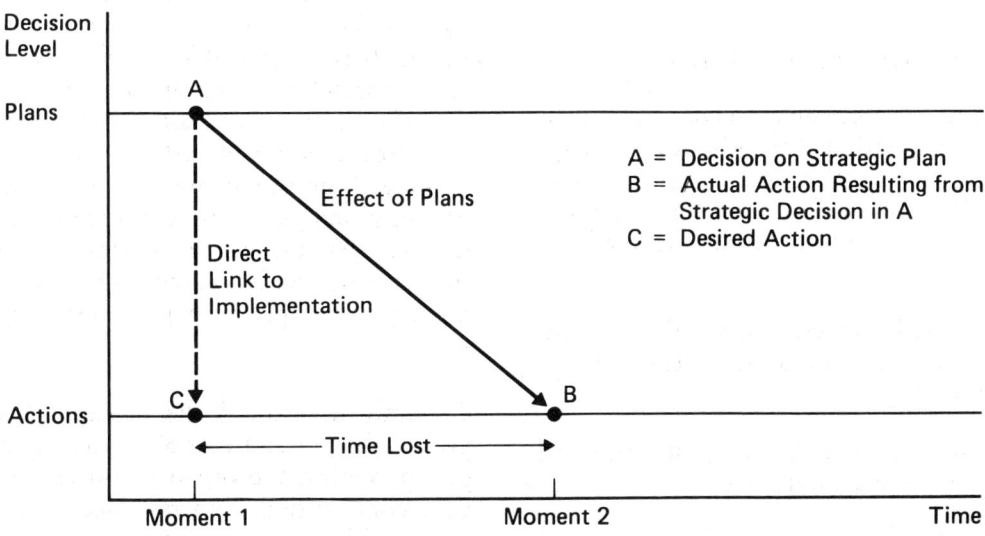

Figure 1. Time lost between the approval of strategic plans and the initiation of actions derived from these plans

committee is then supported by and received information from the staff division. Bodies such as a staff division can ensure that the strategic planning is given explicit attention and that the services of specialists can be enlisted. Bodies such as the committee ensure the contributions of those line officials who are being confronted with reality, whilst the ultimate decisions can be taken by management (not by staff). There remains the question of whether the process is not after all of too exclusive a nature; for one thing, because of the substantial influence of the staff officials and for another because of the limited number of executive officials involved. Incidentally top management cannot altogether delegate the process to a committee, top management itself will also have to be given a considerable say in the decision-making process. The publication *Management van Morgen*[7] deals at length with the question of the formulation, on different levels, of 'objectives,' stating that this concept of determining objectives could contribute to a better functioning of organizations and increase both motivation and involvement of the organization members. This concept implies that first of all the highest level objectives are formulated, thus in fact indicating the marginal conditions for the formulation of lower level objectives. In this way a line of objectives is created, enabling all such acts as are performed to be tested within the context of the objective formulation in question. When formulating the objectives there is, at each level, a cycle of preparatory, executive and controlling actions.

If this concept is applied to the organizational structure, this results in the following picture (see Figure 2), which enables one to indicate, for each individual organization, the line circles one distinguishes. By a line circle in this context is understood the combination of functions, which collectively, formulates objectives

for particular levels. If this structure is to work, a number of conditions should be met. A solution must be found to the reconciliation and the through-put at the various levels of the objectives formulated and the testing thereof. For the process to be kept manageable, the number of objective lines to be controlled, and therefore the number of line circles, in an organization are to be limited. In this way a need is created to flatten off organizations, that is to say a tendency for the number of line levels to be reduced. The need for the number of line levels to be restricted is also reflected in the following diagram (Figure 3).[8] In order not to have organizations lose themselves in too many consultative committees, too much bureaucracy and too little decision making, it is a prerequisite for the number of levels to be reduced.

Participation in Decision Making Regarding Strategic Planning

The question of who are to have a say in the decisions taken within the strategic planning will now be considered. In our opinion this in the first instance depends on the management policy pursued by top management. The top management that, in its decision making, shows a substantial degree of autocracy is likely to be less inclined to allow organization members, except for perhaps some experts and—in some cases—representative consultation participants, to participate in the process of strategic planning. Talking about participation in strategic planning, we should distinguish between the *degree* of participation on the one hand, and the *direction* the development of the participation currently takes on the other. Figure 4 shows that there are two developments: a tendency towards a greater say in matters of decision making (from being informed to jointly determining—jointly deciding) and a development

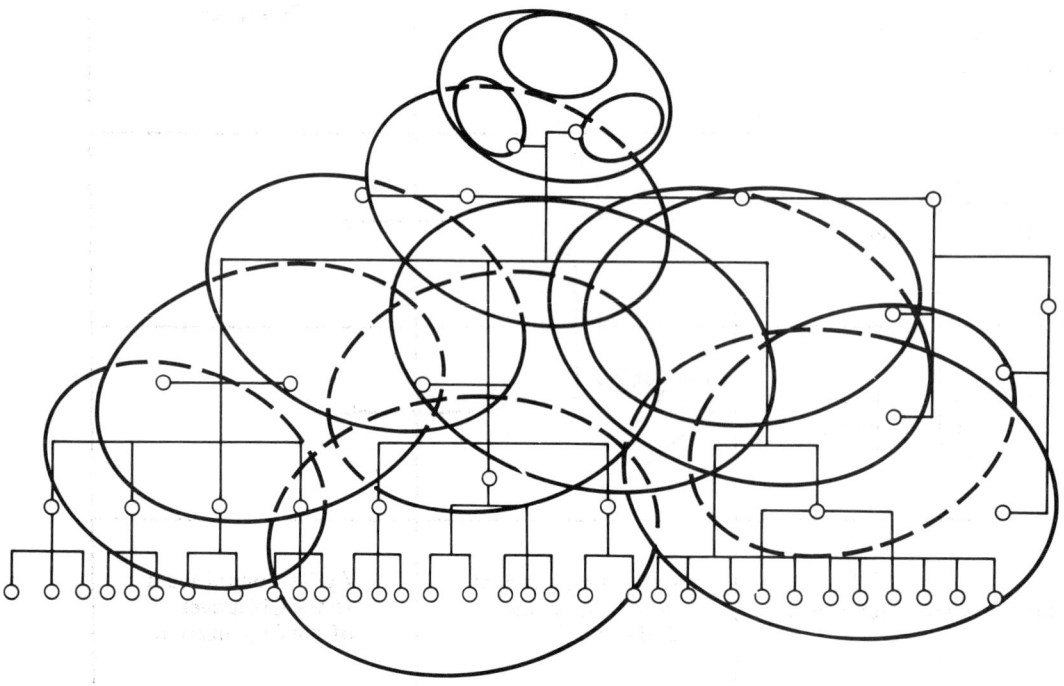

Figure 2. Line of objectives (reconciliation between the steering cycles at and in between the various levels within the context of the objectives formulated and those to be adjusted)

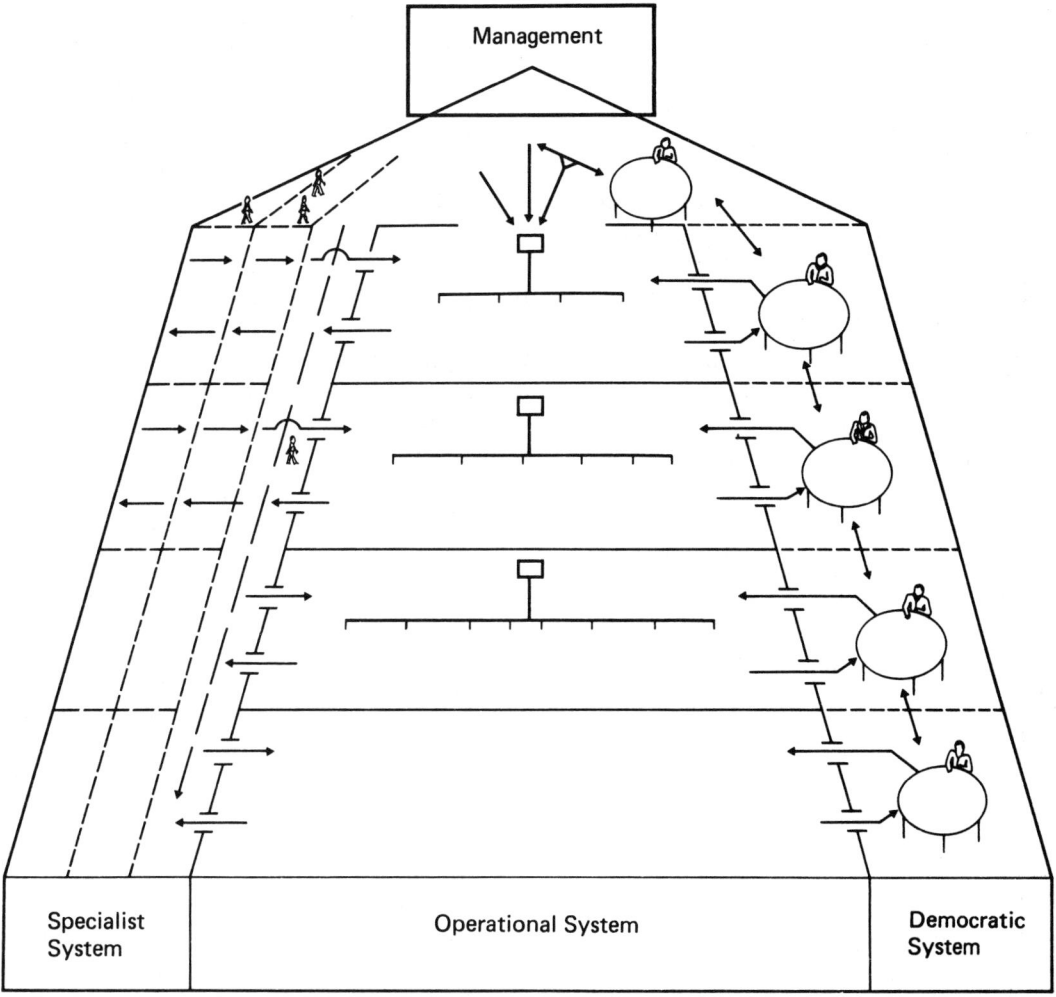

Figure 3. Systems for specialist and representative consultation participants in the organization in relation to the operational system

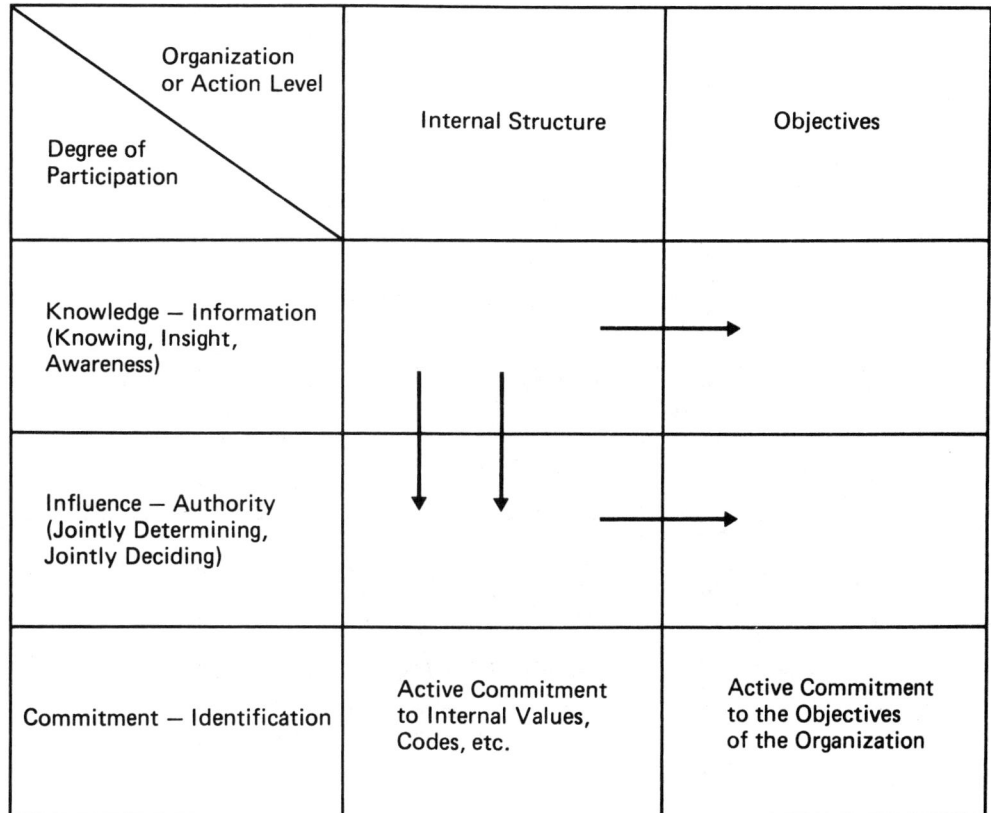

Organization or Action Level Degree of Participation	Internal Structure	Objectives
Knowledge — Information (Knowing, Insight, Awareness)		
Influence — Authority (Jointly Determining, Jointly Deciding)		
Commitment — Identification	Active Commitment to Internal Values, Codes, etc.	Active Commitment to the Objectives of the Organization

Figure 4. Development of participation at decision making levels in organizations

to the effect that participation should to a greater extent be aimed at the issues of the objectives of the organization.

Cauwenbergh[9] works out in further detail the participation in strategic decision making of particularly the various management levels. To do so he avails himself of the division of management into top management (the highest line level within the organization), middle management (heads of large functional divisions, of specialist divisions, of product groups or of sizeable geographical groups) and lower management (such as product manager's, works manager's, divisional head's levels). He gives the following representation of the differences in the contributions of each of these management levels: (Figure 5)

In the first phase—the formulation of the strategy—top management no more than outlines the policy, the actual substance being provided by lower management on the basis of more direct, daily experiences of marketing, environmental or technical developments. Middle management mainly takes care of the co-ordination and the reconciliation between the 'main lines', the 'facts' and the specific proposals. The second phase—the activation of the strategy—is mainly a political phase, namely convincing middle management of the ideas, the proposals and the elaborations submitted by lower management. In the third phase—the organizational strategy—such provisions are made by top management as to make it possible for the strategies chosen to be implemented. After the proposals have been adopted by top management, top management and middle management will take the steering of the plans to be implemented by lower management upon themselves. The development outlined above of increasing participation in decision making affects the organizational handling of the strategic planning process. It is obvious that a higher degree of participation, both on the internal

structure and on the objectives levels, calls for structures other than the current ones and for further participants besides management. If we set out some forms on a line, the development to be anticipated can be represented as follows (whereby we would note that the groups or committees—viewed from left to right—complement rather than eliminate each other).

Strategic Planning in Practice

We would first of all like to dwell on the position of strategic planning in practice by means of some empirical investigations of the situation in the Netherlands, as well as being based on the description of a case from practice with substantial participation. We shall consider in detail some findings from these investigations, dealing with the aspect of the extent to which the various groups participate in this process.

Participation in the process of strategic planning depended on whether or not this process was explicit. Derkinderen[10] and others found that companies with an explicit process considered themselves fortunate that this could occur in a non-polarized environment and organization. Some companies would even return to an implicit process, if polarization set in. Some levels and sections, however, should always be included in the process. Besides the management and managing board these were the divisional managers, the employees' council and the planning staff.

The managing style of (top) management and whether or not it met the views held within the organization, was another important factor. The participation of the representative consultation (RC) in the strategic planning can be seen from the results of the enquiry conducted by Hövels and Nas,[11] which showed that 40 per cent of the employees' councils (EC) examined and 86 per

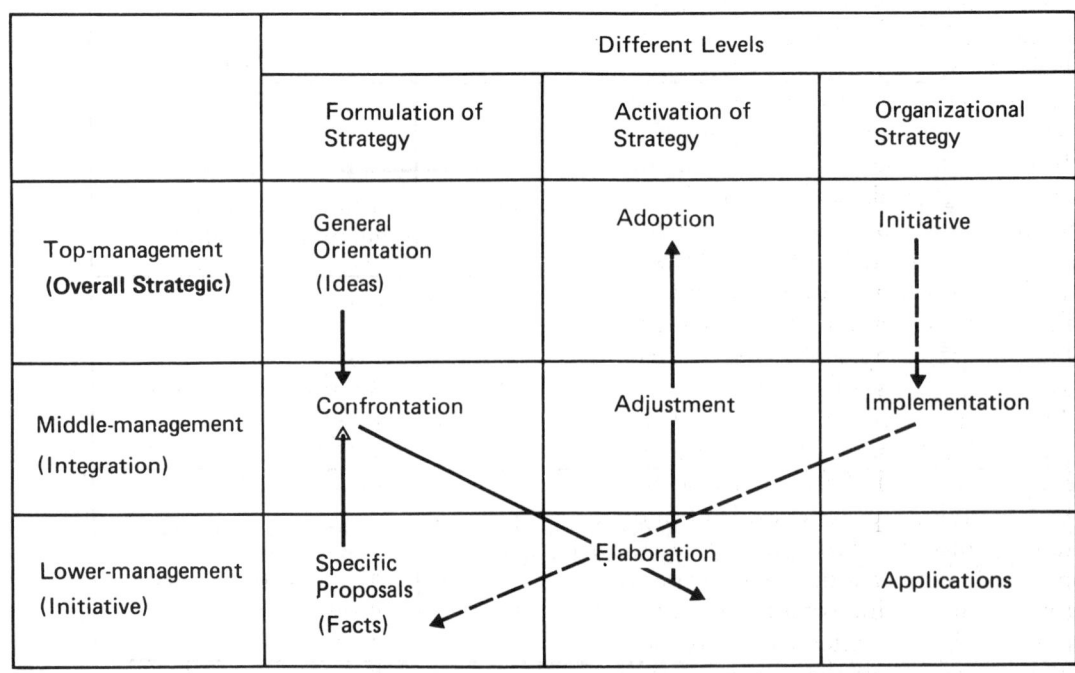

	Different Levels		
	Formulation of Strategy	Activation of Strategy	Organizational Strategy
Top-management (Overall Strategic)	General Orientation (Ideas)	Adoption	Initiative
Middle-management (Integration)	Confrontation	Adjustment	Implementation
Lower-management (Initiative)	Specific Proposals (Facts)	Elaboration	Applications

Figure 5. Contribution of each management level in the different strategy levels

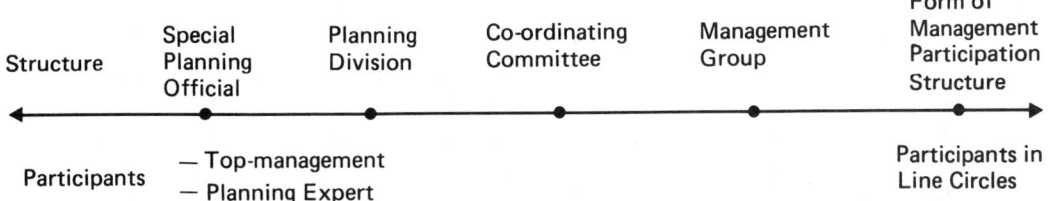

Figure 6. Structure and participants when shifting scope and level of the participation

cent of the Central Employees' Councils (CEC), when meeting, mainly discussed the 'subjects on which their policies centre' mentioned by them, that is to say subjects or fields holding many strategic points for the corporate policy, such as the internal structure and the economic policy, whereby the relative power within the company and between the company and its environment were brought up as well as the internal distribution of means.

Three forms of RC participation were found to occur:

☆ (C)ECs who dealt with strategic issues, however not in the planning phase but in the implementing phase.

☆ (C)ECs who mainly discussed issues which were in an early phase of management planning, that is to say they also discussed 'plans' (50 per cent of the CECs coming within this category).

☆ the (C)ECs who discussed subjects on which their policies centred and more relevant to the EC. However, they waited for management to broach specific subjects. Probably due to their inactivity they did not consider the point of whether there were any further problems within this sphere that should be brought up for discussion.

The following can be stated regarding the opportunities for EC participation: in 34 out of 100 cases the demands put forward by the chosen EC members went beyond the chairman's, especially in the strategic matters of policy and management and internal organization. In 51 out of 100 cases the demands of the members chosen kept pace with the chairman's and in 15 out of 100 cases the members did not push their demands as far. The members chosen themselves believed that they had a greater say in results in the less strategic matters. For the near future the alteration of the Act on the Employees' Councils create openings for the RC to have a greater say in the process of strategic planning in organizations. In the first place, this concerns the ECs power to advise on major decisions of a strategic nature, such as transferring the control of the enterprise or part of it, taking over or giving up the control of another enterprise, entering into or discontinuing a long-standing co-operation with another enterprise, discontinuing activities or an important part of such activities. This power is also extended to reduction, expansion or other alterations of the company's activities, including the related investments, and to major

changes in the company's organization. The new element is that it is no longer possible for the corporate management to use the argument of weighty company interests. Furthermore, the EC can assert its right of appeal in the event of disagreement.

The authors of this article will here consider an advanced form of participation, which was found in a large non-profit making institution in the Netherlands. This institution introduced a new organizational structure aimed at raising the participation level and re-directing participation, a clear distinction being made between policy planning and implementing systems. The policy planning system comprises a number of steering groups on which officials chosen from divisions are represented. Staff bodies and divisions form part of the implementing system. Management acts as an intermediary between the steering groups and further organization staff. This may be represented—in a stylised form—by Figure 7:

Management, although not represented on the steering groups, does in fact submit thoughts and views to these groups, for consideration. It is management which takes the decisions regarding the policies proposed and drafted by the steering groups. The staff bodies' specific duty is to advise on and to test the process of organization control. This is effected within the policy proposals accepted by management. It is especially the procedures connected with the implementation of policy proposals on which advice is given. Management is reported to by a number of management teams representing as many divisions. These divisions have been set up, applying the chief criterion of 'the primary process character'. Within each division various groups (of an interdisciplinary composition) operate headed by a chairman. Management is mainly accountable for the decisions taken.

In relation to the forms, earlier described, in which strategic planning is arranged organizationally, the participation of the various groups of employees permitted by this structure is larger than the participation permitted by staff, committee or policy group structures. A 5-year experience of this structure, when evaluated, raises questions. There are fewer candidates for participation in the steering groups and few people have themselves put forward for nomination. Supplementation by the supporting group seems at least questionable. The influence of the divisions is increasing.

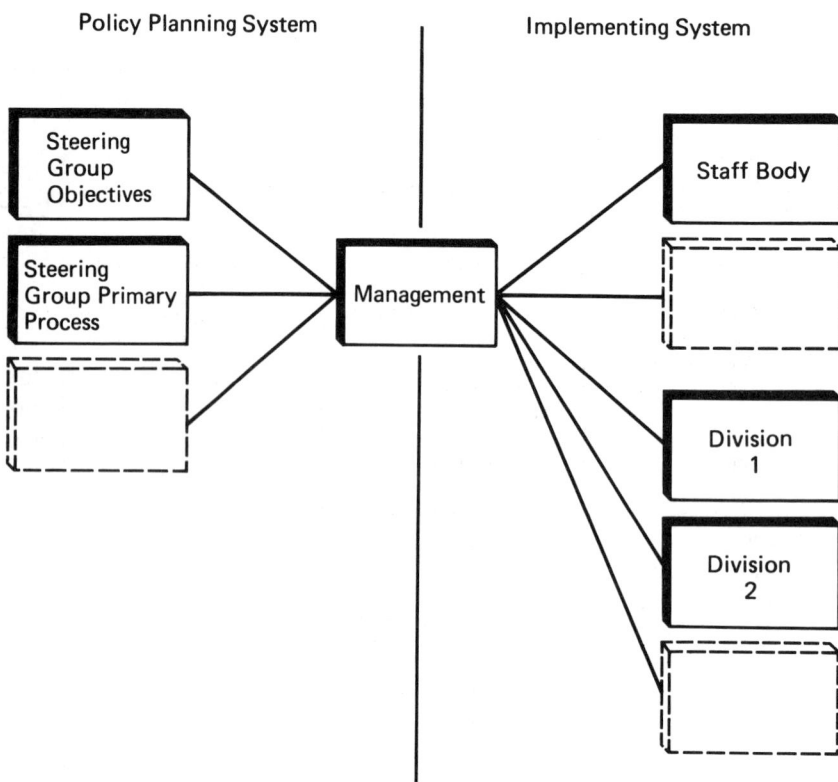

Policy Planning System   Implementing System

Figure 7. A form of participation

The time lost between policy plan and plan of action is sometimes as much as some years, thus only few are motivated to continue making an active contribution to the steady development. Furthermore, views have changed somewhat as to the concept of doing 'everything jointly'. Recently, management has begun to designate in the management teams 'persons bearing ultimate responsibility'. This is at variance with the original concept of participation. Now the chief question is whether there is, in fact, such need for participation in strategic planning. In this connection it would be interesting to investigate what the influence is of the representative consultation, since, if participation is structured into the regular organization satisfactorily, the Employees' Council's role in the process of strategic management planning can be justly expected to change drastically.

A Framework for the Organizational Arrangement of the Strategic Planning

From the foregoing it has become apparent that generally only a limited number of persons or groups are involved in the strategic planning of organizations. Usually, this includes (part of) the top management and—especially—a number of specialists. The degree of the representative consultation's participation in this process depends, *inter alia*, on how the (C)EC functions within the organization (actively or not). It has also become clear that, for strategic planning to produce

results, in our opinion more officials of the various levels and divisions of the organization should be involved. All the employees should have an insight into how the process develops and when and how members of the organization can make a contribution. It is only this that contributes to the process being 'borne' by the organization and to parties being aware, when taking operational decisions, of the strategic principles then applicable. Now the question is how this can be realized or—in other words—what the organizational arrangement of the strategic planning will then be like. From the foregoing it will be clear that it is not possible for a 'standard' organizational arrangement to be given for this. It is, however, possible for a framework to be outlined of steps to be taken. However, these steps are different for each situation. In this way, unique arrangements are created for each individual enterprise. In our opinion, the following steps will subsequently have to be passed through for an adequate organizational arrangement to be reached.

Step A: Letter of Intent
An organization's top management will have to commit itself as to the value attributed by them to the strategic planning process and as to how they expect to recognize the external and internal developments and integrate them into the strategic plans. It should, *inter alia*, be made clear whether

(1) the objectives of the organization and the respective divisions (line circles) are up for discussion; and

(2) creativity and inventiveness at different levels within the organization are honoured.

Phase	Long-Range	Medium-Range		Short-Range
Plans	Strategic Plans	Structural Plans	Operational Plans	Plans of Action
Objects	— Environmental Investigation (Destep) — Internal (Strength/Weakness) Investigation — Development of Possible Strategies In Order to Meet Long-range Objectives; Aspects: · Economic · Financial · Social · Organizational · Technical	Choice from the Alternative Strategies, Elaboration and Refining, Aspects: — Transfer of Authority — Takeover or Disposal of Part of the Company — Termination of Activities — Substantial Reduction, Expansion or Other Changes — Major Investments — Important Changes in the Organization — Changes in the Location Where the Company Carries on its Activities — Group Recruitment or Borrowing of Labour	Preparation of Operational Plans, Aspects: — Budget · Marketing/Sales Plan · Production Plan · Investment Plan · Staff Plan	Preparation of Plans of Action per Function/Discipline Example Plans of Action for Social Function: — Pension, Profit Sharing and Savings Schemes — Working Hours or Holiday Arrangement — Arrangements in the Fields of Security, Health or Hygiene — Arrangements in the Fields of Appointment, Dismissal or Promotion Policies — Training Arrangement — Arrangement in the Field of Staff Evaluation — Company Social Welfare — Arrangement in the Field of Work Consultation — Arrangement in the Field of Handling Complaints
Participation of the Representative Consultation	— Regular Consultation and Reporting to (C) EC	— Formal Consultation Required; and (C) EC Gives Advice	— Budget to be Submitted to (C) EC Prior to Adoption; to be Discussed During a Meeting with (C) EC at Such a Time that it is Possible for this Discussion to Affect the Contents of that Budget Materially — After Publication 1st Half of the Financial Year Soonest Possible General Data Regarding the Company's Results for this Period to be Furnished and to be Discussed in the (C) EC Meeting	— (C) EC has Formal Approval Authority — At Least Once a Year to be Reported to the Employee's Council on the Policies (to be) Adopted

At Least Twice a Year to be Reported to the (C) EC:
— Plans and Expectations regarding the Activities (Strategic Plans)
— The Company's Results, Particularly
· the Investments
· "Structural Plans"

Figure 8. The influence of the employees' council on the process of strategic planning

The attitude of the top management determines the effect of strategic planning on the organization and as such is indicative of the interest and motivation of other organization members.

Step B: Identification of Participants
The various participant groups in the organization will have to be clearly defined and made visible in advance, such as through a structure of line circles, it thereby having to be indicated *when* they can make *what* specific contributions.

As groups could be mentioned bodies such as: the top management, the specialists, the staff divisions, management other than top management, the representative consultation and the primary divisions. Each group could exercise its influence in one or more ways, such as by:

(1) taking initiatives,

(2) making an actual contribution,

(3) taking part in the decision making,

(4) taking decisions and bearing responsibility, and

(5) checking the implementation.

For each phase in the process of strategic planning the contribution(s) will have to be determined per group. To illustrate the foregoing, Figure 8 indicates what could be the influence of the representative consultation—and particularly the Employees' Council. It is necessary for each participant group in this process to be included in such a survey!

Step C: Participants' Perception
Employees of the organization—including representative consultation members—are given the opportunity to acquire a knowledge of and an insight into the theory and practice of strategic planning. This may require specific instruction and training. Within the organization not only should there be some agreement as to aim and utility of strategic planning, but also on the way in which this concept is given substance.

Step D: Participation in the Process of Strategic Planning
During the actual process, tensions may build up as a result of opposing interests between groups within the organization, or deficient information and communication. The strategic and structural plans can become widely divergent from the operational plans and actions. However, it is advisable to avoid any such divergence. The tension field between conceptual strategic thinking on the one hand and operational-implementative thinking on the other, is here called the participative strategic tension field (pstf), see Figure 9.

In this diagram the participant groups distinguished per phase—by means of a participants' chart—are to be represented diagrammatically, eliminating possible line links as being irrelevant. We are in favour of such a chart being drawn up per organization. How can the pstf now be prevented from leading too much to disfunctional effects for the organization? For this to

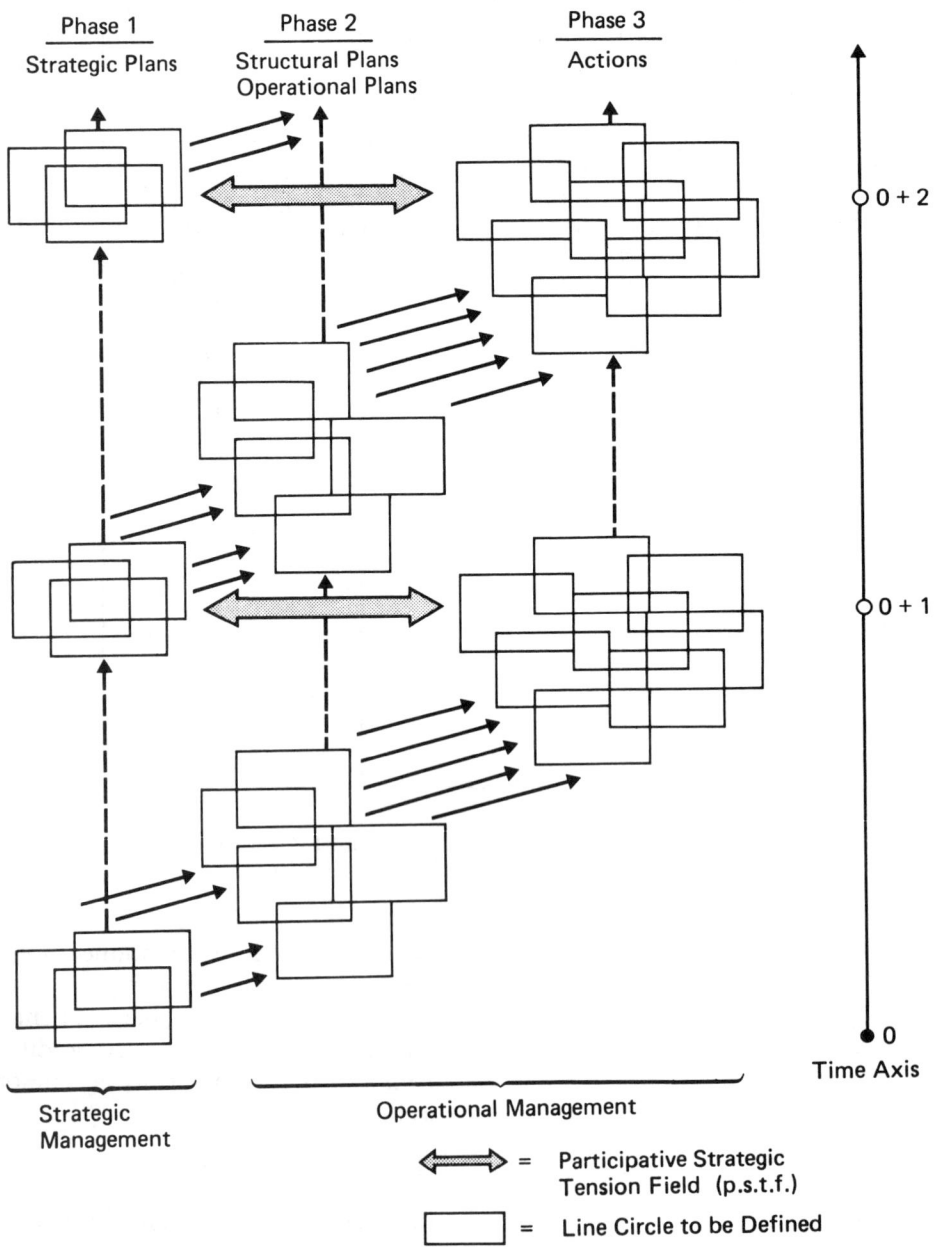

Figure 9. Participants' chart strategic planning

be achieved, the following measure must be taken:

(a) the number of those directly involved must be reduced;

(b) the structure of the organization must be simplified ('flattened off') and

(c) the autonomy of the various line circles must be better defined.

Permitting many to exercise a direct influence on the process of strategic planning on the one hand has a positive(?) effect on the quality and the acceptance of the strategic decisions, but, on the other, causes alertness to be reduced. The number of levels within an organization also strongly determines the complexity of the process. As has already been indicated before in Figure 3, consultative bodies, staff groups and managers operate at each line level. The 'flattened' organization scheme can largely reduce the sources of tension.

The keeping in balance of participation and alertness will be increasingly important to management. The, in this connection specific, challenge is for the strategic planning to be embedded in the organization in such a way as to maintain flexibility and alertness and ensure its controlability and manageability. The framework presented above for the organizational arrangement of the strategic planning may possibly contribute to this.

Acknowledgement—A version of this article was originally published in Dutch in *Maandblad voor Accountancy en Bedrijfsadministratie*, Haarlem, Holland.

References

(1) H. I. Ansoff, R. P. Declerck and R. L. Hayes, From strategic planning to strategic management, John Wiley (1976).

(2) C. E. Lindblom, The science of muddling through, *Business Strategy* (1969).

(3) H. Mintzberg, The nature of managerial work, Harper and Row, London (1973).

(4) H. I. Ansoff, *Corporate Strategy*, McGraw Hill, New York (1965).

(5) H. I. Ansoff, Third generation management and consultancy, lecture, Rotterdam, December (1973).

(6) P. Verburg, De organisatie van de groei, *Besturen en beslissingen*, Kosmos, Amsterdam-Antwerp; undated.

(7) H. Kloeze, A. Molenkamp, F. J. W. Roelofs *et al., Management van Morgen*, Stenfert Kroese, Leiden (1976).

(8) Feaco: The European Federation of Management Consultants Organizations. Professional Conference: *Management for Tomorrow*, Brussels (1977).

(9) A. van Cauwenbergh, *Strategen Buiten Spel?*, TED, August (1976).

(10) F. G. J. Derkinderen and K. de Jong, Besef voor ondernemingsplanning: bevindingen uit Westeuropees praktijkonderzoek, Bedrijfskunde, Volume 48, No. 3 (1976/3).

(11) B. W. M. Hövels and P. Nas, Ondernemingsraden en medezeggenschap, Instituut voor toegepaste sociologie, Nijmegen (1976).

How Planning Works in Practice—
A Survey of 48 U.K. Companies

Dr. Shawki Al-Bazzaz, Kingston Regional Management Centre and Peter M. Grinyer, University of St. Andrews

This paper reports the findings of one of the authors, Al-Bazzaz, on contributions and difficulties perceived in 1974 by corporate planners in 48 large U.K. companies as one aspect of a considerably wider study of the process of corporate planning and its relationship to situational factors. These findings are compared with the results of other studies of the subject and the study is extended to a further analysis of relationships between the planning process and the characteristics of the company and the extent of contributions and difficulties perceived.

Surveys at the turn of the decade, suggested that adoption of corporate planning in the United Kingdom, West Germany and France was later than in the U.S.A.[1-6] Moreover, corporate planning was in no country as sophisticated and 'advanced' as one would imagine from the literature. Subsequent surveys concentrated on the pay off, contributions, pitfalls and problems encountered.[7-13] Within the U.K., verbatim accounts of problems and benefits of corporate planning were given by both Hewkins and Kempner[1] and Irving,[14] although they gave only examples and no quantitative indication of relative importance.

The Companies Surveyed

Companies in the sample were drawn from two sources. First, 11 companies represented on the Organization Study Group of the Long Range Planning Society in London collaborated. Second, 37 companies were drawn at random from those with head offices located in the South East of England and listed in the European Directory of Economic & Corporate Planning (1974). Checks to determine if there were significant differences between these two sub-samples suggested none, and all 48 companies were, therefore, grouped into one main sample.

The frames from which the samples were drawn inevitably influenced the characteristics of the companies in the survey. By design, only companies with an active involvement in strategic planning were included. The companies were large (see Table 1), from 19 industries

Table 1. Characteristics of the sample

(1) Industries included : Chemicals, building and construction, food and beverage, data processing, banking, transportation, petroleum, printing and publishing, insurance, gaseous products, steel, tobacco, automotive accessories, paints, engineering, unrelated activities	

(2) Size:	Variable	Range	Mid point of median category
	Sales (annual)	£5m to over £2000m	£150m
	Net capital employed	£1m to over £2000m	£150m
	Net profit before tax	under £1m to £500m	£12·5m
	Wages (annual)	under £1m to £500m	£17·5m
	No. employees	under 1000 (two companies) to over 300,000	£7500m
	No. of sites	1 to over 2000	15

(3) Dispersion of sites

Per cent with all of 3 most important sites in U.K.	54·2
Per cent with at least 1 of 3 most important sites in U.K.	64·6
Per cent with all of 3 most important sites overseas	35·4

(4) Hierarchical status of company

Status	Per cent of sample
Parent (including 3 nationalized industries representing 6·3 per cent of the total sample)	56·25
Division	20·8
Subsidiary	22·9

(5) Charter

	Per cent of sample
Service company only	25·0
Manufacturing company only	43·1
Manufacturing with service operations	31·9

(6) Organizational structure

	Per cent of sample
Functional	39·6
Divisional product	31·3
Divisional geographic	8·4
Divisional geographic and product	20·7

*S. Al-Bazzaz is at the Kingston Regional Management Centre.
†P. H. Grinyer, Professor of Economics at the University of St. Andrews, St. Andrews, Scotland KY16 9AL.

including both service and manufacturing, had their major plants or operations, on the whole, concentrated in the United Kingdom, but with a large minority operating major plants overseas, ranged from functional to highly divisionalized structures, and from marketing predominantly a single product line to highly diversified undertakings.

Problems of Operationalization

The questions dealing with difficulties and contributions were open-ended to allow full expression by the interviewees. Answers were then classified and tabulated. By this means tables of seven main types of contributions, six types of difficulties, seven types of required changes and nine types of planners' responsibilities were compiled. The subjective nature of the process was recognized and other data collected were used to check the resulting classification.

Functions of Corporate Planners

Over 80 per cent of the respondents identified no more than four areas of responsibilities and no more than 8 per cent more than four. The responsibilities cited are shown in Table 2. Apart from the 46 per cent of companies in which corporate planners perceived themselves as giving advice and making proposals and the 29 per cent

in which special projects were undertaken, the emphasis was on the design and operation of the planning process, including forecasting, evaluation, communicating and collating information and control.

As may be seen from Table 3, the perceived responsibilities of corporate planners varied between the hierarchical level of the organization they served, those in parent companies tending to have more wide-ranging functions than those in subsidiaries. Corporate planners in the former tended to have the responsibilities to propose and advise, provide information and report, analyse and evaluate, collate, co-ordinate and control with significantly greater frequency. However, differences relating to special projects, assumptions and forecasts and the development of planning were not significant. These results are consistent, with Lorange and Vancil's[15] suggestion that, in large companies, one of the main planning tasks is co-ordination of the plans, but there are clearly other responsibilities of equal significance.

The responsibility for actually writing the plans covering the various areas of business activity rested with line management in 85·4 per cent of companies and with the corporate planning function in only 14·6 per cent, a difference so large that there was a probability of less than 1 in 1000 that it was due to the chance of sample selection alone. Our findings confirmed, then, those of Hewkins and Kempner[1] and of Taylor and Irving[5] on the planner's role and the responsibility of operational management in the planning exercise.

Table 2. Extent of prevalence of each type of responsibility

Type	Percentage
1—Design and administration of plans and initiation of planning process	58
2—Proposals, advice and recommendations	46
3—Analysis and evaluation	44
4—Collation and co-ordination of plans	38
5—Monitoring and control	35
6—Ad hoc work and special projects	29
7—Information, data, reporting and communication	27
8—Assumptions and forecasting	23
9—Development of planning concepts and function training	17

Contribution of Corporate Planning Systems

Contributions claimed by corporate planners interviewed were analysed into seven categories.

Some 83 per cent of the sample quoted contributions from four or less categories. None thought that improvements were made in all the seven. Table 4 shows the contributions and their relative frequencies. Under each head, but particularly in the area of profit and growth, the strength of the contribution thought to have been made inevitably varied, but the open ended answers

Table 3

Corporate planners responsibility category	No.	Parent Percentage	No.	Subsidiary Percentage	Significance of difference
Propose and advise	15	55	4	36	Highly significant
Analysis and evaluation	12	44	4	36	Significant
Collation and co-ordination	12	44	4	36	Significant
Special projects	8	29	4	36	Not significant
Information and reporting	7	25	1	9	Highly significant
Assumptions and forecasts	6	22	2	18	Not significant
Control	11	40	3	27	Significant
Development of planning	4	14	1	9	Not significant

Significance levels:
'Highly significant' denotes a probability of less than 1 in 100 that the difference could have occurred by chance.
'Significant' denotes a probability of less than 5 in 100 that the difference could have occurred by chance.
'Not significant' denotes a probability of more than 5 in 100 that the difference could have occurred by chance.

Table 4. Extent of mention of each type of contribution

	Per cent of respondents
Perceived improvement in:	
Type	
1—Awareness of problems, strengths and weaknesses	85·4
2—Profits and growth	47·9
3—Information and communication	39·6
4—Systematic resource allocation	35·4
5—Co-ordination and control	29·2
6—Morale and industrial relations	16·7
7—Quantification	4·2

Table 5. Types of difficulties in formal corporate planning systems

Type	Per cent of respondents
1—Departmental interface	41·7
2—Data and communications	33·3
3—'Culture'	29·2
4—Forecasting	27·1
5—Time and timeliness	16·7
6—Top management attitudes	12·5

obtained did not permit its measurement. This is clear from the examples of verbatim answers.

(i) Yes, I am convinced of it (contribution). If we did not have plans, we would not be nearly as profitable as we are and would never achieve objectives. . . . without planning, we would be lost. I think it most certainly contributes to profits.

(ii) I do really believe it has improved our financial position, that is, the company moved from loss three years ago to profit for the last two years.

(iii) I think it has contributed to profits but I can't quantify it. For example, planning led to raw material substitution to get profit improvement through cost reduction.

(iv) I would like to think that it contributed to profits, growth, etc., but I cannot quantify.

The order of contributions in Table 4 is very similar to that found by Greiner et al.[16,7] However, improvements in information and communication were seen to be more important in the U.S. study. In addition, no direct mention was made of profits or growth in the Harvard study, although 56 per cent of Greiner et al.'s respondents said planning had a 'High Impact on Operating Performance'. Given the difference in methodology, and the precise categories of contributions used, however, the findings of the two studies are perhaps surprisingly consistent. For instance our results provide support for Greiner et al.'s statement that formal planning makes 'educational' and analytical contributions by 'helping managers to discipline their thinking, achieve a clearer focus on specific goals . . .'. This role of planning was further illustrated by the fact that within the virtually 50 per cent of companies with such documents, planning manuals were used not only to provide an extensive description of the planning system, but also to develop a wider understanding of the role of corporate planning and its underlying concepts.

Difficulties in Planning Systems

All the interviewees had encountered major difficulties but only 19 per cent more than two. The most frequently mentioned difficulties were related to the interface with line departments. Table 5 shows that this was alluded to by two in every five corporate planners. Some thought

the difficulty inevitable because of their staff or advisory role. Others thought it resulted from insufficiently clear lines of authority and responsibility. One third of planners experienced difficulties with respect to data collection and communication, complaining of inability to obtain necessary information, uncertainty of its delivery and unreliability on the one hand and excessive quantification by technically-qualified staff on the other. Difficulties in obtaining information were inevitably linked with general attitudes to corporate planning, and style of management, within a number of companies, i.e. to the 'culture' of the company. This was unfavourable to corporate planning in nearly a third of the companies. No doubt the proportion would have been much higher if companies without corporate planning had been included in the sample. This resistance and, possibly, misunderstanding of corporate planning may have stemmed, in part, from its potential threat to existing vested interests. It was encouraging, however, that only one in eight corporate planners thought that lack of trust of new techniques and other attitudes of top management impeded planning. Resistance to corporate planning was obviously concentrated below the chief executive.

Difficulties in forecasting were mentioned by 13 respondents. Unpredictability of government policy and of public expenditure where companies were major suppliers to the state were given as causes. In general, it was suggested that the pace and number of sources of change in the environment were increasing, making long range prediction more difficult and less valuable and, perhaps, requiring bigger and faster systems to evaluate the possible effects of an event. There were indications, therefore, of increased environmental turbulence. Forecasting and planning problems in general were compounded by use of different time scales within sub-units of the company within a number of companies. In others necessary data were not available at early enough times to permit orderly forecasting and evaluation.

Weaknesses of Planning Systems

Forty-four per cent of the respondents expressed satisfaction with their planning system. Some saw no reason to change a system they had designed themselves. Others believed that evolutionary change was occurring anyway and, therefore, no interference was necessary. A third group suggested that it was too early in the system's development to suggest change.

In contrast, over half the respondents thought improvement necessary. The changes thought to be required were not the same in number or in kind. One third of the total sample, and three-quarters of those desiring change, thought that only one weakness needed removal but a further ninth gave two. The required changes mentioned are tabulated in Table 6. Perhaps predictably,

Table 6. Types of changes required in formal corporate planning systems

	Percentage of respondents
More formality	12·5
More quantification and details	12·5
More co-ordination and control	12·5
Changed attitudes and more influence for planning	12·5
Need more time	8·3
Less formality and less sophisticated systems	6·3

the majority of respondents wanting change wished to have greater formality, documentation, co-ordination or control. Others reflected the problems already identified, and quoted by early researchers too, by calling for a change in attitudes towards planning within their companies. Only 8 per cent of the respondents wanted more time, however. A small minority of planners, even as early as 1974, had perceived that their systems had become too formal. The fact that the percentage was as low as 6·3 no doubt reflected the relatively short lives of many of the corporate planning systems, for Lorange and Vancil[17] detected that formality of planning was tightened in the early years of a system, became less necessary once the discipline of planning was widely accepted by line management, and was then reduced as it appeared increasingly burdensome and unnecessary. Among our sample, too, the cry for greater informality was from companies with a longer experience of corporate planning.

In general, the results on difficulties and required changes, which also indicate areas of dissatisfaction, are largely consistent with those of Vancil, Ringbakk, Steiner and Schollhammer,[10,12,18] all of whom suggested that top management's support is critically important, that line management involvement in planning is essential, but that a lack of sympathy and understanding of planning concepts militates against these conditions in many companies.

Interrelationships Between Responsibilities, Contributions, Difficulties and Changes Required

Statistical analysis showed that the numbers of responsibilities, contributions, and difficulties perceived by corporate planners in the 48 companies were significantly, positively correlated, i.e. vary together. Similarly, the number of changes required in the planning system and difficulties encountered were positively correlated, as might have been expected.

There are a number of possible explanations. The correlations may reflect real associations between the numbers of responsibilities, contributions, difficulties, and required changes. However, because the questions were open-ended the apparent relationships may merely reflect the fact that some respondents were more articulate than others, giving a fuller account of just every aspect.

One way of seeking to determine whether the correlations reflect more than differences in loquacity of the interviewees was to examine relationships between individual responsibilities, contributions, difficulties, and required changes and total numbers cited in the other categories. Not only is it inherently interesting to know, for instance, the tasks associated with a greater number of perceived difficulties, any relationships found can be examined to determine whether they are reasonable. If found to be so, the case for suggesting that the positive correlations between numbers of responsibilities, contributions and difficulties, for instance, reflect real associations is greatly improved.

To this end, statistical analysis was undertaken, results being presented in Table 7 and in Figure 1. The relationships suggested by the analysis seem to make sense. Corporate planners assuming the more active roles of proposing, advising, controlling and inducing their colleagues to accept planning concepts tended to encounter more difficulties. Where more difficulties were perceived by corporate planners some wanted more co-ordination and control, others more time, and yet a third group wished to back out of an apparently overly formal and complex system. Those who chose the first response seemed to have more responsibilities. In turn, those with more responsibilities tended to identify difficulties with forecasting, which might be resolved by more co-ordination, and management 'culture'. Somewhat paradoxically, however, it was those with fewer responsibilities who tended to both complain of lack of time and demand more time.

Relationships with the number of desired changes are also intuitively reasonable. Where corporate planners were conscious of difficulties in obtaining data in a timely manner, of having enough time to carry out their responsibilities adequately, and of obtaining good working relationships with line departments, they tended to suggest more changes in their planning process. High numbers of such changes were, in turn, associated with the tasks of co-ordination, collation, setting planning assumptions, and producing forecasts which might well generate precisely such difficulties.

Again, it was precisely where corporate planners assumed more active roles, taking the tasks of proposing and advising as well as developing planning upon themselves, that they believed their contributions to be greater. Thus the positive correlation between the numbers of difficulties and contributions, which seem to make no immediate sense, could well be due to both the problems and contributions such influence seeking corporate planners create, i.e. the apparent statistical relationship

Table 7. Correlations between individual items and total numbers of responsibilities, contributions, difficulties and changes required

Changes required	No. of responsibilities	No. of contributions	No. of difficulties	No. of required changes
(1) More formality	NS	NS	NS	0·41*
(2) More quantification and details	NS	NS	NS	0·41*
(3) More co-ordination and control	0·26*	NS	0·22†	0·33*
(4) Need time	−0·21†	NS	0·26*	0·38*
(5) Need more money	NS	NS	NS	0·24*
(6) Changed attitudes and influence	NS	NS	NS	0·27*
(7) Less formality and more simplicity	NS	0·24*	0·19†	0·30*
Responsibilities				
(8) Production of plans	0·22†	NS	NS	NS
(9) Propose and advise	0·37*	0·24*	0·22†	−0·15§
(10) Analyse and evaluate	0·49*	NS	NS	NS
(11) Collate and co-ordinate	0·29*	NS	0·14§	0·31*
(12) Special projects	0·42*	NS	−0·13§	NS
(13) Infn. and reporting	0·15§	NS	NS	NS
(14) Assumptions and forecasts	0·39*	0·13§	NS	0·31*
(15) Control	0·20‡	NS	0·23*	NS
(16) Devt. of planning	0·30*	0·23†	0·17‡	NS
Contributions to				
(17) Awareness and analysis	NS	0·19†	0·27*	0·17‡
(18) Profit and growth	NS	0·61*	0·24*	0·14§
(19) Systematic resource allocation	NS	0·46*	NS	NS
(20) Co-ordination and control	NS	0·35*	0·28*	NS
(21) Quantification	0·21†	NS	−0·16‡	NS
(22) Infn. and communication	NS	0·52*	0·19‡	0·17‡
(23) Morale and ind. relations	0·24*	0·46*	NS	NS
Difficulties of				
(24) Data and communications	NS	0·14§	0·21†	NS
(25) Culture	0·18‡	NS	0·43*	NS
(26) Deptal interface	NS	0·20‡	0·42*	0·17‡
(27) Timeliness	−0·18‡	NS	0·33*	0·24*
(28) Forecasting	0·18‡	0·31*	0·30*	NS
(29) Top mgt	NS	NS	0·14§	0·14§

*Denotes very highly statistically significant, i.e. a chance of less than 1 in 1000 of the result being due to chance alone.
†Denotes highly statistically significant, i.e. a chance of less than 1 in 100 of the results being due to chance alone.
‡Denotes statistically significant, i.e. a chance of less than 5 in 100 of the results being due to chance alone.
§Denotes strongly suggested, i.e. a chance of less than 1 in 10 of the results being due to chance alone.
NS Denotes not statistically significant.
The coefficients shown are Kendall's tau.

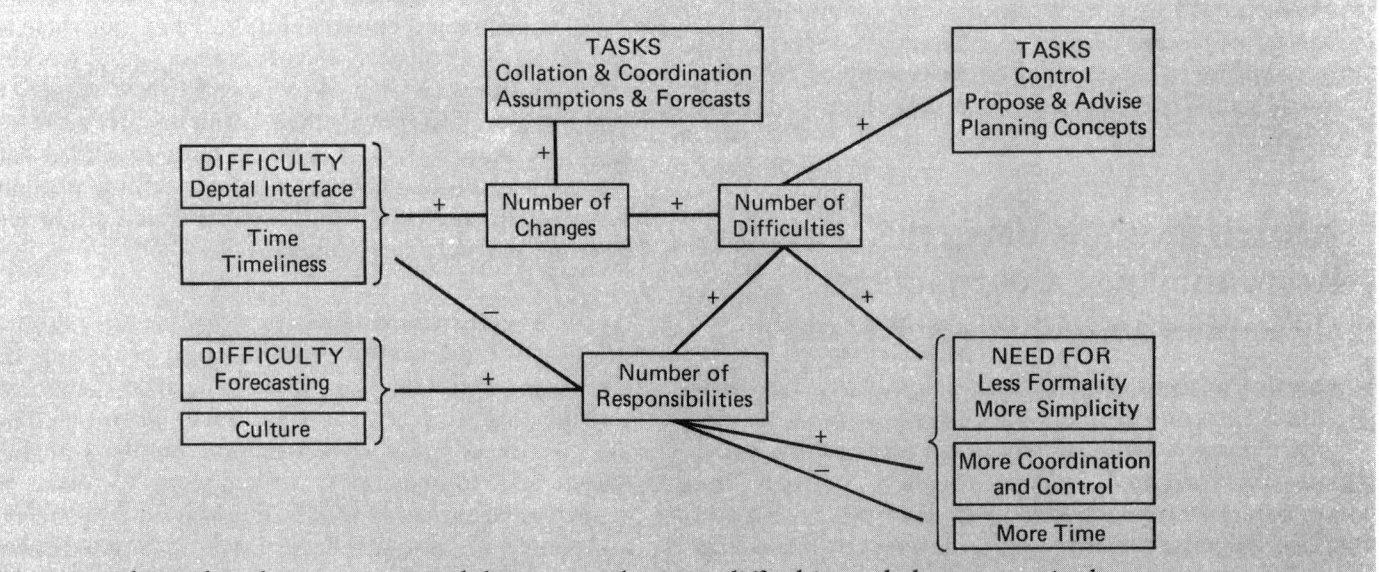

Figure 1. Relationships between responsibilities, contributions, difficulties and cheques required

between them is a reflection of a common dependence on a more active corporate planning role.

Thus the additional statistical analysis strengthens the case for believing that the relationships between total numbers of responsibilities, contributions, difficulties, and required changes reflect real associations within the companies in the sample.

Relationships with the Planning Process and its Context

Although research to which earlier reference has been made investigated benefits and pitfalls of corporate planning, there is a conspicuous absence of systematic analysis of the relationships between each of tasks, contributions, difficulties and changes required and the context of the planning process. Vancil[18] did suggest that success is heavily dependent on the formality of the company as a whole, as well as the status of the chief planner. Ringbakk, Steiner and Schollhammer[10,12] and much of the prescriptive literature have also stressed the importance of the corporate planner's reporting level. With a quite different emphasis, Thune and House[9] suggested that corporate planning pays particularly in industries with faster rates of change, but did not use measures of the rate of technological change, for instance. A thorough analysis of the relationship between percep-

tions on responsibilities, contributions, difficulties and required changes on the one hand and major characteristics of the planning system, company, technology, and its market environment on the other remains to be done. To meet this need, statistical analysis was undertaken using the data collected by Al-Bazzaz[19] and results are reported in Table 8. Full descriptions of the scales may be found in Grinyer and Al-Bazzaz[20] but for the purpose of this article they be taken as largely self-explanatory. Where this is not so their meaning is clear from the text.

Factors Influencing the Breadth of Corporate Planning Responsibilities

No causal relationships may be inferred from these correlations for the direction of causality can only be hypothesized and significant associations may be due to common dependence on other variables. None the less, by drawing on experience it is possible to suggest a causal model which would explain the statistically significant relationships. This is done in Figure 2. Detailed analysis of the design of the planning process and its context,[20] shows that the former is strongly related to the size of the company, age of the planning process, and technical inflexibility and complexity, these technical characteristics being, for instance, highly significantly linked to the number of forecasting and evaluative techniques used. It is consequently no surprise that these very

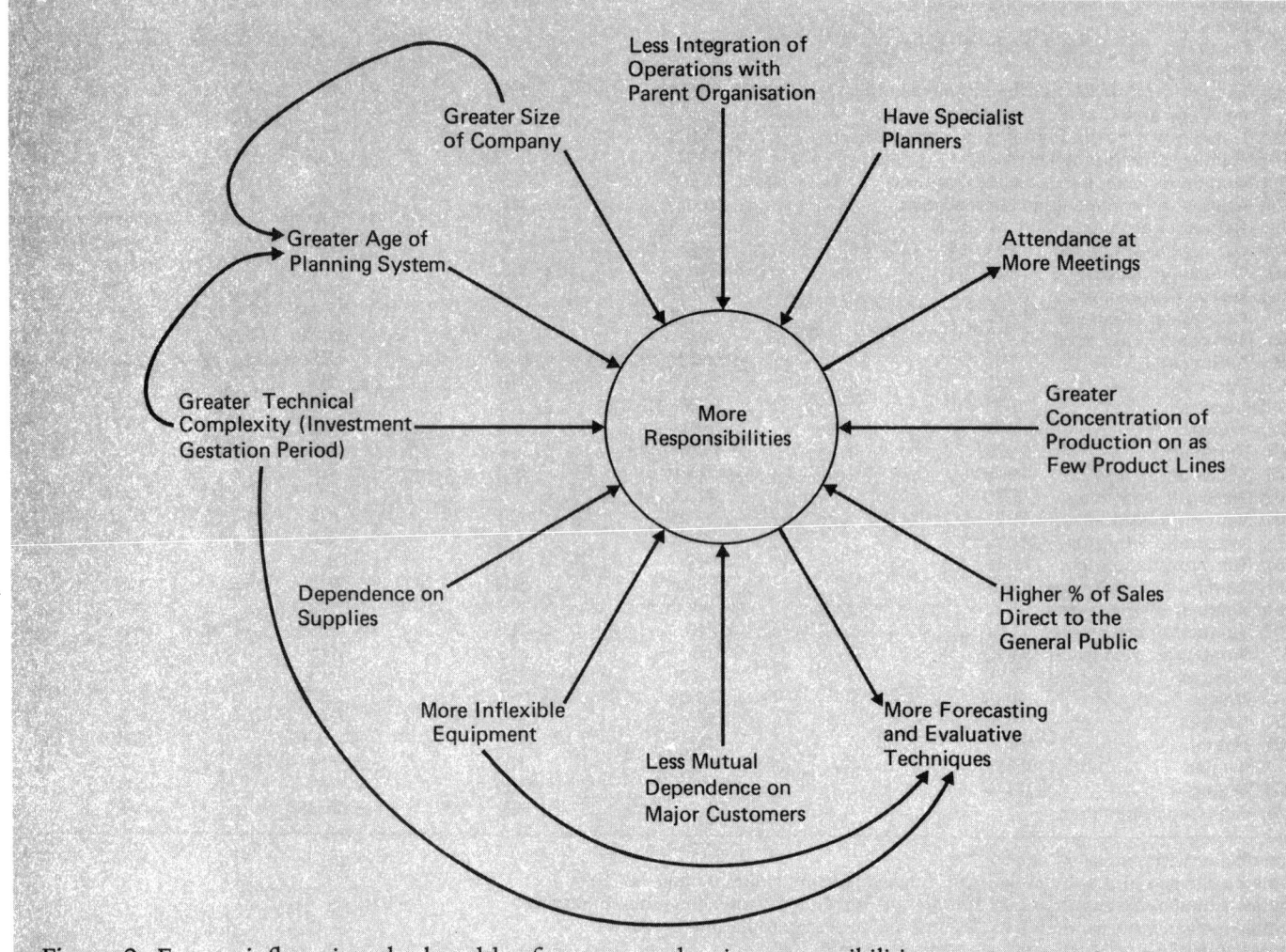

Figure 2. Factors influencing the breadth of corporate planning responsibilities

Table 8

	No. of responsibilities	No. of contributions	No. of difficulties	No. of changes required
(1) Co. charter	NS	−0·25*	−0·22‡	NS
(2) Co. status	NS	0·17‡	0·37*	NS
(3) Structure	0·14§	0·20†	0·28*	NS
(4) Strategy	NS	−0·22‡	NS	NS
(5) Vertical span of control	NS	NS	0·20‡	0·18‡
(6) Lateral span of control	−0·14§	NS	0·19‡	NS
(7) Number of sites	0·24*	NS	0·20‡	−0·15§
(8) Geographic dispersion	NS	NS	0·23†	NS
(9) Country of ownership	NS	NS	−0·23†	NS
(10) Dependence on suppliers	0·29*	NS	−0·18‡	NS
(11) Dependence on 10 largest customers	NS	NS	NS	NS
(12) Dependence on parent's products/services	−0·41*	−0·29‡	−0·42*	−0·36†
(13) Per cent of sales to 5 largest customers	−0·39*	−0·24‡	−0·31†	NS
(14) Per cent of sales to general public	0·18‡	0·17‡	NS	NS
(15) Per cent of sales to wholesalers/agents	NS	NS	NS	0·21‡
(16) Per cent of sales to ind. users/govt.	NS	NS	NS	−0·17§
(17) Per cent of sales to retailers	NS	NS	NS	0·15§
(18) Ranking in 1st market	NS	NS	NS	NS
(19) Ranking in 3rd market	NS	0·22‡	0·27†	NS
(20) Share in 1st market	NS	−0·16§	NS	NS
(21) Share in 2nd market	NS	NS	NS	NS
(22) Share in 3rd market	NS	−0·17§	NS	NS
(23) Past market turbulence	NS	NS	NS	NS
(24) Future market turbulence	NS	NS	NS	NS
(25) Production concentration	0·23‡	NS	NS	NS
(26) Investment gestation period	0·23†	0·18‡	NS	NS
(27) Technical inflexibility	0·25†	NS	NS	−0·16§
(28) Need for product innovation	0·15§	NS	−0·16‡	NS
(29) Rate of technological change	NS	NS	NS	NS
(30) Planning specialism	0·18‡	NS	0·14§	−0·28*
(31) Age of formal planning system	0·23†	NS	NS	−0·28*
(32) Formal post of chief planner	NS	−0·21‡	−0·20‡	−0·19‡
(33) Number of planning staff	NS	NS	NS	NS
(34) Meetings attended	0·16‡	0·26*	0·20‡	0·21‡
(35) Frequency of board meetings attendance	NS	0·21‡	NS	NS
(36) Frequency of group planning meetings attendance	0·23‡	0·25*	0·48*	0·19‡
(37) Frequency of capital budgeting meetings attendance	NS	NS	0·38*	NS
(38) Frequency of divisional/functional planning meetings attendance	0·34*	NS	NS	0·19‡
(39) Number of types of planning documents used	NS	NS	NS	NS
(40) Number of written plans used	NS	0·26*	0·21†	0·35*
(41) Number of forecasting techniques used	0·31*	0·24*	NS	0·15§
(42) Number of evaluative techniques used	0·26*	NS	NS	NS
(43) Rate of return percentage in 1973	NS	NS	NS	−0·18‡
(44) Net capital employed 1969	NS	NS	NS	0·25‡
(45) Net capital employed 1970	NS	NS	0·15§	0·30*
(46) Net capital employed 1971	0·22‡	NS	NS	0·16§
(47) Net capital employed 1972	0·23†	NS	0·14§	NS
(48) Net capital employed 1973	NS	NS	0·17‡	NS
(49) Turnover 1969	0·23†	NS	NS	0·29*
(50) Turnover 1970	0·26†	NS	NS	0·24‡
(51) Turnover 1971	0·26*	NS	NS	0·20‡
(52) Turnover 1972	0·24*	NS	NS	NS
(53) Turnover 1973	0·25*	NS	NS	NS
(54) Net profit before tax 1969	NS	NS	NS	NS
(55) Net profit before tax 1970	NS	NS	0·15§	NS
(56) Net profit before tax 1971	0·15§	NS	NS	−0·18‡
(57) Net profit before tax 1972	0·14§	NS	NS	−0·16‡
(58) Net profit before tax 1973	NS	NS	NS	−0·29*
(59) Number of employees 1969	0·24‡	NS	NS	NS
(60) Number of employees 1970	NS	NS	NS	NS
(61) Number of employees 1971	NS	NS	NS	NS
(62) Number of employees 1972	NS	NS	NS	NS
(63) Number of employees 1973	0·20‡	NS	NS	NS
(64) Wages 1969	0·18§	NS	0·26‡	NS
(65) Wages 1970	NS	NS	NS	NS
(66) Wages 1971	NS	NS	0·19§	NS
(67) Wages 1972	0·22‡	NS	NS	NS
(68) Wages 1973	0·26*	NS	NS	NS
(69) Planning committee	NS	NS	−0·13§	NS

The coefficients shown are Kendall's tau.
*Denotes a chance of less than 1 in a 1000 that the result is due to chance.
†Denotes a chance of less than 1 in 100 that the result could have been due to chance.
‡Denotes a chance of less than 5 in 100 that the result could be due to chance.
§Denotes strongly suggested but not statistically significant.

factors are related to the number of tasks assumed by corporate planners. Large companies have greater problems of co-ordination and control, particularly where involved in diverse businesses (see Grinyer and Spender[21] for an analysis of such problems), and respond more slowly to environmental threats and opportunities due to more extended chains of communication and greater bureaucracy (Grinyer[22] refers to research which has shown the relationship between company size and bureaucracy). Under these circumstances, the needs met by corporate planning may be wider, and the number of responsibilities of the corporate planner correspondingly greater.

The relationships with technical factors make equal sense. Where the investment gestation period is long, a characteristic usually associated with complex, special purpose, and expensive plant, the investment decision can be justified only in terms of forecast conditions several years at least ahead. Not only forecasts but also careful evaluation of alternatives are important, for major investment decisions on new plant create substantial hostages to fortune, as illustrated by the history of overcapacity in the chemical industry in the last decade. Risk cannot be avoided by careful forecasting and analysis, but it may be reduced, and even where this is not so a sense of greater security may be induced. Where plant involved is not only large, complex and expensive but also highly inflexible, i.e. special purpose, and production is concentrated on a narrow band of products, the risks attendant on investment are obviously increased because the range of possible future conditions in which its operations would be profitable are by definition restricted. Lack of alternative supplies of raw materials or bought in parts (dependence on suppliers) increases the risk inherent in such investment. It is scarcely surprising therefore that planners have wider responsibilities, and use more forecasting and evaluative techniques in discharging them, in companies with long investment gestation periods, less flexible production equipment, and a greater dependence on existing suppliers.

From Table 7 and Figure 2 it may be seen that planners tend to assume more responsibilities as the corporate planning process becomes more mature. This may signify growing acceptance, and wider participation by planners in the decision making process, but could also be due to other factors on which both the age of the process and the number of responsibilities are both dependent. For instance, size of the company and inflexibility of its production technology may account for both, for they are positively correlated with the age of the planning process too.[20]

The remaining factors bearing on the number of responsibilities of the planner are dependent on parent organizations for goods and services, on the one hand, and on major customers (in terms of their share of total sales), on the other. Dependence on parents for goods suggests integration into the logistic flows of a larger enterprise, which is vertically integrated, with the corollary that major decisions relating to the business may be taken at a much higher hierarchical level. Not only this, the dependence on the parent gives a higher degree of security, buffering the company from at least one part of a potentially hostile environment. Perhaps strangely, the same is probably true of heavy dependence on major customers among our sample, for reasons analysed more fully by Grinyer, Al-Bazzaz and Yasai[23] and Grinyer and Al-Bazzaz.[20] Stripped of the statistical analysis, the argument is quite simple, but accords well with both our own and others' personal experience. The companies in the sample were very large, those heavily dependent on their major customers also tended to have high market shares, and hence the dependence was mutual. Rather than being subject to buffeting at the whim of major customers, these companies had a relationship which economists have called bilateral monopoly,[24] in which each party has considerable bargaining power. Whilst theorists like Coddington see this inducing competition between the parties for the best terms, a condition which can be observed in some cases, a frequent situation among large companies is collaboration to achieve a mutually advantageous outcome. This is a situation described by Rhenman,[25] on the basis of his Swedish research, as 'joint optimization and joint consultation'. New products are designed in consultation with, and to meet the needs of, the major industrial customers who also provide forecasts of future requirements and even tentative delivery schedules. Under these circumstances, the supplier is buffered from the uncertainties of the final market place by his major customers, who bear the managerial burden of responding to market fluctuations and threats. It follows, then, that dependence on major customers, just as much as upon parent organizations, reduces the need for, and so the width of responsibilities of, corporate planning.

Factors Influencing Extent of Contributions

Factors influencing the extent of contributions of the planning process, i.e. the number of types of contributions claimed by the interviewee within the company, are illustrated in Figure 3. In this case the direction of causality can scarcely be in doubt since the contributions are by definition those of operating the planning process within the context of the company and its environment. Hence the independent variables may be analysed into three categories, the planning process, company characteristics, and the market environment.

Four aspects of the planning process seem to be related to the extent of its contributions. It is perhaps scarcely surprising that the number of areas of the business for which there were written plans, the number of forecasting techniques used, and attendance at more meetings more frequently led to wider contributions. Contributions are clearly related to the extent of involvement and effort to some extent at least. What did surprise us was that the extent of claimed contributions tended to be negatively related to the status of the most senior planner. This reverses the orthodox, normative, views to which reference has already been made. Although it could be

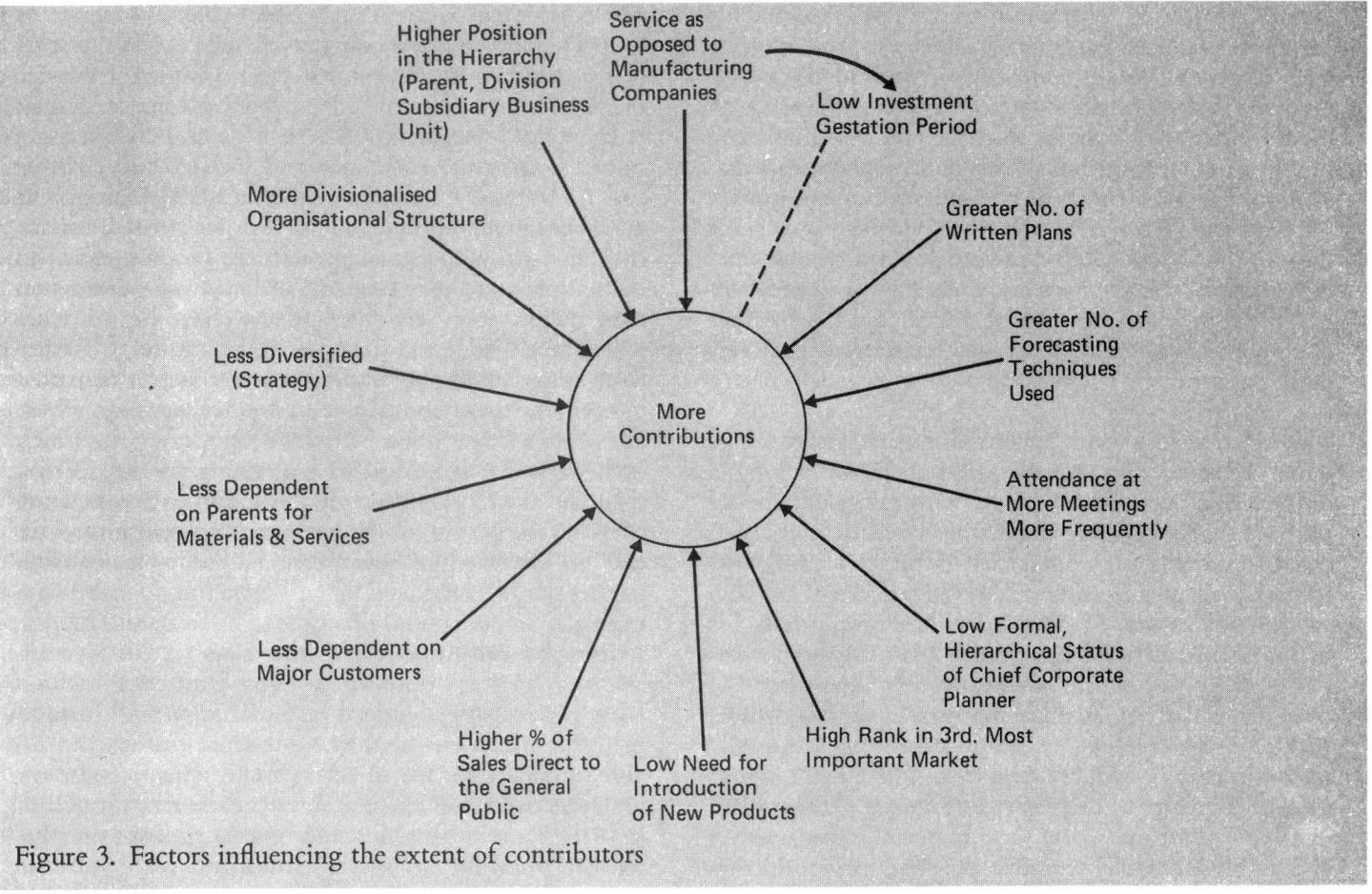

Figure 3. Factors influencing the extent of contributors

argued that, strictly, there is no contradiction because earlier literature related to 'success' or 'pitfalls' (conditions leading to lack of success), whilst our focus here is upon breadth or extent of contributions, the prescriptive implications are quite contrary. Considerable caution must be used, however, for the size of the coefficients were so small that the status of planners could account for no more than 4 per cent of the variability in contributions. Moreover, low status of planners was also associated with recognition of more difficulties and need for more changes in the process, to which we turn later. None the less, it is quite possible that there is a tendency for planners reporting to line executives to become more fully integrated into the operational planning process, and so to contribute more fully than if located at more elevated levels. If this is so, however, the tendency is weak, and should not be allowed to dominate other considerations.

Surprisingly, size and technology, the main influences on the number of responsibilities of corporate planners suggested by the statistical analysis, had no significant relationship with the number of contributions (with the apparent exception of the investment gestation period). Company characteristics found to be associated with this number were charter (service, manufacturing, or both), hierarchical status of the organization (parent, division, or subsidiary business unit), the divisionalization of the organizational structure, and the extent of diversification (strategy). Only the first of these four causes surprise. We had expected that, because of their greater logistic complexity and technological factors

discussed in the last section, manufacturing companies would be perceived to have obtained wider contributions.

This was especially so in view of the fact that manufacturing companies tended to be more diversified.[19] An explanation may be in the different roles that corporate planners play in service and manufacturing companies. In the former, corporate planners were more involved in generating proposals and control, but senior and line management tended to initiate reviews of plans and evaluate alternatives more frequently. An impression is given, therefore, of corporate planners taking a more creative and influential a role within a collaborative approach to planning within the service companies as opposed to manufacturing ones. If this is so wider contributions might be expected from corporate planning. Given that service companies tended to have low investment gestation periods the greater number of contributions cited by them would explain the otherwise inexplicable association between the latter two.

Status of the organization, divisionalization of organizational structure, and diversification of product lines may all be seen to be related to difficulties of communication, of understanding the constituent businesses, and of co-ordination. Because of its functions of co-ordination and control,[20] corporate planning could be expected to meet a substantial need in parent companies, with long vertical chains of command. However, in diversified companies planners tended to emphasize control rather than participation in proposal generation and evaluation[20] which could explain their lower number of reported contributions.

Among the environmental factors, those that bear upon contributions of corporate planning are largely the same as those related to responsibilities, in particular dependence on a parent and major customers. The greater security that such dependence is assumed to induce may equally be expected to limit the contributions that corporate planning can make. Since dependence on major customers tends to be negatively correlated with the percentage of total sales direct to the general public, which necessarily involves sales to many customers, this second factor's relationship with contributions may be seen as another expression of the same theme. Two environmental factors remain. First, where the company has a high rank, i.e. a lower share, in its third most important market the contributions of corporate planning were seen to be wider. Share or rank in the first and second markets have no significant relationship with contributions, however, possibly because most of the sample had strong positions in these but in their third markets the spread of market shares and ranks was wider. There may well be greater scope for an effective contribution from planning where the market rank is relatively high, in that greater penetration can often be achieved without attracting retaliation from market leaders, which would suggest that this could be an important factor. Less explicable is the tendency for *more* contributions to be claimed where the need for introduction of new products was thought to be low. No intuitively reasonable explanation occurs to us. The apparent relationship is probably attributable largely to the fact that service companies perceived both more contributions from corporate planning and less need for introduction of new products.[20]

Factors Creating Difficulties

The number of types of difficulty recognized by corporate planners can also be reasonably regarded as dependent on the planning process, the company, and its environmental linkages. Results of the statistical analysis suggest then the causal model illustrated in Figure 4.

Similarities with Figure 3 are immediately apparent. Greater involvement by planners, in terms of attendance at more meetings more often and use of more written plans, is seen to generate more difficulties as well as more contributions. Passive planners, with little involvement, may be expected to avoid many difficulties! Low status of the chief planner also leads to difficulties, as suggested in earlier literature, and noted above.

Again, the company characteristics associated with contributions seem to be largely related to difficulties, too. Size of company, higher vertical and lateral spans of control, divisional structures, higher status of the company in the group hierarchy (where appropriate), and the number and dispersion of sites all, it has been argued, contribute to greater difficulties of communication, coordination and control, and of rapid response to environmental changes. They consequently influence both the responsibilities and contributions of corporate planning. Yet the argument has been in terms of the difficulties they generate and which corporate planning may help to overcome. These very difficulties must be confronted by

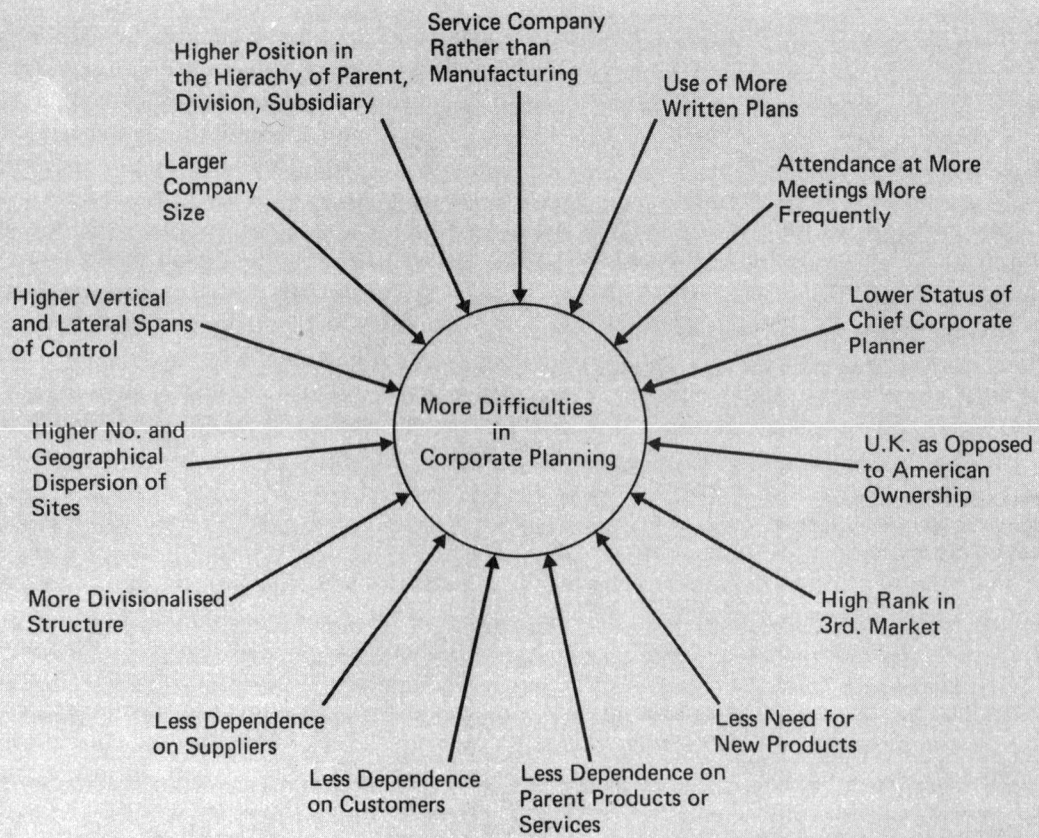

Figure 4. Factors creating difficulties

the corporate planners themselves and are therefore likely to be reflected in their statements on this score.

These arguments have already been rehearsed, the difference being one of emphasis or slant, but this is not so where the new company characteristic, country of ownership, is concerned. From Table 8 it may be seen that this factor bears significantly only on difficulties but that in this case there is a probability of less than 1 in a 100 of the result occurring by chance. Hence although country of ownership accounts for only about 5 per cent of the total variation in the number of difficulties it is still a significant factor. Given that the scale runs from U.K. (low) through continental Europe to U.S.A. (high), the analysis suggests a clear tendency for companies with American parents to perceive less difficulties in corporate planning. This could well be a cultural phenomenon. North American companies tend to employ more business graduates, espouse management techniques more quickly and ardently, and adopted corporate planning earlier and more enthusiastically than those in the U.K. By means of exchanges of personnel, visits, and implantation by the parent of formal planning systems within the subsidiaries as one level of a hierarchical process of co-ordination and control, it is very likely that the American culture permeates the U.K. subsidiaries which are consequently more favourably orientated towards corporate planning than their U.K. owned counterparts. Again, the fact that corporate planners in service companies perceived more difficulties than those in manufacturing ones may be in part a matter of culture, but it is more likely to be related to the more active role they tend to play and the reactions and problems this generates.

Environmental factors too follow the now familiar pattern. Mutual dependence on customers, and now suppliers, buffers the company against environmental turbulence and so reduces the difficulties of corporate planning, as well as the tasks and contributions of the planners. Again the rather paradoxical relationship between need for new product innovation and difficulties of planning may be attributed to a common dependence on organizational charter (i.e. whether or not the company is involved in manufacturing).

Factor Influencing Changes Required in the Planning Process

As with contributions and difficulties, it is assumed that the desire for changes in the planning system is created by its features, the company characteristics, and environmental linkages. Given this assumption, we may derive the causal model illustrated in Figure 5 from the statistical correlations in Table 8, always with the proviso that some of the relationships might possibly be due to common dependence on other factors.

Because of the number of types of changes desired in the planning process is a measure of dissatisfaction, like the number of perceived difficulties, one would expect similar factors to bear upon it. Indeed, it could be argued that the proposal of changes is a response to difficulties. This expectation is largely confirmed. More types of changes are suggested where corporate planners are more fully involved, in terms of both attendance at meetings and the number of areas with written plans, where the

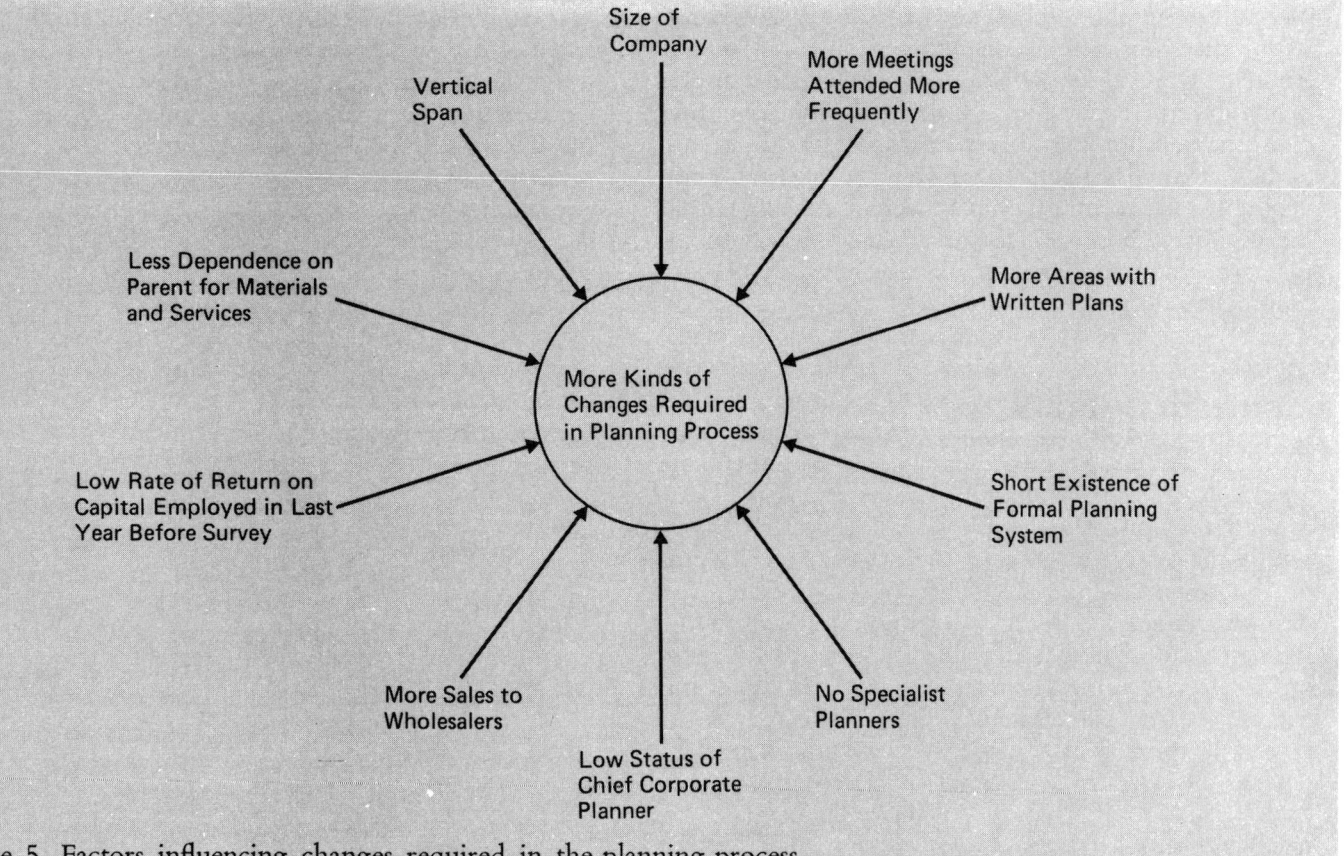

Figure 5. Factors influencing changes required in the planning process

status of the chief corporate planner is low, the size of the company is high, the vertical span of control is great, there is less dependence on the parent for materials and services, and there are more sales to wholesalers (and hence less to government and industrial users with whom there is a relationship of mutual dependence).

New factors entering Figure 5 also make considerable intuitive sense. Where the planning system is relatively young, in our sample at the time of the survey frequently under 2 or 3 years old, many difficulties had still to be ironed out. On the other hand, as suggested in the earlier descriptive section on required changes, others with newly designed systems were unwilling to contemplate changes before they had been given a chance to work. It is quite possible that the relationship found was, then, largely dependent on the large number of relatively new systems within the sample. In addition, since the statistical methods used assumed a one directional relationship, and involved data collected at one point in time as opposed to over a longer period within a smaller sample of companies, they cannot illuminate the possibility of a cyclical pattern of dissatisfaction and change. As indicated earlier Lorange and Vancil[17] suggest that increasingly formal procedures and tight planning discipline are often rejected once line managers have acquired the habit of planning and as irritation with the bureaucratic aspects of the system grows. We would hypothesize that when the formal planning systems are dismantled, an erosion of the planning discipline created among line managers by their operation will commence. In time the very needs for systematically addressing strategic issues, co-ordinating and controlling within the corporate whole which led to the initial adoption of formal systems will reappear. An appropriate response may then be a greater formality of corporate planning. If this speculation is right, rather than an increasing satisfaction with a planning system as it matures, one will be confronted by a cyclical pattern of change, satisfied implementation, perception of weaknesses and mounting dissatisfaction, leading to further change. At the centre of this cycle will be fluctuating emphasis on centralization as opposed to decentralization of decision making within the corporate body, on formalized as opposed to informal methods, and on systematic as opposed to more judgmental decision making.

Concluding Points

From the descriptive and statistical results presented here a number of general points emerge clearly. At the time of the survey, in 1974, there was considerable variability within the sample of 48 large U.K. companies in terms of the responsibilities, contributions, difficulties, and changes required of corporate planning. Yet on the whole the descriptive findings are consistent with those of earlier researchers despite differences in time and national location of their studies. Since 1974, we perceived a swing towards greater dissatisfaction with formal systems as the environment became uncertain in the economic crisis of 1974–1975 and more informality in strategic decision taking, a trend which could well be beneficial.[26] In time, however, we suspect that this may be reversed as problems created begin to outweigh advantages.

Having said this, clearly the role, contributions, difficulties, and dissatisfactions expressed as required changes were related to the planning process itself and the status of the corporate planner. Greater involvement, in terms for instance of more written plans, more meetings attended, and more forecasting techniques used, led to both wider contributions and difficulties. If the cyclical model hypothesized in the last section is correct, this relationship with the extent of involvement could lead to a cyclical pattern of greater and less involvement of corporate planners as designers and operators of formal systems.

Company characteristics also bear strongly upon the extent of each of responsibilities, contributions, difficulties and required changes. Size of company, organizational shape, charter, degree of diversification and country of ownership all enter into the pattern of influence. Similarly, technology has a very strong bearing on the responsibilities of planners in particular. All of these influences are nested in a wider pattern related to dependence on parents, suppliers and customers as well as place in the market. Taken together, these factors can be seen as creating needs that shape the responsibilities and so the extent of contributions of corporate planners, but at the same time confront the corporate planners with difficulties. The very forces which drive a company to set up a corporate planning system may undermine it so leading to the cyclical pattern hypothesized in the last section.

The better the design of a corporate planning system matches the needs of the situation which stimulates its creation, i.e. the better it meets the situational needs, the less intense these difficulties should be compared with its contributions and the longer it should survive before the adverse effects it inevitably creates mount to an insupportable level. As Lorange and Vancil[17] suggest, experiences of the 1960s in the U.S.A. left planners wiser if more cautious, and we can reasonably assume that where a large number of companies respond to given contingencies with specific characteristics of the process this may well reflect a learning process. A contingency approach to the design of corporate planning systems is clearly required, as suggested by Lorange and Vancil.[17] Interested readers will find an account of such an approach in Grinyer and Al-Bazzaz.[20]

References

(1) J. M. W. Hewkins and T. Kempner, Is corporate planning necessary? *British Institute of Management*, London (1968).

(2) K. B. Brown *et al.*, Longe range planning in the U.S.A.— National Industrial Conference Board survey, *Long Range Planning*, **1** (3) (1969).

(3) W. H. Strigel, Planning in West German industry, *Long Range Planning*, **3** (1) (1970).

(4) H. Schollhammer, Corporate planning in France, *Journal of Management Studies*, **7** (1) (1970).

(5) B. Taylor and R. Irving, Organised planning in major U.K. companies, *Long Range Planning*, **3** (1) (1976).

(6) K. A. Ringbakk, Organised planning in major U.S. companies —A Survey, Stanford Research Institute (1969).

(7) F. J. Aguilar, R. C. Howell and R. F. Vancil, *Formal Planning Systems 1970: A Progress Report and Prospectus*, Harvard University Press (1970).

(8) H. I. Ansoff, J. Avner, R. G. Brandenberg, F. E. Portner and R. Radosevitch, Does planning pay ? The effect of planning on success of acquisitions in American firms, *Long Range Planning*, **3** (2), December (1975).

(9) S. S. Thune and R. J. House, Where long range planning pays off, *Business Horizons*, August (1970).

(10) K. A. Ringbakk, Why planning fails, *European Business*, Spring, (1971).

(11) D. M. Herold, Long range planning and organizational performance—a cross-validation study, *Academy of Management Journal*, March 1972).

(12) G. A. Steiner and H. Schollhammer, Pitfalls in comprehensive long range planning : a comparative multinational survey, *Long Range Planning* (1973).

(13) J. C. Camillus, Evaluating the benefits of formal planning systems, *Long Range Planning*, **8** (3), June (1975).

(14) P. Irving, Corporate planning in practice : a study of the development of organised planning in major U.K. companies, M.Sc. dissertation, Bradford University (1970).

(15) P. Lorange and R. F. Vancil, How to design a strategic plan-system, *Harvard Business Review*, September/October, (1976).

(16) L. E. Greiner, *Integrating Formal Planning into Organizations*, Aguilar *et al.*, *op cit*.

(17) P. Lorange and R. F. Vancil, *Strategic Planning Systems*, Prentice-Hall, Englewood Cliffs (1977).

(18) R. F. Vancil, See Vancil's contribution to Aguilar *et al.*, *op. cit.* (1970).

(19) S. J. Al-Bazzaz, Contextual variables and corporate planning in 48 U.K. companies, Ph.D. Thesis, CUBS (1977).

(20) P. H. Grinyer and S. Al-Bazzaz, Corporate planning in 48 U.K. companies : a contingency model, Working Paper of the City University Business School, London (1979).

(21) P. H. Grinyer and J.-C. Spender, *Turnaround: Recipes for Managerial Success*, Associated Business Press, London (1979).

(22) P. H. Grinyer, Organizational structure : The Aston Programmes I, II and III, *Long Range Planning*, **11**, 89–92, December (1978).

(23) P. H. Grinyer, S. Al-Bazzaz and Ardekani Yasai, Strategy, structure, the environment and financial performance in 48 U.K. companies, Working Paper of the City University Business School (1978). Accepted for publication in the *Academy of Management Journal*.

(24) A. Coddington, *Theories of the Bargaining Process*, George Allen and Unwin, London (1968).

(25) E. Rhenman, *Organisation Theory for Long Range Planning*, Wiley, London (1973).

(26) P. H. Grinyer and D. Norburn, Planning for existing markets— perceptions of executives and financial performance, *Journal of the Royal Statistical Society*, Series A, **B8** (1) (1975).

Human and Organization Problems in Corporate Planning

A. C. B. Wilson

Guest, Keen & Nettlefolds Ltd.,
Smethwick, England.

Any management method which is to work in practice must start by recognizing man as he really is, and not what he ought to be. The typical textbook company of the 1960's was peopled by obedient, logical, profit-oriented, ox-like employees— sterilized and faceless characters with£'s signs in their thought bubbles, but the study of Behavioural Science in recent years has taught us that man is a rather more complex animal than we used to think. Simple observations tell us that in practice no business is as tidy, flawless and rational as a 1960's textbook. The reason is that we are people—difficult as individuals for a start and infinitely more complex still when we combine in groups. "Businessman" must be accepted in his full glory, with his ungovernable motives, his intelligence, creativity, his desire for a quiet life, his intuition, his private needs, fears and ambitions and his paradoxical self-seeking ability to cooperate. Everybody who has worked in a company knows the gloriously complicated muddles which "businessman" can get himself into; the misused routines; the convoluted organization structures; the dreadful panics during which all the rules are broken, and the peculiar thing is that, in spite of all these untidinesses, things seem to get done just the same. My point is that management and planning is an extremely complicated business, it is complicated because it is a matter of handling people, it is an art not a science.

CAPITAL INVESTMENT OPTIMIZATION contains several good examples of the complexity of business management and I will digress for a moment in an attempt to demonstrate this.

Group Capital Investment is to Corporate Planning what scoring a goal is to football; it is the 'doing' bit. Invest wisely and your business will succeed. Discounted cash flow techniques for investment appraisal are well known; using DCF one can, assuming correct data have been used, classify all projects according to various criteria. The main ones are internal rate of return, net present value and payback period.

Complications Start to Arise

Each project will have been prepared on the assumption that if it is good and if it 'fits' it will get the capital it deserves, but, of course, capital is not limitless and now things start to get a little complicated, because the amount of capital that will be available in 2 or 3 years' time will itself be influenced by the financial characteristics of the projects selected today for go-ahead.

So we are caught in a loop; we have say 15 major projects which satisfy the chosen criteria (internal rate of return and so on). Maybe the projects are so good that the cash flow in years one and two permits us to start number 16, a more controversial project, as well, or rather than number 16 perhaps number 17 and 18 are preferred instead. Possibly, on the other hand, the 15 best projects taken together retard group cash flow so much that we can no longer be sure of raising finance in year three, so that we must think again and eliminate say numbers 3, 4, 6 and 10 and put in 17, 18 and 20.

Then throw in the possibility of a recession next year and it is obvious that one should, in theory, go round and round the loop many times. One should do so to make sure of choosing the one combination of projects which, when they are added together, has the best future characteristics. These, which include the method of finance, concern such things as cash flow, dividend cover, group return on investment, sales growth and 'fit' with group objectives.

Human Nature Exaggerates the Complexity

The most important job of any top management group is to plan investment wisely, to deal with this theoretical loop which I describe and to choose the best combination of schemes each year when capital expenditure authorizations are approved.

A top management group will typically consist of say four or five key people. When faced with this complex and vital job, some will tend to understand it intuitively, some mathematically, and some will not really accept the problem at all. Put them together on this problem with their different mental processes, their fears and their imaginations, their personal inter-relationships, their private prejudices and ambitions and you begin to understand that the use of DCF is not quite so simple after all. There are many other such complex inter-relationships between the way that decisions are taken in the different parts of a business; I believe that in solving these relationships the universal truths that must be respected can only really be taught and understood as rules of stylishness. They cannot be laid down like computer logic, as it were, in the form of set techniques or rules of procedure.

Stylishness

Set techniques such as budgetary control' management by objectives, costing systems, accounting systems, decision trees, stock control techniques and similar business methods are obviously valid and useful. In fact, they are essential in the efficient running of the business, but they are not enough in themselves. They do not constitute an overall business framework. In designing the overall framework you need to use these and a thousand other procedures, but the question of when to use them and how and why to use which ones is essentially a matter of style, comparable for example to a conductor's style, which is expressed in the way he uses the different instruments of the orchestra. To be successful, a businessman's style must accept the rather earthy and ignoble characteristics of creative man doing business.

Most things that are very complicated are taught in terms of stylishness, particularly games: how to play golf, cricket, or chess. The reason is that the variety of situations which the player will meet is almost infinite, he cannot be taught or be expected to remember exactly what to do each time, so he is taught how to be stylish instead; keep your elbows in, keep your bat straight, keep your eye on the ball, do not use your pawns in the early game, and so on. The great rowing coach Steve Fairbairn used to say "if you can't do it easy, you can't do it at all". A beautifully succinct statement on style.

Style gives no exact instruction. It indicates a way of thinking and moving, a framework in which the creative individual, the star footballer, the exceptional businessman, can do a complex thing.

In the case of the business manager, I believe that the stylish thing for him to do at all times is so to arrange his procedures that when he is trying to solve a problem, or to have it solved within his organization, these procedures can concentrate on presenting all the relevant data in the best possible way, but that they leave the actual decision taking and the solution finding to the intuition of the decision takers themselves.

In the same way that an ocean-going yacht and everything in it is designed with a healthy respect for the sea, the particular brand of corporate planning, which I favour, is designed with a healthy respect for the human environment and its rich complications. It aims to focus the component parts of the company on to the future in an integrated way, it makes them peer forward and it leaves the path finding to them. It does not aim to yield a solution It gives no exact instruction, but it aims to constitute a framework within which the creative businessman can use his intuition to do a complex thing—plan ahead.

BEWARE OF BEHAVIOURAL SCIENTIFIC IDEALISM

The whole concept of corporate planning is quite closely linked with what behavioural science is trying to say. To oversimplify the thing perhaps, behavioural science as I see it, works to release the latent enthusiasm and creativity of people at work and this, of course, is a very fascinating subject, because so often an organization has human problems of all different sorts within itself, which prevent it from reaching its full potential in terms of output.

Behavioural science is so very much in keeping with the trend of our modern permissive society, that it is wise to sound a note of warning: we must not go overboard on behavioural scientific idealism. There are many organizations which, quite rightly, value other attributes more highly than inventiveness and creativity. The degree of innovative creativity and experiment required is not at all high in the Army, the Church or the Civil Service, nor indeed in Law, Accountancy and Insurance Firms. Obedience and iron discipline is about the most important thing in the Army, where it is often necessary to order men to go and risk their lives.

Acceptance of dogma is essential in the Church, and Law and Accountancy firms require that their employees give an impression of faultless ethical behaviour and being able to keep their mouths shut at all times. In these organizations creativity and inventiveness are secondary and must be abandoned if the conditions necessary for their release might be harmful to the primary values of the concern.

Now most corporate planning methods depend on and require a large measure of participation for their success. That is to say that many of these systems would wither away, and in fact do wither away, in an autocratic or a paternalistic environment. Corporate planning usually requires a high degree of democracy in business. Where democracy cannot be tolerated, for one reason or another, then 'ivory tower' planning ought to be the order of the day.

THE RIGHT CLIMATE FOR CORPORATE PLANNING

It is undoubtedly true that corporate planning is much easier in some circumstances than in others and a few observations on suitable and unsuitable climates will be interesting, either as pointers to ways in which the climate should be altered, or to help diagnose why a certain organization may be having difficulty with planning.

The 'entrepreneur' is often referred to as a businessman whose style is opposed to the concept of corporate planning. The word entrepreneur evokes the image of a successful businessman who has flair and intuition, who can and does take decisions on his own, who knows what he wants and knows how to get it.

It is not necessarily true that this sort of man has no use for planning, but if this is the case it gives a further clue to his character—it indicates that he is selfish about his business; he will not let others in on what he really hopes and intends to do. He is a closed-off sort of man, who is not good at discussing and consulting with others. He plays his cards close to his chest.

Thus, in fact, it is not the success, the flair, the intuition, the creative side of him that rejects planning. It is the autocrat in him. He rejects planning because it is too slow and ponderous. If he can absorb all the necessary facts, he, in his own single brain can do the analyzing, thinking, guessing and speculation and take a decision. All the necessary facts mean those which he needs for his own special purpose.

Managing a big company in this way requires fanatical energy, almost to the point of obsession. The entrepreneur must be brilliant and he must also work extremely hard. Furthermore, he must limit himself to key decisions; these are the ones that are usually to do with the selection of top personnel and with overall strategy. The success of such a management method depends essentially on the ability of the top man, by definition the organization cannot support him, it is a one-way traffic, he feeds them. If he makes a few mistakes, or his health fails, he is likely to find that his next line of management is made up of unimaginative acolytes, or of truly able men who stayed in times of success but who have none of the loyalty or sense of belonging that could help to carry the company over a bad patch, because they were never given the rights of ownership in the real decisions or in running the company.

Autocratic Management Needs Ivory Tower Planning

An autocratic or paternalistically managed company should tend towards ivory tower planning. This is the sort of system where you have a few intelligent statisticians, economists, analysts, etc. who predict the future and the technology of chosen markets and who distill their findings into written plans without much reference to the rank and file of the company.

This applies whether the company is successful or not: a failing paternalistic company should not, in my view, try and resort to an open participative method of method of planning, because it cannot really be expected to work in such an environment.

THE SIGNIFICANCE OF SIZE

Another factor which has an important bearing on the design of a corporate planning system is the size of a company, both in itself and in relation to the market.

Small companies of, say, a thousand employees or less, have little need for formalized corporate planning because the top managers being few in number can carry the essentials of their objectives, ambitions and future intentions around in their heads. Whereas one of the secondary advantages of planning in a big company is its value as a communication network, the managers of a small company do not usually need this medium. They should indeed cover the topics dealt with by corporate planning, but they need not formalize it.

Smaller Companies Must be Opportunist

A smaller company, moreover, can do little to influence its market or the sources from which it must get its supply of capital, raw materials and manpower. The company that is small in relation to its industrial environment is swirled around by the turbulences of business, like a leaf in a whirlpool, whereas the large company floats serenely through short term turbulence like a large log. The large company has problems of giganticism which can be clarified and solved by long range planning adopted as a management style. A small company learns to live with turbulence and its management style is suited to this way of life. It fills the gaps in the market, the short runs, the repair business, which big companies leave uncovered.

Thus, the small company must seek to be expert in the short term. In personal contact and in limited influence survival, whereas the big group needs long term planned survival. As the successful small company grows big it should keep modifying its planning methods to keep pace with its growth.

There are, of course, infinite grades between big and small. One that comes to mind is the thousand-employee company set up to make and sell a brilliant new invention which is protected by a worldwide licence: cat's eyes for example. Such a company would be wise to indulge in some sophisticated long range planning.

How Far Into the Future Should One Plan?

There is a connection between turbulence (a factor of absolute and relative size) and the distance into the future which a company should look. I can't pin this connection down and I don't think that it is important to do so, but each company has its natural focus, beyond which management finds it unrealistic to look. When times are good they will dream more and look further out, when times are bad they wisely become more short-sighted. Corporate planning systems should recognize this natural focus and try to extend it somewhat, but they should not court disaster by doggedly insisting on planning 3 or 4 years beyond this natural focus point.

There is a further point here; that in any company's future there is usually one thing, or set of connected things, which looms large say 2 or 3 years out, or maybe 7 or 8 years out. It looms large in the corporate imagination while other unrelated things which could also occur at about the same future date are still not yet being thought about. Practically all companies will have these coming events; a new factory; a known forthcoming market shift; the lapse of a patent; the probability of a new breakthrough and so on.

The planning system, like the radar screen, should be scanning the future at a distance ahead which will allow the company time to spot, plan for, and handle these events. Furthermore, as I have learnt often to my cost, the planners must expect the future to be unevenly lit up by their long range planning system. You can get people's enthusiasm and cooperation on a significant event foreseen 4 years out, but you can arouse little interest in the mundane event even 1 year out.

TYPES OF PEOPLE

Human and organization problems must include some of the typical reactions one gets from different types of people and an organization. The first type that I have found particularly frustrating are the dyed-in-the-wool accountants. The problem here is two-fold. Not only do these people have a firm and often miserly grip on the financial figures that are the life of any planning system, but also by their training and by their understandable obsession with always being precisely right in what they do and say, they command a certain respect in the organization. They straddle many of the areas which need to be involved in corporate planning and can often be quite obstructive, often not on purpose, but rather as a sort of absent-minded, negative habit.

What I find rather tantalizing is the fact that of all the business training that is available I am convinced that the accountant has a training which is the most relevant to the disciplines required in corporate planning. The main reason for this is that by his training the accountant is taught to see the overall inter-relationship of all the parts of the business. For example, the salesman knows little about production and the manufacturing man knows little about selling. But the accountant has the opportunity, and indeed if he is to be a good accountant and if he is interested in his job, he is obliged to get to know all the parts of the business. Furthermore, all plans must eventually be set down in financial terms and so I think that on the whole the planner should be an accountant. I have often seen cases when the corporate planner is kept strictly out of the mysteries of financial control, and this I think is usually disastrous, because budget setting and financial control is the essential bridge between planning and doing.

The Theoretician

Another person worth talking about is the theoretician. Every company has its theoretician, and some have several. He is usually a menace to the corporate planner, he will button-hole you and talk to you endlessly on an abstruse point. treading his way delicately and logically through chicken-and-egg problems, semantics, questioning definitions and so on. I have found that the only thing to do is to develop a nose for these types and when you smell them coming run for cover. Cynical advice perhaps, but quite valuable.

THE ORGANIZATIONAL DILEMMA OF PLANNING vs. CONTROL

Plans must be flexible, and the planning system must allow for this, but there always comes a point in time when you must go firm. For better or worse you must decide which way to go. From this point on, planning as such ceases, and budgets take over. Ideally this point arrives at a specific and different moment for each decision. To establish this moment you merely have to work out how long it takes for the decision to be acted on—the lead time—and count backwards in time from the action moment. When the lead time starts it is the same as the start of the 'count down' for a rocket launch.

Unfortunately, it would be immensely complicated to manage a system where each different decision was individually switched from plan to budget when its lead time (or count down) started to elapse. Progress needs to be measured against budget, so that the need for corrective action can be spotted; for this purpose the budgets must be inflexible because if they were changing all the time they would become hopelessly confusing. I have known this happen in practice—you find yourself comparing actual with original budget (which everybody sweated tears over last August and knows very well) updated by a recent set of revisions which did not go below operating division level (because it would be too complicated changing all the detailed budgets) and therefore the variances cannot be investigated in detail.

Herein lies one of the major dilemmas of corporate planning. Plans must be flexible and budgets must be inflexible. Often the worries caused by this dilemma are blamed on the accountants, but the simple truth is that because the thousand different decisions being taken at any one time have different lead times, the disciplines of deciding what to do on the one hand, and working out what went wrong on the other, are perpetually in conflict. The one requires flexibility, the other inflexibility.

The solution that most companies sensibly adopt is the crude one of treating anything planned to happen in the next financial year and thereafter as a plan (flexible) and anything planned to happen in the current financial year as the budget (inflexible). Every planner will come up against this dilemma and I am sure that there never will be a way around it. One just has to admit that it is there and get on with it.

THE STRUGGLE BETWEEN HEAD OFFICE AND OPERATING PEOPLE

Corporate planning, I have found, can contribute a very major benefit in helping to alleviate the age-old struggle between Head Office and operating people.

When Nelson put a telescope to his blind eye as he is said to have done at the Battle of Copenhagen, he was acting out the classical struggle that has been going on between Head Office and the 'doers' since the beginning of human history.

Head Office know that the operating people are the arms and legs, the 'doing' part of the enterprise, but they do not trust them to take an overall view which is good for the organization, and at the slightest cause Head Office people start to suspect the quality of work being done at operating level. Head Office instinctively want to have complete control right down, not only as to what should be done, but also as to exactly how it should be done. But, of course, they cannot physically do so; in the first place it

is not their job and they are not there all the time. Furthermore, good operating people won't really accept instructions in this way. They like to have proper guidance but they do not want detailed action instructions.

The problem is that Head Office cannot really give proper guidance if it does not have a good grasp of what is going on at operating level. If, in fact, they do not know quite a lot of the detail.

Operating Paranoia

The operating people, for their part, see things in quite a different way. They instinctively feel the need to hold back the more significant details. This is because they want the maximum freedom of choice in their daily decision taking. They are afraid, often quite rightly, that if Head Office knows all the details then the natural thing would be for them to start issuing detailed instructions, thus effectively usurping the leadership and control of local affairs.

The operating people feel misunderstood. "Head Office doesn't understand our problems. Head Office", they say, "are always interfering. Head Office hasn't enough to do, come to think of it, what do they do there all day anyway, apart from drinking cups of tea while we earn enough money to pay their salaries?" With these conditions only just below the surface most of the time, the question of achieving true and effective contact between Head Office and operating people is a very delicate matter, and one of the main questions is how should they work together? What formal methods, committees, procedures and timetables should be set up to make them understand each other, and to make them work smoothly together?

How should the executive directors at Head Office run the business? Should they fly by instruments acting as analysts and seldom getting out to see what is happening at the sharp end? Or should they dash about from factory to factory, customer to customer and supplier to supplier trying to see everything for themselves? Clearly neither extreme is satisfactory, and a compromise is needed. Corporate planning elegantly provides the answer. Planning cycles should be widely publicised within the company, so that Head Office and operating people know what they must do and when. Thus, they can see how the different jobs fit in logically with each other and how each job is a necessary part of the proper management and guidance of the company, and most important of all, they can see how these jobs cannot be done either by Head Office or by operating people on

their own. They are essentially jobs which involve both sides.

Very simply, then, corporate planning constitutes, as it were, a super agenda for the management of an organization, by giving the executive directors specific and regular homework to do on each of the operating divisions, and by giving them specific tasks to perform at different times of the year, it enables these Head Office people to get below the polite but tough skin of divisional affairs. It gives them a co-ordinated and integrated annual timetable. No longer do they have to rely on unconnected figures and reports from different parts of the organization which land on their desks, more or less at random and on *ad hoc* fire-fighting visits, to the operating divisions.

THE ANATOMY OF AN INNOVATION

Finally those who are about to put in a corporate planning system and those who are still struggling with the early stages will be comforted to know that their problems are universal. The stages I have been through are listed below:

1. *Advance*
   Management announce launch of new system. 'Intelligenzia' master concept. Worthies brace themselves; all bright new stuff; brave new world.

2. *Setback*
   Little annoying things go wrong, true system snags spotted when live running starts. Progress is seen to be slower than planned. The more idealistic euphoria of the innovators is now seen to be naive. New system gets blamed indiscriminately—it is on trial—guilty until proved innocent. If there is to be sabotage it will occur now.

   Intelligenzia jeer, worthies outraged, their genuinely loved company being ruined by damned consultants or young upstarts. Worthies are an easy convert to the cynical intelligenzia point of view.

3. *Advance*
   Management recover—more attention now paid to training needs. The snags found in live running get ironed out. The organization structure is altered, lines of reporting change. People in favour—keen innovators, progressives, get promoted.

   It is realized for the first time that the new system actually does work in real life—a great morale booster to the innovators. Progress now starts to be visible and optimism shines bright again.

4. *Setback*

Deeper resistances and secondary snags. The deeper resistance persist; old habits, worn paths, established ways of thinking and doing things, old names, old code numbers, etc.

People admit new system is in and working but are too set in their ways. Language and terminology, older people slow, group attitudes not yet changed. People reluctant to make the effort to master the spirit of the new system. In the minds of the more reactionary die-hards the system is still on trial.

Deeper weaknesses in the system in system design now appear: things that look right on paper but will not work because they violate the basic rules of human nature.

Intelligenzia resort to the miserly process of using knowledge as power. Systems backlash puts strain on system—better is the enemy of good.

Administrators versus innovators. Administrators are needed now but are sulking in the shadows with their noses out of joint, out of favour since step 3 above.

5. *Advance*

The method grows at last. Progress happens and jerks forward unevenly. Some sections do surprisingly well, others are surprisingly sticky. Training begins to pay off at last. New people taken on from outside to replace those who have left (naturally or in a huff) begin to count in favour. They have no personal investment in the old system. The old system starts to be forgotten The wiser people begin to see how the new system paves the way for still better things. Attainment of new plateau, reveals new vistas, new possibilities. Worthies have now got used to the new system and are proud of it—they talk about it at the 'local'. Faults of the new system can be lived with and compared objectively with those of the old: they are different sorts of faults altogether. The price of progress to better information is, for example, an occasional gigantic computer error and can be compared with the insipid slowness and lack of information of the old methods. (Knowledge is power, so there will be some who liked the old system for the monopoly it gave them on the source of investigated information.)

The introduction of new ideas that were greeted with howls and discarded at step 2 is now demanded from below. People get used to the idea of change—the first change is always the hardest to make.

6. *Setback*

Further setbacks will continue, but now it becomes a question of proper maintenance. The setbacks will include the intelligenzia using the new technique as an offensive weapon with which to beat the stupid and they will thus warp the spirit of the technique.

The knowledge is power 'weakness' and other behavioural problems will continue to occur from time to time.

Reactions will occur to the extent that the new system is ahead of its time—ahead of the average level of training and general education in the organization. For example, DCF or network analysis would have been pretty impossible in the 1930's. Reactions will occur to the extent that the new system is out of step with developing political and social thought, e.g. autocratic and paternalistically based attitudes and methods may have to wait for a back-swing of the pendulum before they have much chance of permanent success. ∎

Participation in Planning

H. H. Berschin*

Brown, Boveri & Cie AG (BBC), W. Germany

In this article Mr. Berschin shows that a company must and can find a balance between a centralized and a decentralized approach as to planning and control in order to optimize employee motivation, thus increasing productivity. The findings of this article are based on research and experience.

INTRODUCTION

THIS ARTICLE CONCERNS ITSELF WITH 'participative planning and control'. It shows, how the planning and control approach emerged and what it can achieve for a corporation.

Participative planning and control is a planning and control approach in which all management levels, headquarters and divisions, staff and line, are involved. This approach eliminates the strong hierarchical distinction between those managers who develop goals and strategies, and those, who specify the detailed operations to achieve these targets.

It will help to make sure, that ambitious, but realistic goals are set and achieved through appropriate strategies and detailed operational programmes.

The emerging of today's large and multinational companies very often followed a path from a strongly centralized organization to an organization with rather independent divisions. Seen from a corporate viewpoint, however, both forms do not constitute the optimal solution as to planning and control.

A strongly centralized organization basically lacks the flexibility to define and re-define strategic goals and to develop necessary strategies fast and market-oriented. An organization with very independent divisions, on the other hand, very often stresses mere divisional goals, therefore neglecting the interest of the whole corporation.

To get the planning process rolling, especially in larger, multinational corporations, a formal planning procedure with established schedules and time-tables has to be set up.

The task consists of the following steps:
(1) To set goals.
(2) To develop strategies to achieve them.
(3) To translate strategies into detailed operational programmes.
(4) To ensure that these plans are carried out.

This approach to planning and control is widely accepted. Theoretically, management knows very well what has to be done. But in reality, during the day-to-day business, roughly knowing the approach and successfully applying it are two different stories.

The crucial question and problem is: How to apply—step by step—these basic principles of doing business.

The discussion of these problems is by far not yet closed.

Planning work is full of experiments. Some experiments brought good results, whereas others did not always live up to their expectations. And the pressure of continuously searching for more sustained growth and profitability continuous.

Planning does help management to achieve sustained growth and profitability, if a basic principle is constantly adhered to.

Own experience has shown that there is one aspect which is often forgotten or under-utilized when developing and executing plans: *The full motivation and involvement of both line and staff personnel.*

Unless *both parts* are fully involved in the *whole planning* process, there will always be a discrepancy between headquarters' goals and divisions' operations.

Participative planning and control will help to close that gap.

Participative planning and control capitalizes on the human factor. People want to feel being important. While goals and strategies are developed, they want to be involved, too. If final agreed upon goals and strategies do differ from theirs, they do at least understand why. Corporate 'higher order needs' then become theirs. By controlling that the plans are carried out they are then controlling themselves.

By stressing that human factor, frustrations will be kept to a minimum.

Participative planning and control is capitalizing on the following aspects:
(1) More people get personally involved in all planning and control aspects.
(2) The hard process of continuous new thinking and continuously being challenged will be intensified.
(3) Communication between line and staff, headquarters and divisions, will be stepped up.

Successfully implemented, participative planning and control is the best available approach for today's corporations in achieving sustained growth and profitability.

HISTORIC DEVELOPMENT

Large and multinational companies very often followed a path from a strongly centralized organization to an organization with relatively very independent divisions. As to planning and control, these corporations did change their approach from being 'autocratic' to being 'democratic'.

In short, 'autocratic corporations' do strongly emphasize corporate needs. '*Autocratic planning and control*' calls for specialization at a low level and for co-ordination and control centrally.

'*Democratic corporations*' on the other hand, do strongly emphasize divisional needs. '*Democratic planning and control*' calls for independent divisions, with headquarters coordination and control being kept to a minimum.

'Autocratic corporations' put all the main decision making and controlling power into the hands of top management in

*Mr. Berschin is Planning Manager in the Headquarters of Brown, Boveri & Cie AG (BBC), W. Germany. He has held controllership and planning posts with multinational companies in the U.S.

95

headquarters. The idea is to have as tight a control as possible, concentrated way up in the organization hierarchy.

Only the chief executive, or a small group of top executives, are entitled to plan ahead and to ensure that their wishes are carried out. This small executive group, therefore, is setting all the goals for the corporation. Likewise, they develop all the necessary strategies to make sure that these goals are really achieved.

Only headquarters, aided by a small central staff, actually does all the thinking ahead.

When the goals and the necessary strategies are developed and agreed upon, these strategies then have to be translated into detailed operational programmes.

That is accomplished by pushing the further detailing and executing of these strategies further down the line of the management hierarchy.

Lower levels of management, in headquarters and mainly in the divisions, now have to develop and implement detailed operational programmes in order to achieve the appropriate goals set by top management.

The responsibility for these detailed operational programmes now lies with the management in factories and sales offices. But management in the factories and in the sales offices do *not* have the power to question or change the objectives of top management in headquarters. They have to adhere to the directives of top management. That means, they may have to develop operational programmes for strategies which are not optimal for their division.

Afterwards, top management closely follows the execution of these detailed operational programmes. Deviations between planned and actual achievements are immediately detected and corrective steps can be taken.

This approach, however, now forces top management in headquarters to get fairly much involved in day-to-day operations, and that on a continuous basis.

'*Democratic corporations*' put the main decision making and controlling power out of headquarters into the divisions. The idea here is to have as loose a corporate control as possible, therefore mainly concentrated in the hands of the divisional management.

Now it is the divisional top management which mainly plans ahead and ensures that their wishes are carried out.

Goals are developed and set by these divisional executive groups. Headquarters is only involved in giving rough profitability targets. The necessary strategies to achieve these goals fall under the divisional responsibility, too.

In 'democratic corporations' the divisions do most of the thinking ahead.

Once the divisional goals and strategies are developed and agreed upon by the divisional executive group, these strategies have to be translated into detailed operational programmes.

For that purpose, the executing of the strategies is now being further pushed down the management hierarchy. This time, however, it is done within the divisions, and not from headquarters to the divisions.

Lower levels of management in the divisions now have to develop and implement detailed operational programmes in order to reach the appropriate goals set by their own divisional management.

Because the goals and strategies were set by the divisions and not by headquarters, these targets will probably be more realistic and more feasible. Lower levels of management in the divisions will now be able to more easily comply with the wishes of their superiors.

The same applies for the control. Lower levels of management are responsible to their divisional executive groups that the agreed upon plans are really carried out within the given time-span. The control now lies in the hands of the divisions.

Headquarters, on the other hand, is mainly being informed. They still have to prepare consolidated balance sheets and profit and loss statements. The entire corporation as a legal entity still has to comply with government laws and regulations.

This information has to be put together and consolidated by headquarters, before being given to the proper authorities.

But the idea here is more of a recording of facts which did occur in the past. These facts, however, can not be changed any more.

The planning, executing and controlling for better results now rests mainly in the hands of the operational management.

MAIN SHORTCOMINGS

Both centralized and decentralized planning and control approaches show a number of advantages. They will be discussed later when explaining the synthesis of the two systems.

The following section concerns itself with the shortcomings of the centralized and the shortcomings of the decentralized planning and control method.

In *centralized corporations* the difficulties start when companies grow bigger and expand into new markets and products. Top management will then find it more difficult to oversee and comprehend all operational aspects.

Therefore, central coordination and

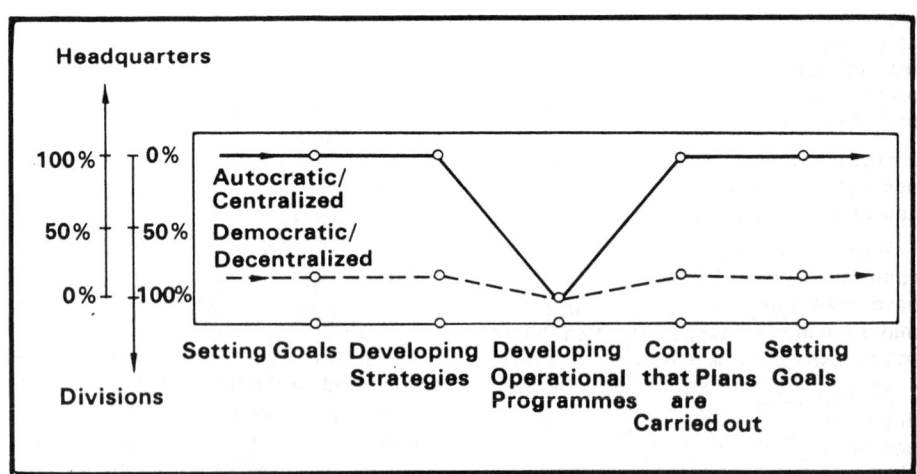

Figure 1. Centralized and Decentralized Planning and Control.

Figure 1 shows the involvement of headquarters and the divisions during the different steps of the planning and control cycle.

In general, the operational management is then controlling itself.

priority setting will not be optimal.

At the present time the technology of computerized management information systems is not far enough advanced and still too expensive to solve these special problems.

Bigger and more complex organizations realize the ever-increasing difficulties in defining and re-defining corporate goals. It also takes too much time to define and re-define market-oriented strategies.

Very often, physically and mentally, headquarters is too far away from the customer. As a result, headquarters cannot act flexible and knowledgeable enough.

Corporate needs, mainly conceived at headquarters, then tend to lack the practical touch. Goals and strategies will merely be the outcoming of theoretical wishes, and can hardly be implemented.

Detailed operational programmes, which should be the translating of these goals and strategies into workable approaches, then are very often not feasible, and sometimes even outright impossible.

When operational programmes are not very feasible, then it will be very difficult to make sure that these plans are carried out.

It is not difficult to find examples of incurred shortcomings of the centralized/autocratic system.

Assuming, a major competitor changes his market strategy, by changing prices, discount policies or other special advantages given to the customers. Then, in a centralized organization, the divisions have to report significant changes back to headquarters. They will ask for advice, approval of adaption strategies, and the go-ahead to apply these strategies.

It happens very often that such a request has to pass several levels of corporate hierarchy. By the time it has reached the decision making level, the original request and information may have been distorted.

Often the word comes back to the operational divisions asking for further and more detailed information.

When finally a more or less agreeable compromise is found, valuable time may have been lost. By then the competitor may have already strengthened his market position quite considerably.

As these disadvantages of the centralized organizational set-up became severe, corporations sought new approaches as to planning and control.

The result was the creation of strong, independent divisions.

The *decentralized organization* did eliminate the above-mentioned shortcomings. However, new problems became obvious.

In short, strong, independent divisions tend to stress their own divisional goals, thereby neglecting corporate goals.

When a countervailing power in headquarters is missing, necessary and important aspects of the corporation as a unity are too easily overlooked.

The corporation as a unity has to be confronted with optimal allocation of resources, and that according to corporate goals and strategies, and not according to mere divisional desires.

Furthermore, corporate management will find it difficult to change corporate directions quickly, if necessary. If the control is mainly lying with the operational divisions, and corporate management is merely being informed—after the fact—corrective steps cannot be taken any more.

Incurring losses or missing opportunities are the results.

The following example demonstrates the shortcomings of such a decentralized/democratic system.

Country organization A and country organization B of the same international organization are both selling almost the same products in country C.

At this point, now too late, the two suborganizations realize that they did develop and market similar and/or substitution products at the same time. This could happen because headquarters' co-ordination was lacking.

The increase in production capacities in countries A and B now leads to an output capacity bigger than the market can reasonably absorb. Over-investment with all the negative aspects is the result.

To sum up, both forms of planning and control do not constitute the optimal solution.

In a nutshell, a strongly centralized organization basically lacks the flexibility to define and re-define goals and to develop necessary strategies fast and market-oriented. An organization with very independent divisions, on the other hand, very often stresses mere divisional goals, therefore neglecting the interest of the whole corporation.

Corporations, therefore, have to look for a balance between centralized and decentralized planning and control.

PARTICIPATIVE PLANNING

The concepts of mere centralization and decentralization do incorporate many shortcomings. But partially, where one concept failed, the other one did often show good results.

The aim of those companies who apply advanced planning and control techniques is to find a compromise between both concepts. This new synthesis of autocratic and democratic planning and control should capitalize on the advantageous features of both methods. At the same time, it should avoid the shortcomings and pitfalls inherent in the pure approaches.

Following positive features of the centralized approach have to be incorporated:

(1) Scarce resources have to be allocated according to corporate goals.

(2) Corporate efforts have to be combined in crucial areas like research and development, procurement, production, distribution, finance, marketing and personnel. Duplication of work has to be avoided, combined efforts have to be stressed.

In addition, the following positive features of the decentralized approach have to be incorporated:

(1) Goals and strategies have to be developed as market-oriented as possible. They will then be more realistic and feasible.

(2) The process of re-defining goals and strategies, whenever deemed necessary because of changed market conditions, has to be done fast, flexible and knowledgeable. The same applies for the detailed operational programmes supporting the goals and strategies.

It is possible to reconcile the centralized/autocratic with the decentralized/democratic approach.

This *new synthesis* may be called '*participative planning and control*'.

Experience has shown, that participative planning and control can be applied effectively.

Common practice in business, applying to both centralized and decentralized as well as to participative organizations, is the development of two plans. First, the strategic plan, in general put together in the spring. Second, the operational plan, also labelled as budget, worked out in the fall.

Whereas the strategic plan evaluates long-range objectives—covering several years—and possible opportunities and threats, the operating plan does cover in general the following 1 or 2 years, with more detailed programmes being developed.

This operating plan clarifies how the goals and strategies are being accomplished, covering a shorter and better overseeable time-span.

Although the development of both strategic and operational plans is also done in '*participative corporations*', with '*participative planning and control*', there is

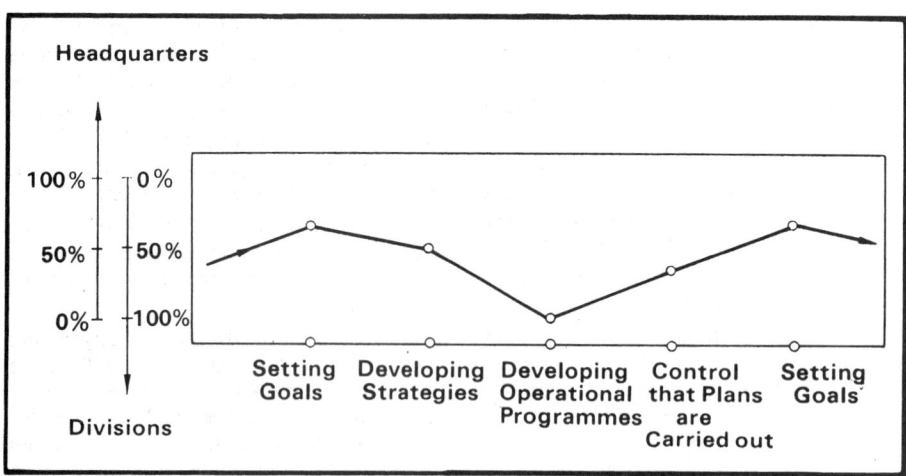

Figure 2. Participative Planning and Control (Synthesis).

one basic difference to the previously described historic approaches.

The first and most important step for achieving the new synthesis is that all managers, those in headquarters and those in the divisions, are working very closely together, and that on all planning and control aspects.

Only participation of *all management levels*, covering *all planning aspects*, can really achieve the best results in the long run.

But how should all management levels, in headquarters and in the divisions, be actively involved in all planning aspects?

There can be no longer a strong hierarchical distinction between those managers who develop goals and strategies, and those, who specify the detailed operations to achieve these goals and strategies.

Both parts of management, headquarters and divisions, should develop goals, strategies, and operational programmes, and should make sure that these plans are carried out.

In setting goals and developing strategies, *both* headquarters' top management and all divisional top executives are part of the main goal setting and strategy formulating team.

More detailed operational plans are basically formulated and carried out by lower levels of management, but with 'inherent' involvement of higher management. This is accomplished by effectively communicating 'higher order' needs down the line.

The controlling process of plans being carried out is basically again the responsibility of all management levels. Further up the organization only main aspects get priority, whereas at lower management levels more detailed aspects have to be considered.

This system can only work, however, if there are formal guidelines to define the communication flow up and down the organization.

and evaluating of forecast data is *mutually* done by the staff of headquarters as well as by the line personnel, and consists of:

(1) Forecasting sources of income (e.g. markets, products, customer acceptance, industries) and

(2) Technological forecasting, evaluating the possible conception and further development of technologies not yet associated with a market forecast.

This forecast data then serves as special input with guidance character for developing the strategic plan, which is basically a headquarters exercise.

Having accomplished that step, the divisions do get—through guidances from headquarters—special input for developing their operational plans, which is mainly a divisional exercise.

The experience gained with developing of the operating plans does again serve as input for the forecasting exercise. By accomplishing that, the yearly planning and control cycle is closed.

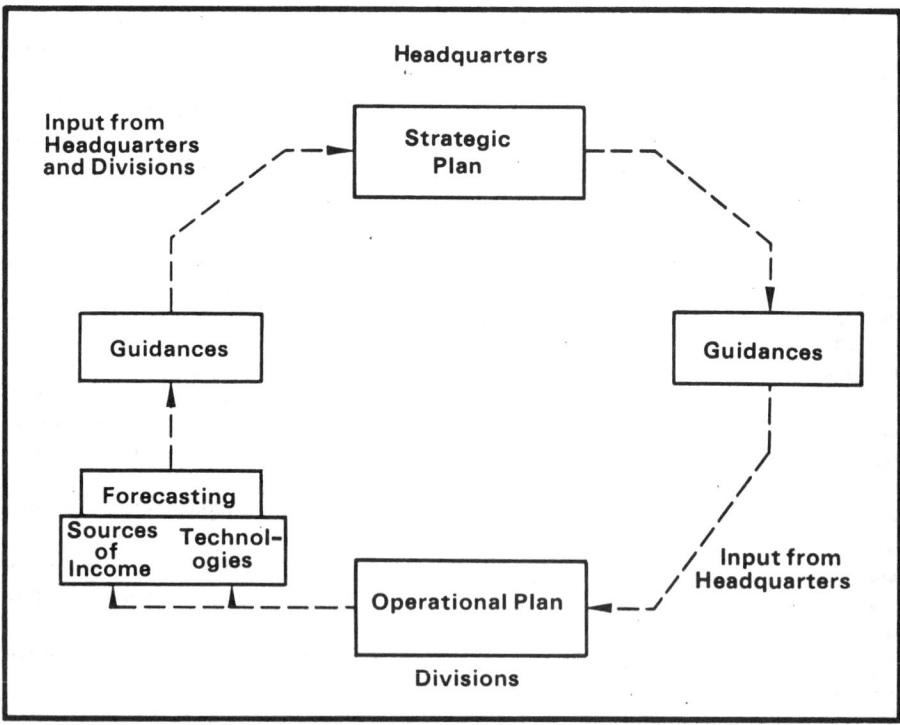

Figure 3. Planning Cycle with Mutual Participation.

In addition to that, special *guidances* do act as *links* between the strategic and the operational plans. They ensure that both headquarters and divisions are involved in all planning aspects.

The first step in developing the strategic plan is a forecasting system. Compiling

Figure 3 shows how the steps of the planning and control cycle are linked together.

Both parts, headquarters and divisions, staff and line, can now participate in a continuous, all year long effort of influencing the other part, and *mutually communicating*.

All parties involved do feel as being part of one crew, helping to develop corporate goals and strategies, and making sure, that these goals and strategies are met and accomplished. The old antagonism of thinking on one side, and merely executing on the other side, then does not exist any more.

THE HUMAN ASPECT

Participative planning and control also utilizes the human resources of the corporations more effectively than it is being done in centralized and decentralized corporations.

The job of a successful, aggressive company will not only be to get people to work, but to get them *to think, to improve*, and to communicate their ideas effectively to the proper levels of hierarchical management.

That thinking ahead and the communication to other levels of management can only be achieved, if the company personnel does identify itself with the basic goals and strategies of their corporation.

That will only happen when everyone, including all management levels, is more or less actively involved in helping setting goals and strategies. The company then becomes their company, and corporate ideas and wishes theirs.

That implies, that *both* staff and line are allowed to see and understand why their original wishes may have been changed in order to satisfy the needs of the whole corporation. These corporate objectives may differ from theirs.

These needs then become modified 'higher order' needs. But that information has to be effectively communicated first.

Participative planning and control, because of its formal set-up of information flow, does ensure that.

This participative planning and control approach is that effective, because all managers are allowed to participate, including line and staff, headquarters and divisions.

In practice, this involvement will be more or less comprehensive, depending on the level of corporate hierarchy. Details have to be delegated. But there has always to be some sort of visible involvement of all management levels in all planning aspects.

People want to *feel being important*. This participative approach is going to help them being important.

Defining and re-defining future actions and making sure that the plans are carried out, will then be done with more personal involvement of theirs.

Every executive getting involved in these aspects knows that there are a lot of hidden resources in the overhead. This overhead should be and can be more effectively utilized.

Staying competitive does not always depend on absolute cost advantages, but very often merely on a relatively small motivation advantage of the personnel.

Executives have sometimes lost sight of this fundamental knowledge.

In structuring these ideas more, and getting a first-hand knowledge of where a company is standing right now, it may be useful to answer the following two questions:

(1) Do all the personnel know the basic company goals and the main strategies?

(2) Are they motivated towards these goals, e.g. are they personally interested in helping achieving them?

OVERCOMING FRUSTRATIONS

The ambitious goal of an effective planning philosophy is to utilize all hidden resources for the basic goals of the corporation.

This way, one can *avoid* to some extent *human frustrations.*

People merely being on the payroll, just doing repetitive work and being frustrated, create twofold problems.

First, they under-utilize all resources inherent in them.

Second, they influence other people who are still motivated. This is like creating a 'rats-leaving-a-sinking ship effect!

To get people involved, and to get them actively participating in the process of formulating goals, strategies and operational programmes, helps to avoid that lack-lustre, passive attitude.

It also helps personnel to define their own future in the company.

Getting the strive and zeal out of an organization is the first step for difficulties ahead.

If a person is unhappy in his present job, he will have three choices:

(1) First, he can try to change positions within the company.

(2) Second, he can quit the company, if more rewarding opportunities are found on the outside.

(3) Third, if he does not have such an option, and if he has to stay in the same job, he will try to avoid all risks, especially personal ones. But that avoids capitalizing on possible opportunities. These people will

not show new ideas nor enthusiasm, and will not bring anything more than what is just required of them.

In the beginning, maybe, that will not be seen as being too dangerous. But such an attitude keeps organizations just going, and not striving ahead any more.

The underlying side-effects of a participative approach in planning—thereby avoiding frustrations can show the following example:

If ambitious goals and strategies are agreed upon by line and staff, more detailed operational programmes have to be developed to achieve the desired results. At this stage, management does very often not yet know exactly how—in all aspects—these goals can be met through detailed programmes.

But if line personnel was actively involved in this goal-setting process, and if they did agree on helping to achieve the targets, they will be eager to look for the results which they proclaimed they can get. They are going to prove it, without already knowing exactly at this point how to do it step by step.

But they are constantly thinking of how to fulfil the expectations set in them by others, and also set in them by themselves.

How can such a thinking be effectively further developed?

For that, the following steps can be taken:

(1) Getting people personally involved in all aspects of the planning and control cycle.

(2) Continuously stressing the hard process of new thinking.

(3) Putting more emphasis on life-long, continuous education.

(4) Stepping up the explaining and selling of these ideas down the executive ladder.

(5) Initiating more flexibility to train, to retrain and to expose management personnel to participative planning and control.

Getting people involved in all planning and control aspects can be achieved through initiating a system of guidances. They will act as links between headquarters and divisions, line and staff.

Continuously stressing the hard process of new thinking will create an atmosphere of continuous business awareness. It will create a lively organism, fast and comprehensively reacting to opportunities and threats.

Life-long, continuous education will help to create a more competent and self-confident management. The thinking should be developed towards a thinking in general management terms, even if the managers have not yet reached that stage of their career at this moment. Universities are in many cases not able to do that. The emphasis will, therefore, still be on in-house training sessions or on special institutions, specialized in this field.

More executive time has to be devoted in explaining and selling above ideas to lower levels of management. The rewards will compensate for that approach and executive-time giving.

Exposing of management personnel to participative planning and control has to be stepped up. That includes especially for planning departments the revolving of personnel from staff to line and back. The dialog and the understanding of quite different planning approaches will be intensified.

All questions are never completely answered and solved. One cannot classify human beings that easily and motivate them accordingly. But thinking these problems over, and making this a way of corporate life, will be more rewarding as it is anticipated right now.

Peter Drucker's term "the age of discontinuity" is widely known. That means that less life-long repetitive work will be done, and more thinking ahead with more changes will be necessary.

People will only give their best, if they have some personal interest in the matter they are working on. Stressing participation in planning and control and continuously looking for better ways of how to do that—by satisfying personal, corporate and divisional needs—will be a gain for the company. ■

Strategic Planning for Public Affairs

Thomas G. Marx

This paper attempts to advance the integration of business and public affairs planning. The original concept of strategic planning envisioned a comprehensive, integrated process through which the firm would develop plans for responding to the opportunities and threats in both the economic and socio-political environments. In practice, however, business planning and public affairs have evolved into distinct and separate activities within most companies. The paper traces the reasons for this bifurcation of the planning process, and describes the actions necessary to develop the analytical capabilities and management systems needed to integrate these two critically interdependent functions.

Introduction

The classic purpose of strategic planning is to relate the company to its external environment—to match the company's internal strengths, weaknesses and basic values with the opportunities and threats present in the external environment in the pursuit of sustainable competitive advantage. This classic concept of strategic business planning is illustrated in Figure 1.

As this figure shows, the key to successful strategic planning is a thorough, integrated analysis of the external environment and assessment of the firm's internal competencies and values. In particular, strategic planning, from its origins, has called for analyses of both the economic and socio-political environments facing the firm and for the inclusion of values in the formulation of company strategy. The reality of strategic planning, however, is that it has focused almost exclusively on the economic environment and that the incorporation of company values into the planning process has been narrowly limited to those business values which constitute the company's 'culture', and which contribute directly to the company's financial

success (e.g. being the technological leader or providing the best customer service).

The assessment of the company's external socio-political environment and consideration of social values are primarily the responsibility of public affairs specialists who operate largely in isolation from those developing the business plans in most companies. Thus, what was originally conceived of as a comprehensive, integrated business planning process has developed into two distinct activities within the majority of companies.[1] The need for management to comprehend social values and expectations fully in their business plans is, perhaps, most spectacularly evidenced by the past controversy which embroiled Nestlé and the infant formula industry, and, currently, by the Valdez incident which has coalesced environmental opposition to the oil industry.

The purpose of this paper is to advance the integration of strategic business planning and public affairs management. The next section examines and dismisses the most common explanation heard in the business community for the bifurcation of business planning and public affairs—the need to decentralize strategic planning while maintaining centralized control over public affairs. The third section of the paper explains the separation of the two functions as the result of the very narrow, 'reactive' missions originally adopted for most public affairs activities when they first appeared in the early 1960s. The fourth section describes the steps necessary to integrate effectively strategic business planning and public affairs. A summary of the major conclusions closes the paper.

Decentralized Business Planning and Centralized Public Affairs

The most frequently cited obstacle to the integration of business planning and public affairs voiced by practitioners in the business world is the need to

Dr Thomas Marx is the General Director of Economic Analysis on the Economics Staff of General Motors Corporation.

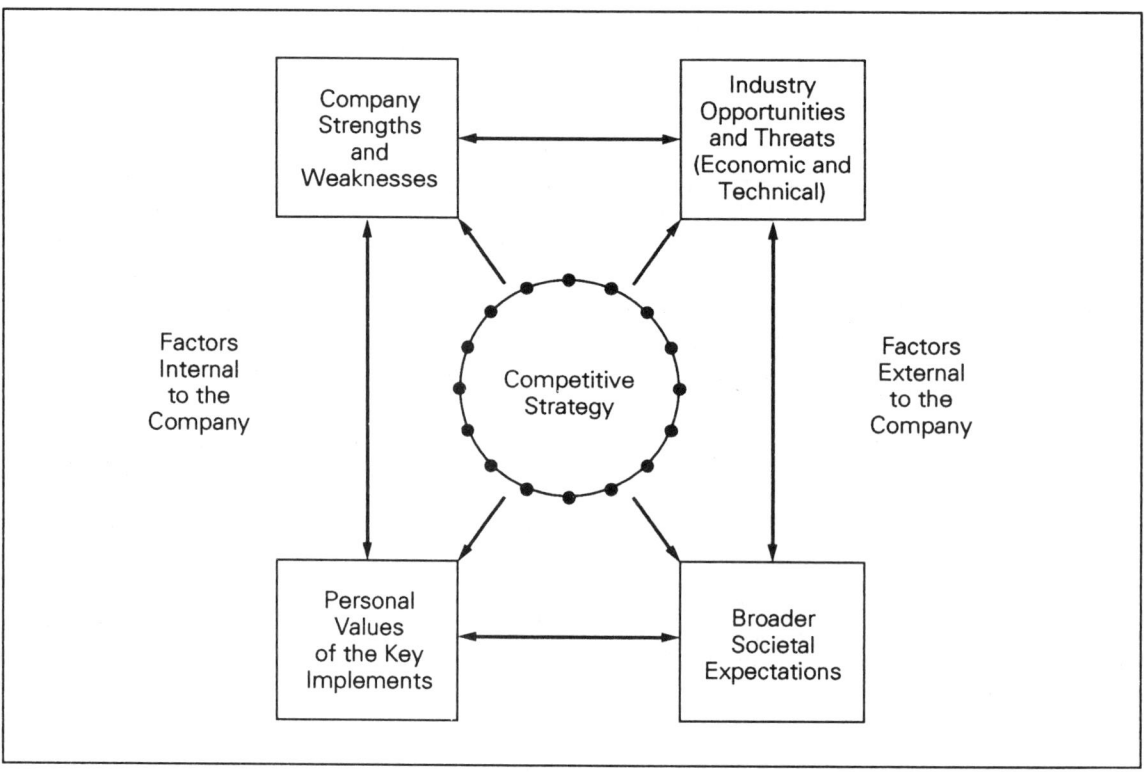

Source: Michael E. Porter, *Competitive Strategy*, p. xviii, The Free Press, New York (1980).

Figure 1. The concept of strategic planning

centralize public affairs while decentralizing strategic business planning. This argument is not heard nor debated nearly as much in academic circles where there is less research emphasis on implementation issues. But, it is an issue which immediately surfaces when business and public affairs planners meet, and one which must be resolved if further progress is to be made.

There are compelling economic reasons for placing the responsibility for strategic planning with the strategic business units (SBUs) throughout the firm, and for centralizing the responsibility for public affairs at the company's headquarters. The SBU concept was developed by General Electric in recognition of the need to develop individual business plans for each product line or group of strategically interrelated products. Centralized planning for the diverse products of most large companies by top executives far removed from the market and not responsible for carrying out the plans has proven to be too slow, too standardized and too unresponsive to the changing needs of the dynamic marketplace.

At the same time, it is recognized that the responsibility for public affairs cannot be located within the SBUs. The SBUs are needed to develop differentiated marketing, manufacturing and distribution strategies to meet the varying conditions of their markets and the needs of their particular customers. These strategies are subject to overall conformity with corporate policy and objectives, but must be tailored to the specific needs of the SBU's markets to be effective.

Public policy, on the other hand, must be consistent throughout the entire company to be effective. The company can produce a variety of products to meet different customer demands, but it must obviously take but one position on a public policy issue, which is unlikely to be the preferred position of every SBU within the company, and it must comply uniformly with any resulting legislation or regulation. Public affairs management must therefore be centralized to ensure the internal uniformity and consistency needed to be effective. Economies of scale in the implementation of uniform policies across the entire company (just as in the production of standardized products) further dictates a high degree of centralization.

The fact that the responsibility for public affairs cannot be decentralized to the SBUs does not mean, however, that strategic business planning and public affairs cannot be integrated. Lodging the responsibility for business planning and public affairs within different organizational units within the firm does impose an extra burden of coordinating across, rather than within, sub-organizational boundaries within the firm. But this is neither a unique nor insurmountable obstacle to an effective integration of the two activities. SBUs have always had to coordinate their strategic business plans with numerous other centralized activities, including personnel, research, finance, legal and, frequently, purchasing and sales. In addition, the plans of individual SBUs must often be coordinated at a group or sector level to capture broader technological or managerial synergies which span several SBUs. Thus, the need to coordinate SBU plans with a centralized public affairs activity raises no unique or unmanageable obstacles to effective, integrated planning.

The Bifurcation of Business Planning and Public Affairs

What then is the reason for the separation of strategic business planning from public affairs if it is not explained by the need to decentralize the former while centralizing the latter? The separation of business planning from public affairs is directly traceable to the original missions of the public affairs offices which were created in the 1960s in response to a wave of social regulations affecting safety, health, energy and the environment. This onslaught of social regulation made the importance of social values, attitudes and objectives to the firm's economic success crystal clear, as it did the importance of an effective public affairs program. Unfortunately, the fundamental nature of the socio-political changes which were occurring was less evident, and the long-term consequences of these changes little understood, perhaps, by all. As a result, the missions of the newly created public affairs functions were narrowly limited to the insulation of the company from what were thought to be sporadic governmental intrusions into traditional business planning and decision making.

This mission for public affairs was reinforced by unrealistic expectations about the extent to which these efforts could hold back the tide of changing social values which was sweeping the nation, and which would affect the conduct of business for decades to come. Because of this misreading of the changing socio-political environment, the original missions of public affairs were, in a word, 'reactive' —to react to the flood of new and proposed regulations and social controls in defense of the status quo. With such a mission statement and great confidence in their ability to carry it out, companies saw no need to integrate business planning and public affairs. Indeed, the mission of public affairs was to ensure that such an integration would not become necessary. Public affairs would ensure that the strategic business units could proceed with their business plans largely unencumbered by public policy concerns.

Now that the fundamental nature of the changes in the socio-political environment which began in the 1960s has become clear, the original public affairs missions are changing rapidly from 'reaction' (reacting to social change to preserve the status quo) to 'pro-action' (anticipating social change so as to be able to respond more effectively and constructively) and, in some companies, even to 'inter-action' (working with external constituencies to bring about positive social change).[2] These expanded mission statements have brought with them a clear recognition of the need to integrate strategic business planning and public affairs for it is only through such an integration that a 'pro-active' or 'inter-active' public affairs mission can be realized. Unlike the original missions, which attempted to shield the strategic business units from social demands, the accomplishment of these broader missions requires their active participation in the development and implementation of strategies that are responsive to social demands without unduly jeopardizing, and perhaps even enhancing, their competitive position in the market.

These broader missions for public affairs, however, only began to appear in the late 1970s.[3] As a result, most of the companies which have adopted a broader mission for public affairs still lack both the capability to analyse the external socio-political environment and the internal organizational mechanisms needed to effectively integrate business planning and public affairs, neither of which was necessary to carry out the original 're-active' missions. Thus, much additional progress in public affairs analysis and management must be made before the clarion calls for an integration of strategic business planning and public affairs can be answered. This has not been adequately appreciated by those often making the loudest calls. The advocates of integrated planning who are bewildered by the lack of progress must come to realize that they have the cart before the horse. Substantial further progress in integrating public affairs and strategic business planning awaits the development of the analytical and managerial foundations needed to support a 'pro-active' or 'inter-active' public affairs mission.

The lack of adequate analytical and managerial foundations to support a 'pro-active' or 'inter-active' public affairs mission can, perhaps, best be illustrated by reference to the following figure which contrasts the state of strategic business planning with progress in public affairs using the four classical phases of business planning.

The strategic planning process at most major companies has progressed from Phase I, rudimentary financial planning focused on meeting the annual budget (with only top management knowing what the company's strategic plan is, if there is one) to phase II and, in many cases, phase III planning where there is a comprehensive analysis of the external (economic) environment. The comprehensive analysis of the economic and competitive environments and the formulation of strategic responses to detected opportunities and threats in phase III planning goes well beyond the multi-year forecasts of select economic variables in phase II. This comprehensive external environmental analysis lies behind the sharp increase in planning effectivness shown in phase III. It is also in phase III that strategic business units first appear, and that contingency planning becomes an integral part of the planning process. A smaller number of firms

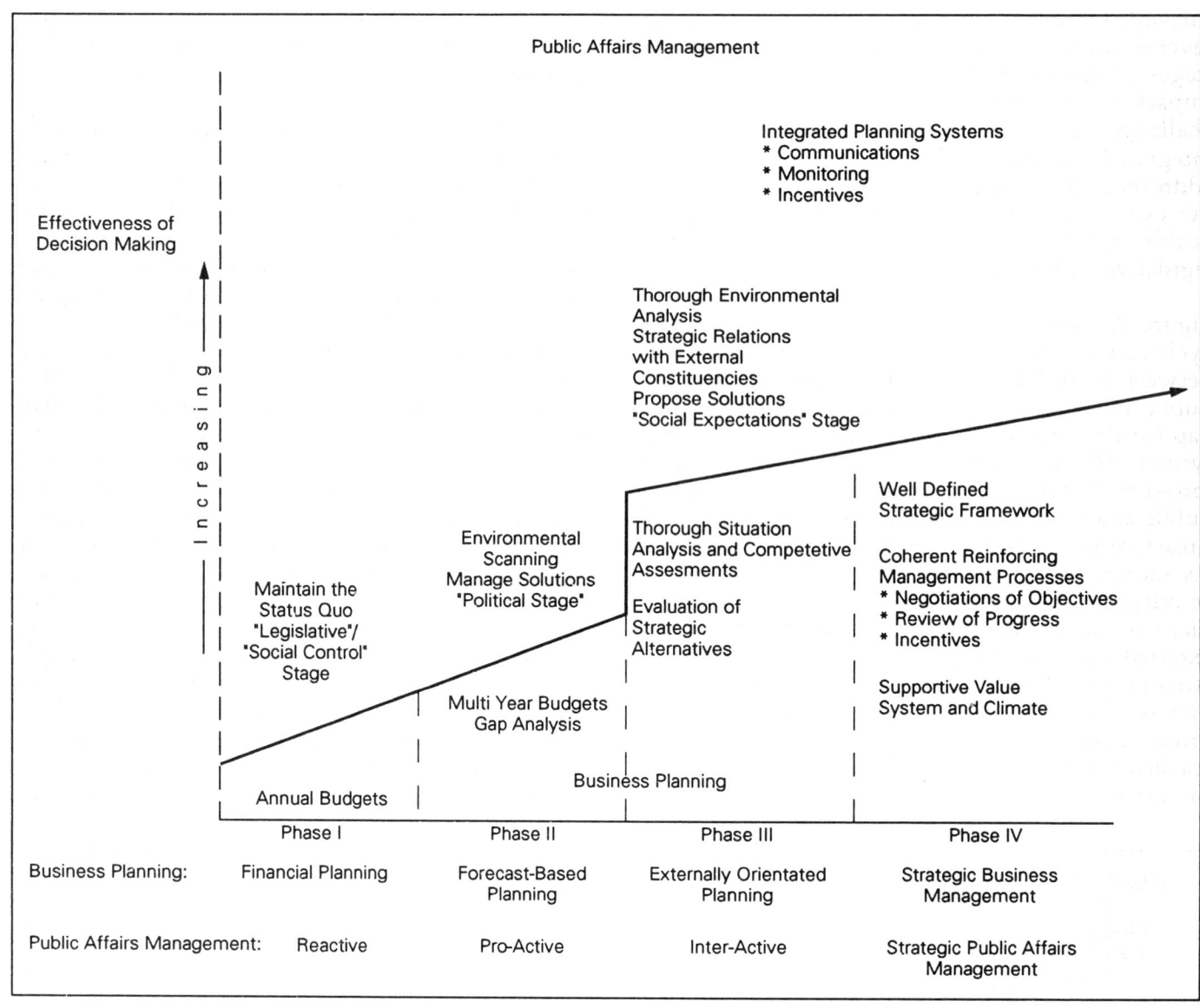

Source: Adapted from F. Gluck, S. Kaufman, and A. S. Walleck, The four phases of strategic management, *The Journal of Business Strategy,* p. 11, Winter (1982).

Figure 2. Phases in the evolution of business planning and public affairs management

have reached the pinnacle of strategic business planning (phase IV) where the plans are thoroughly linked to operating management through the appropriate organizational structures, incentive systems and management processes, and where the firm is actively attempting to 'create its own future' through its strategic initiatives.

Public affairs can also be modelled as moving through the same basic phases as strategic planning with the same ultimate goal of actively creating its own future. As stated by Ray Ewing: '. . . senior management has to understand that it must decide to create its own future, rather than try to embalm the present'.[4] The key concept in integrating strategic business and public affairs planning is the public issues life cycle which is patterned after the product life cycle concept used by strategic planners. The public issues life cycle concept has been most vividly described by Ian Wilson: 'The social expectations of yesterday become the political issue of today, and the legislative requirement of tomor-

row, and the litigated penalties of the day after.' The passage of public policy issues through these four stages—social expectation, political, legislative and social control—is critical to the integration of strategic business and public affairs planning because, as shown in Figure 3, the effectiveness of integrated planning declines markedly as an issue advances through its life cycle.

The integration of strategic business and public affairs planning is most effective during the early stages (social expectation and political) of the issues life cycle when alternative solutions can still be advanced and there is sufficient lead time to modify business plans. Once an issue reaches the legislative and social control stages, the opportunities for responding to the issue pro-actively by effectively integrating private and public goals in the company's business plan are very limited. In these later stages of the life cycle, the firm can do little more than react defensively to the interpretation of legislation, and to the social control mechanisms through which it is enforced. Figure 3 also shows several important public policy issues at different stages of the issues life cycle which have a major impact on planning in many industries.[5] The challenge facing the affected industries is to develop integrated business and public affairs plans for addressing those issues still in the early stages of the life cycle, such as global warming, day care and health care reform, before they advance to the legislative and social control stages.

Figure 2, with the incorporation of the issues life cycle concept, also clearly shows the analytical gap between the different phases of strategic business and public affairs planning, and the implications of this gap for the effectiveness of an integrated planning system. Many companies today have adopted a 'pro-active' (phase II) or 'inter-active' (phase III) public affairs mission, but most still have a phase I ('reactive') or, at best, phase II public affairs activity. As shown in Figure 2, in a phase I public affairs activity, like in a phase I strategic planning activity, there is no analysis of underlying trends in the external (socio-political) environment nor any attempt to identify strategic opportunities and threats. The firm in this phase simply 'reacts' to those mature public policy issues which have reached the 'legislative' or 'social control' stages of the issues life cycle and which, therefore, pose an

obvious and immediate threat to the firm. In this phase, the opportunities for effective, integrated planning are very limited.

In phase II, there is an initial attempt to identify issues in the earlier 'political' stage of the issues life cycle through a variety of more or less sophisticated environmental scanning techniques. Coalitions are formed and plans are laid for influencing the political debate on the most important issues before they reach the 'legislative' stage of the life cycle. Much of the emphasis in this phase II activity is on managing the proposed solutions so as to minimize their adverse impact on the firm. Very few firms, however, have undertaken the comprehensive analysis of the socio-political environment; very early identification of emerging issues in the 'social expectations' stage; and development of strategic relationships with external constituencies for proposing and bringing about the social changes needed to meet those expectations which define an 'inter-active' (phase III) public affairs program. It is during this 'social expectations' stage of an issue's life cycle that integrated business and public affairs planning is most productive for both the firm and society. Still fewer firms have a phase IV strategic public affairs management (or strategic business management) process characterized by both a comprehensive analysis of the external environment and the

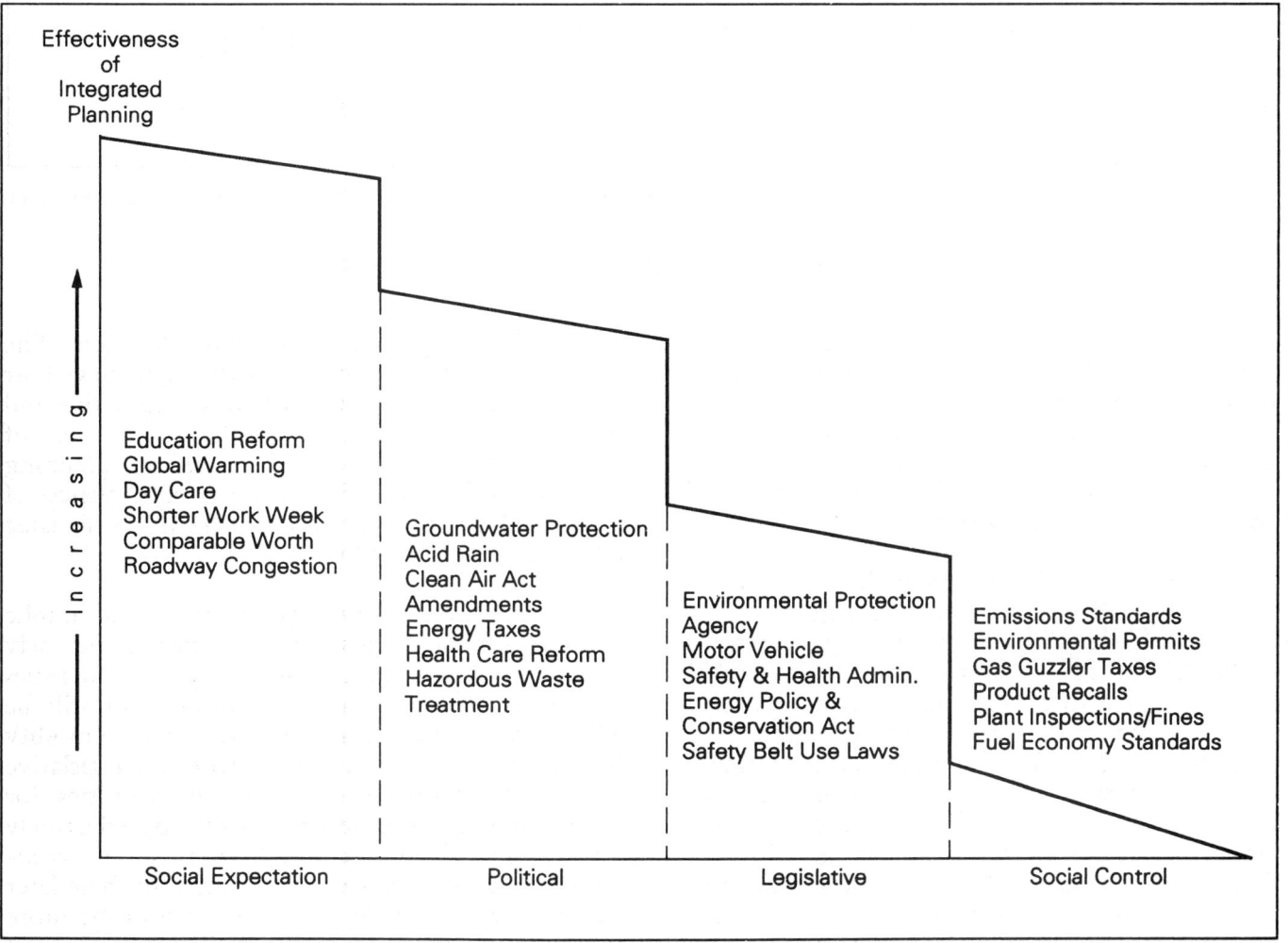

Figure 3. The public issues life cycle

supporting management structures and systems needed to forge the links between business and public affairs planning.

Some of the major companies in the more advanced phases of public affairs management where they are able to integrate public affairs and business planning effectively include Allstate, Monsanto, Champion International, General Motors and General Electric, which was also a pioneer in strategic business management. The increasing integration of strategic business and public affairs planning at Monsanto is clearly evidenced by the changes in the focus of their issues management process which began in the early 1980s, and by the direct involvement of their top operating management in this process. Prior to these changes, Monsanto's Issues Identification Committee identified numerous broad issues which could effect the company, and a higher-level Emerging Issues Committee kept top management abreast of the most important long-term issues and social trends. A closer integration of public issues and strategic business planning began when the top-level Executive Management Committee took direct responsibility for prioritizing the identified issues on the basis of their impact on Monsanto's competitive position. Only a handful of short-term issues (their impact likely to be felt within 2 years) which directly affected the achievement of Monsanto's strategic objectives were selected for the development of action strategies. In addition, and very importantly, only issues which could still be influenced by Monsanto's action strategies were selected, i.e., issues which were still in the earlier stages of the issues life cycle where integrated business and public affairs planning is most effective.

Each of these issues is assigned to a top executive at Monsanto, including the chairman and the CEO. These executives are responsible for developing and implementing an action strategy for the issue assigned to them. Since these top-level executives are also ultimately responsible for the company's operations, this process creates an effective organizational link between public affairs and strategic business planning at Monsanto.

Allstate Insurance was one of the first companies to place responsibility for public issues management with its top management, including the chief operating officer. Allstate's public affairs strategies are the responsibility of the Issues Management Committee. This committee is chaired by the chief planning officer and includes the chief operating officer and all other officers responsible for major activities at Allstate. The plans and policies of the Issues Management Committee are carried directly to the operating companies through the chief operating officer. This committee deals only with the four or five most critical issues which will effect Allstate over the next 12–36 months. These issues are brought to the committee by a Steering Committee which is chaired by the chief operating officer.

To further integrate public issues and strategic business planning, the Issues Management Division at Allstate, originally a part of the Corporate Relations Department, was made a part of a new Corporate Planning Department which also includes strategic and marketing planning. Thus, there is a thorough organizational integration of strategic and public affairs planning throughout the company.

The management of public affairs at General Motors is the responsibility of the Public Affairs Group. This group includes the Environmental Activities Staff, Industry-Government Relations Staff, Public Relations Staff and Economics Staff. Collectively, these staffs are responsible for identifying, prioritizing and assessing most of the public policy issues affecting the company. A major effort is made to identify issues early in their life cycle so that a thorough analysis of their impact on the company can be conducted, and the most effective solutions can be developed in an uncharged environment. Through the Group Executive for the Public Affairs Group, direct contact is maintained with the highest-level Executive Committee, and with the Administration Committee which includes all of the operating executives.

The linkage between public affairs and strategic business planning at General Motors has been strengthened through a number of initiatives. The introduction of formal staff planning at General Motors was a major step towards the integration of public affairs and strategic business planning. Each of General Motors' staffs are required to develop long-term business plans in a format which closely parallels the strategic plans developed by the operating units. The corporate review of both operating and staff plans then provides an effective mechanism for ensuring that the company's business strategies respond adequately to both private and public demands. This process is particularly critical when these demands severely clash as they do, for example, when fuel economy standards necessitate smaller vehicles than consumers are willing to purchase at prevailing gasoline prices.

Another initiative to foster the integration of public affairs and strategic business planning at General Motors is the inclusion and quantification of the impact of major public policy issues on the cost and demand for motor vehicles in the company's business outlook review which provides the backdrop for the development of the business plans. More recently, executives from each of the four staffs in the Public Affairs Group have begun joint meetings with the business planners to review the major public policy issues which could significantly affect the corporation prior to the launch of the company's business planning cycle. These meetings provide an opportunity for a direct exchange of information between public affairs and strategic business planners within the context of an integrated planning process.[6]

The common elements among these three companies, and others which are in the advanced phases of public affairs planning, are the identification and assessment of public policy issues early in the life cycle; the prioritization of public policy issues in terms of their impact on the company's strategic objectives; the development of organizational structures and management systems for linking public affairs and strategic business planning; and direct top and operating management involvement in both public affairs and strategic business planning.

The bottom line is that until companies progress to these more advanced phases of public affairs management, there is no opportunity for meaningfully integrating a phase I, and little opportunity for meaningfully integrating a phase II, public affairs activity with the significantly more advanced phase III strategic business planning systems found in many major companies. It is not until public affairs also reaches phase III that there is sufficient understanding of the socio-political environment and adequate strategic interactions with external constituencies that a meaningful integration of strategic business planning and public affairs becomes possible. Thus, the first step towards achieving the much sought integration of strategic business planning and public affairs is to advance public affairs management to phase III. Ultimately, further progress to phase IV is required to realize the full potential from an integrated strategic business and public affairs planning process.

Integrating Business Planning and Public Affairs

To advance to phase III, public affairs must be able to conduct comprehensive analyses of the current and future socio-political environment. It must be able to detect and assess the changing social values, attitudes and emerging 'social expectations' from which tomorrow's legislation will derive and ultimately take its form. The task is not just to 'predict' the future, but to understand, in a timely fashion, the forces causing change, the potential policy implications of that change and the opportunities and risks it creates for the firm.

Phase II companies, which have introduced environmental scanning activities, are capable of identifying hundreds of 'emerging' social issues which could, conceivably, have a substantial impact on the company. The distinguishing characteristic of phase III companies is their ability to assess the probability of these issues evolving to the point

where they actually do impact the company; to estimate the timing and gauge the magnitude of those impacts on the company's financial and competitive position; and to be able to formulate and negotiate positive solutions with other affected constituencies. Without such capabilities, the identification of endless potential issues for which the company has no solutions provides little basis for incorporating public policy issues into the company's planning process. This often only leads to disdain for the initial attempts at pro-active issues management in phase II.

Once the analytical foundations and external relationships necessary to support a phase III public affairs activity are in place, some integration of public affairs management and strategic business planning will result from the normal interactions among public affairs and operating management. Public affairs planners will be anxious to find ways to bring their greater understanding of and capacity for effecting the external environment to bear upon corporate decision making. However, the amount of integration which can be achieved through professional zeal is seriously limited by the lack of continuous, formal contact between business and public affairs planners throughout the planning cycle. The next major task, therefore, is to develop the phase IV communications, monitoring and incentive systems needed to integrate systematically business planning and public affairs management. This effort should begin with a requirement that the annual strategic planning cycle commence with a comprehensive, joint review of both the economic and socio-political aspects of the external environment by the public affairs and business planning staffs. This would ensure that both the competitive and public affairs issues affecting the SBU are fully evaluated. Management should then require that plans incorporate strategies for responding to the social as well as competitive issues facing the SBU before they are submitted for corporate review. The opportunities for modifying SBU plans to avoid adverse social impacts or to propose strategies for addressing emerging social issues are greatly reduced once plans have been developed and submitted for management approval.

The next step in the integration of public affairs and business planning is for management to demonstrate its commitment to the integrated planning process by instituting systems to measure, report and monitor, in the quarterly or annual business plan reviews, the SBU's progress in responding to the social as well as business challenges confronting the unit. Finally, and perhaps most importantly, SBU managers must be explicitly rewarded for meeting social as well as sales and profit objectives. Without this monitoring by top management and the provision of adequate incentives, SBU managers will have little interest in the socio-political consequences of their business plans.

Conclusions

The missions of public affairs in many companies have been changing since the late 1970s from 'reaction' to 'pro-action' and even to 'inter-action' in some companies. With these changes in mission comes a clear recognition of the need to integrate strategic planning and public affairs. Such an integration would facilitate the achievement of legitimate social goals with less economic disruption to the firm's business plans. The basic reason for the lack of integration today is the absence of an adequate analytical foundation to support these recently adopted 'pro-active' or 'inter-active' missions for public affairs, and the integrative management systems.

The necessary next step towards achieving an integrated strategic business planning process thus lies with the public affairs community which must advance public affairs to Phase III where integrated planning can begin, and ultimately, to phase IV where it becomes fully effective. In responding to this challenge, the public affairs community should be inspired by the importance of its role in the planning process.

Reginald H. Jones, the former chairman who led the development of strategic business planning at General Electric, is among those who clearly recognize the importance of meeting this challenge: 'Public policy and social issues are not peripheral to business planning and management today: Today they are the mainstream of it.'[7]

References

(1) For a discussion of the relationship of public affairs to corporate business planning in a broad sample of companies see, James E. Post, Edwin A. Murray, Robert Dickie, and John F. Mahon, Managing public affairs: the public affairs functions, *California Management Review*, **26**, 135–150 (1983). For an assessment of the relationships between public affairs and operating line management, see S. Prakash Sethi, Moving social responsibility down a peg, *Public Relations Journal*, **38** (8), 25–27, August (1982).

(2) The evolution of public affairs management from reaction to pro-action to inter-action is reviewed in, James E. Post, Public affairs and management policy in the 1980s, *Public Affairs Review*, Public Affairs Council, Washington, DC (1980). A broad overview of this evolution is provided in Rogene A. Buchholz, *Business Environment and Public Policy*, pp. 463–497, Prentice-Hall, Inc., Englewood Cliffs, New Jersey (1982). The public affairs strategies (reaction, pro-action and inter-action) of different companies in the chemical industry are contrasted in John F. Mahon and James E. Post, The evolution of political strategies during the 1980 superfund debate, in A. Marcus, A. Kaufman and D. Beam (Eds), *Business Strategy and Public Policy*, pp. 61–80, Quorum Books, New York (1987).

(3) For a discussion of the origins and development of public affairs, see Raymond P. Ewing, *Managing the New Bottom Line*, pp. 12–13, Dow Jones-Irwin, Homewood, Illinois (1987). The organization, administration and development of issues management in a sample of eight companies from different industries is analyzed in Steven L. Wartick and Robert E. Rude, Issues management: corporate fad or corporate function? *California Management Review*, **29** (1), 124–140, Fall (1986).

(4) Ewing, p. 4.

(5) For a discussion of the passage of several critical issues in the motor vehicle industry through the issues life cycle, see Thomas G. Marx, Integrating public affairs and strategic planning, *California Management Review*, **29** (1), 141–147, Fall (1986).

(6) Public affairs management at Monsanto and Gulf Oil are analyzed in detail in, Stephen E. Littlejohn, Competition and cooperation: new trends in issue identification and management at Monsanto and Gulf, in A. Marcus *et al.* (Eds), *Busines Strategy and Public Policy*, pp. 19–30. Public affairs at Champion is described by Robert Colodzin, Positioning the company in society: implementing a public affairs strategy at champion international, in A. Marcus *et al.* (Eds), *Business Strategy and Public Policy*, pp. 211–222. Public affairs management at General Motors is described further by Thomas G. Marx in, Social legitimacy and strategic issues management at general motors, in A. Marcus *et al.* (Eds), *Business Strategy and Public Policy*, pp. 81–94.

(7) Joseph Coates, *Issues Management*, p. 21, Lomond Publications, Inc., Mt. Airy, Md. (1986).

PART THREE

Cases in Successful Implementation

Creating a Productive Culture at Shell Chemicals

Ian A. Thornley

This article is based on a briefing to Shell personnel with the objective of describing operations within the organization where ideas and changes are being generated and major human resources and organizational developments that are occurring in Shell companies around the world. This paper describes the operational and cultural changes at the Shell Carrington site near Manchester.

The Carrington site near Manchester, U.K., is a major manufacturing facility of Shell Chemicals U.K. (SCUK), producing petrochemicals from ethylene, propylene and styrene (see Figure 1).

In 1985 it had a turnover of about £200m, based on sales of 400,000 tonnes of petrochemicals, with a total workforce of 1150.

The site was established in the 1940s, had grown rapidly in the 1950s and 1960s and was poised for another major expansion in the early 1970s. The cancellation of the expansion projects following the first oil price shock in the early 1970s left the site with a high overhead burden and production facilities based largely on early 1960s state-of-the-art technology. The second oil shock in 1979 found Carrington in a poor competitive position and from the period 1980–1984 it made losses of £146m.

During this period Carrington undertook several phases of a rationalization programme which:

☆ shut down the oldest, least competitive plants and, with minor expenditure on those remaining, retained both the overall production capacity and almost all of its products portfolio;

☆ reduced manpower by over 57% (2700–1150) through successive voluntary severance campaigns;

Ian Thornley is Personnel Director of Shell U.K. Limited.

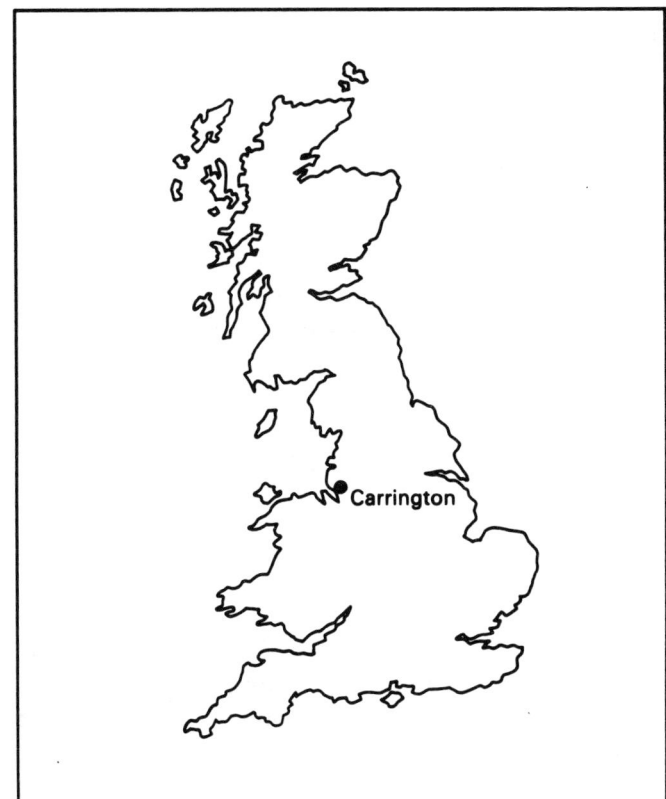

Figure 1. The Carrington site

☆ removed 'fat' within the organization and increased flexibilities within traditional employee trade groups (supervisory, foremen, process operators, maintenance craftsmen).

In 1985, with ethylene becoming available to SCUK from a new jointly owned ethylene cracker in Mossmorran, Scotland, and the expectation of continuing fierce market conditions, a reassessment of all SCUK's operations at Carrington was undertaken. The conclusion was that, to survive, the site had to reduce its fixed costs and its manpower drastically from 1150 to below 500 (see Figure 2).

111

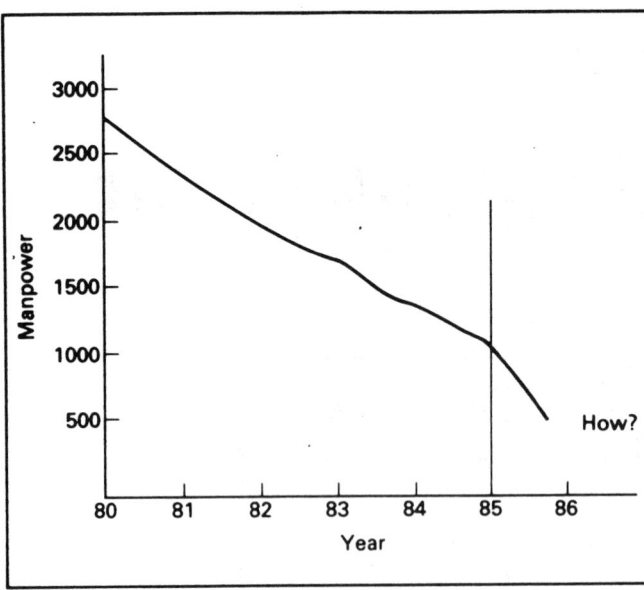

Figure 2. Manpower reduction 1980–1986

The Problem—The Culture Determines Productivity

Carrington had had 5 years of continuous retrenchment and through this experience management had come to recognize that, despite reduction of the site to under half the 1980 numbers, and despite improvements in productivity, the culture had remained unchanged. This culture was felt to be a restricting force on Carrington's potential to be a winner.

An in-depth analysis of the way the site was organized convinced the Carrington management that conventional 'pruning' would only reduce manpower to about 700 and that, to achieve the reduction to 500, with the productivity improvement that this would imply, would require a change in site culture.

Equally serious, straight manpower cuts would not re-establish the confidence of senior Shell management, and the employees, of Carrington's determination not only to survive, but to become the best in an intensely competitive business. The question was, how to produce a lot more from a lot less?

The 'greenfield' Shell plants at Sarnia, Canada and Mossmorran, Scotland have manufacturing organizations and multi-skilled working practices very different from those traditionally found in the oil/petrochemical industry. The Carrington management believed these to be potentially more productive in the tasks of operating, maintaining and quality controlling the plants and they used these examples as the start point for organization and job design changes. The simple question Carrington management asked themselves was 'How would we run the site if we were starting out all over again?'

The Vision—To Create a Productive Culture

The management was convinced that the only competitive edge that could be achieved with the Carrington asset base was through the knowledge and commitment of its people. They were also convinced that the employees wanted to contribute and become part of a successful team, and that the measures of success they were determined to champion were bottom line financial performance and the satisfying of customer needs. The management were committed to aim for, and reward, excellence in both personal and team performance. The keys to achieving a productive environment were seen to be those of having consistency and re-enforcement of these and allied values in all facets of organization design, job design, working practices, reward systems and training/development programmes (see Figure 3).

The Changes Made—A New Life for Carrington

The old organization had a six layer structure. This was 'flattened' to four layers to improve communications and allow each job a bigger scope, with people being fully responsible for their jobs and the way they perform them.

The new Carrington is smaller and leaner with whole layers of organization removed and with those plants which could not be made profitable shut down (see Figure 4).

The site is changed from a functional based organization to one based on four performance accountable plant centres, each operated and maintained by six teams of multi-skilled *technicians* (an amalgamation of the conventional foreman, operator, craftsman positions) working a 6-month cycle rotating between shifts (4 months) and days (2 months). While on shift they run the process operations and attend to minor maintenance as necessary. While on days *these same technicians* are largely involved only on plant maintenance. The key role of co-ordinating each team is carried out by a shift manager to whom the teams report. This manager stays with his team throughout the shifts/day cycle (see Figures 5 and 6).

Within the teams the technicians, on all occasions, do any required operating and maintenance work which they have the knowledge and skills to tackle safely. There is also a small group of dedicated day technicians on each plant who carry out the most highly skilled diagnostic and specialized work.

The focus is on the main business activity and all support functions are actively questioned. The plant teams are supported by two service groups which

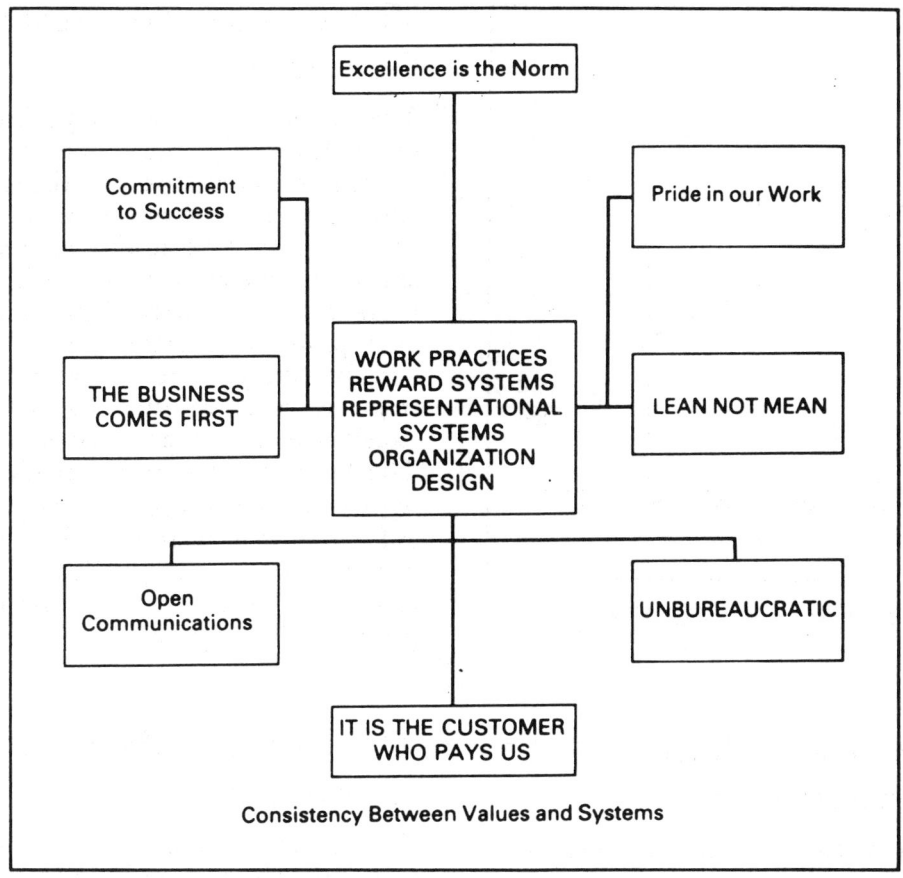

Figure 3. The new Carrington vision

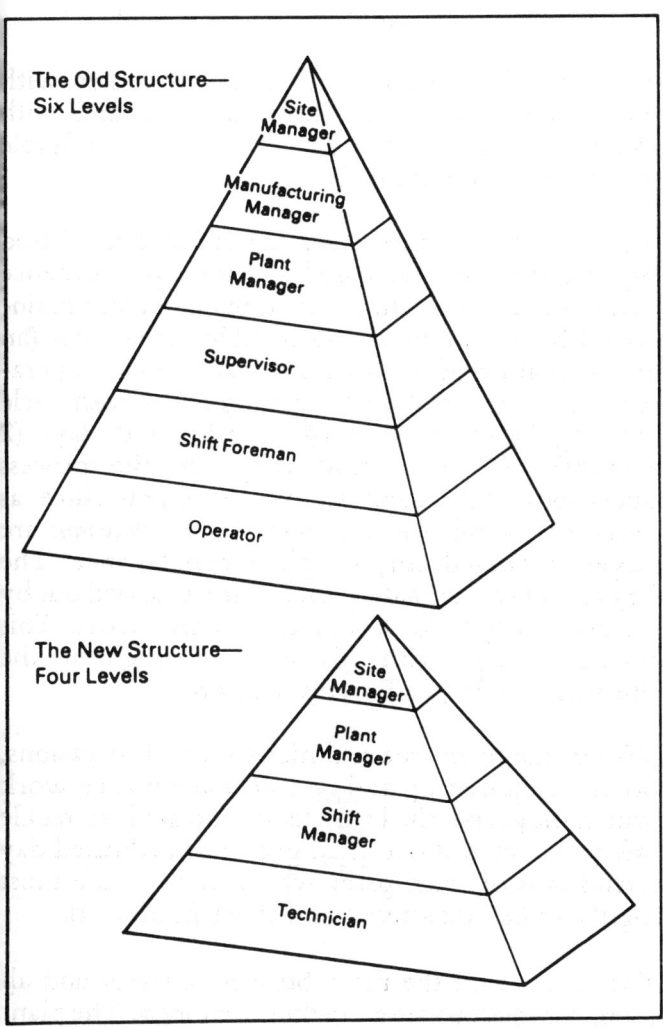

Figure 4. The change to a flatter structure

supply essential technical and administrative back-up to the four plants.

To achieve the full range of skills in the plant teams, a personal training programme is being carried out for each technician, depending on existing skills and job background (see Figure 7).

Divided into individual modules covering theory and practice this training leads to qualifications against the nationally recognized standards of the City & Guilds Institute of London. These modules are in two blocks, each taking approximately 6–9 months. Successful completion of each block is recognized by a salary increase (see Figure 8).

The new Carrington is lean but not mean. Salaries are highly competitive reflecting the value of the jobs and the gaining of extra skills.

There is a single monthly staff status for all employees. For all technician grades there is now only one union agreement with a single set of terms and conditions. Previously there had been three separate, demarcation-based union agreements, with distinctions between 'blue collar' hourly paid workers and 'white collar' monthly paid staff.

The pensionable 'rate for the job' will cover a planned $37\frac{1}{2}$ hour week and some committed hours to manage unplanned absences and peak workloads.

Every employee is paid a regular monthly distur-

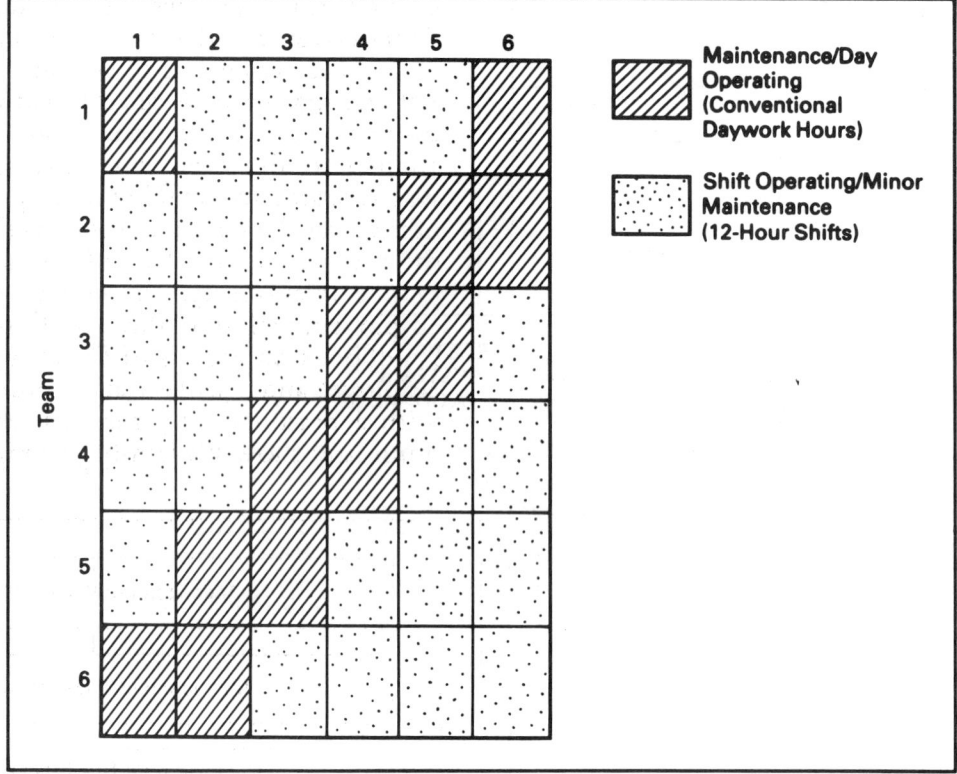

Figure 5. The six shift pattern

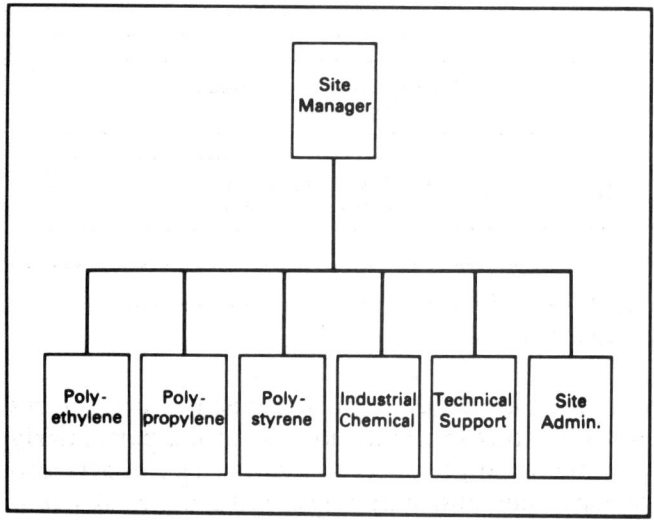

Figure 6. The site manager's team

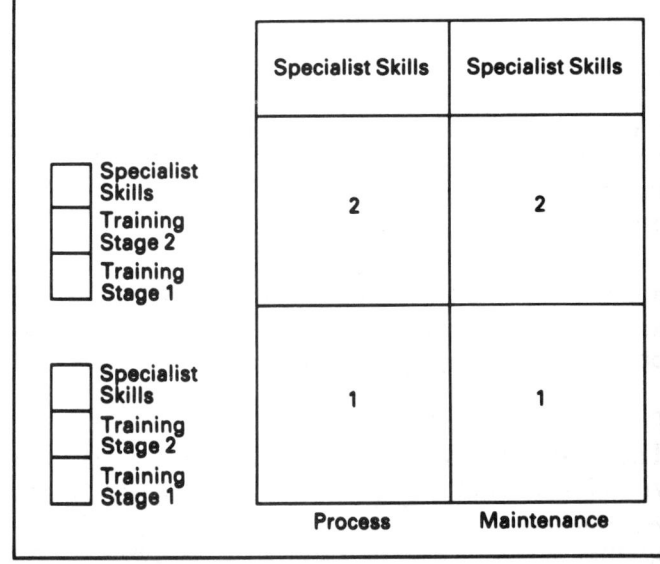

Figure 7. Technician training blocks—training emphasis depends on background

bance allowance, instead of the many incident payments that previously existed (see Figure 9).

Everyone in the new Carrington has the opportunity to earn an annual bonus based on their performance and contribution in the job and on the site results. Employees establish their performance targets jointly with their manager as part of the regular cycle of performance appraisal.

The Change Process—Fair, Firm and Fast

The key aspects of the change process itself were:

High integrity, High resolve
There was an open bias on all information—as soon as possible, as much as possible, to as many people as possible. In the context of significant job loss there was a clear commitment to maintain the company's caring tradition via the establishment of a Redeployment Unit. In addition however there was a clear resolve on the part of the company to see the change programme through, even where this involved enforced redundancy, in the firm belief that there was no viable alternative to secure the future of the site. From the outset, and particularly with regard to the trade unions, clear limits were

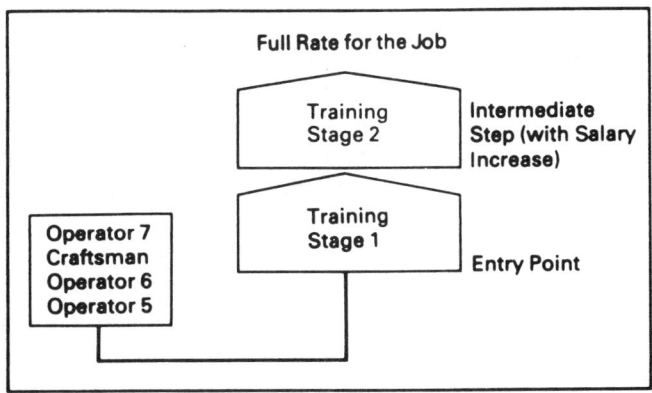

Figure 8. The senior technician ladder

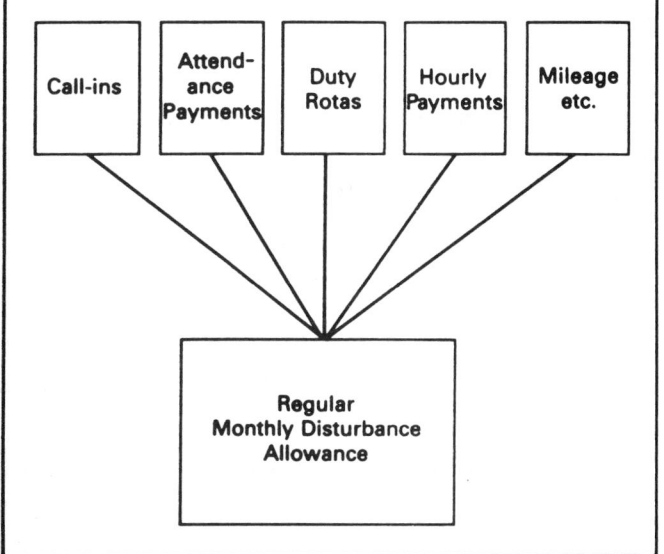

Figure 9. Consolidating many incident allowances into one

of you must go, the others must change their demarcation-based ways of working and there must be a complete change of attitudes and site culture'. All line managers were retrained in effective 'one-to-one' communications and were regularly audited. A full-time senior management resource was allocated to the sole task of producing and co-ordinating the communications effort. Building on the revitalized solid base of the line manager–employee relationship, all modern techniques were employed, including three professionally produced handbooks on aspects of the change plan for each employee and a professionally produced video, also with a personal copy for each employee to take home and show his family (see Figure 10).

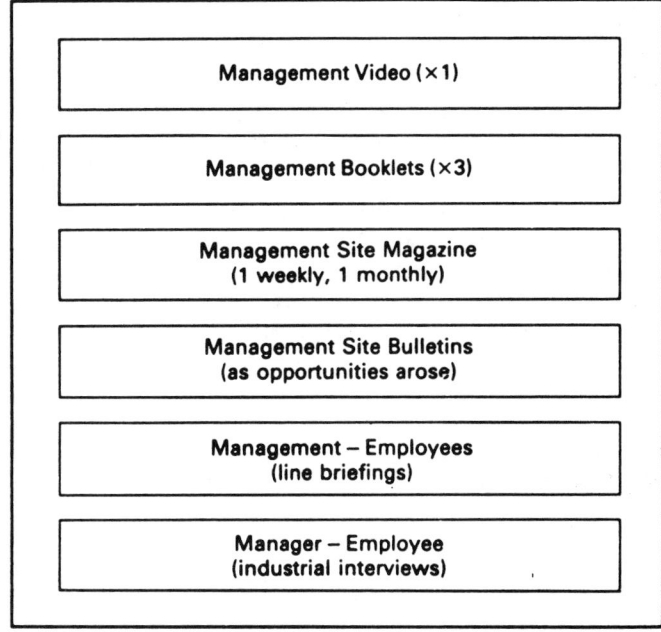

Figure 10. The employee communication programme

The simple belief which shaped Carrington's approach to communications was that, particularly in times of high uncertainty, the space between management and employees must be totally and quickly filled, otherwise, rumour and third party communications will fill the remaining vacuum.

defined beyond which the company would not alter its position as this could compromise the main objective of an overall culture change.

Primacy of the Individual

The personal uncertainty surrounding each individual was removed at the earliest opportunity. His wishes had to be established, and then considered against the company's requirements, prior to an unequivocal statement as to whether he had or did not have a job in the new organization. This process took a maximum of 4 weeks. Each individual was personally counselled at least once a fortnight by his line management focal point, specially trained in counselling techniques. Throughout the communications exercise endless stress was put on the need for each employee to consider his position on the change proposals as an individual. In addition, no information was ever given to third party union bodies which had not previously been communicated via line channels to each employee.

Effective Communications

The precise use of communications as a strategic management tool was essential in getting across and gaining support for a difficult message—'60 per cent

Tight Schedule

While the full implementation of all aspects of the change programme would take 18 months, the company adopted the tightest of schedules for the formal consultation and decision-making process, involving both individual employees and third party union bodies. This schedule was published in advance and was never deviated from (see Figure 11). The prior informal individual consultation with employees on each and every detail of the change proposals meant that a momentum had already been generated such that the formal consultation phase (4 weeks) was more than adequate.

Visible Management Leadership

Whereas the original vision for change was shared

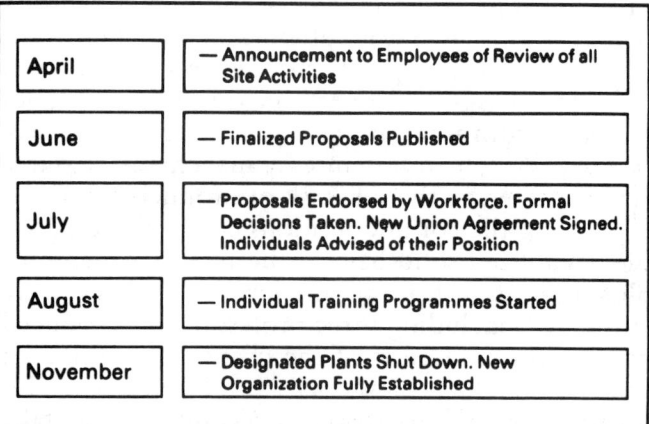

April	— Announcement to Employees of Review of all Site Activities
June	— Finalized Proposals Published
July	— Proposals Endorsed by Workforce. Formal Decisions Taken. New Union Agreement Signed. Individuals Advised of their Position
August	— Individual Training Programmes Started
November	— Designated Plants Shut Down. New Organization Fully Established

Figure 11. The change schedule (1985)

initially by a few managers, it was essential that the change programme was visibly 'owned' by all management. This process was reinforced by exclusive use of line channels to discuss every aspect of the programme. Line management were given the clear responsibility for, and were seen to manage, industrial relations without any competing influence from the personnel function. It was crucial that, to convey confidence and trust, there was a total investment of personal credibility by management as leaders in the programme.

The Redeployment Unit—Life after Carrington

As a central feature of the high integrity and innovative emphasis of the change programme, the company set up a full-time Redeployment Unit (RDU) manned by four managers and six nominees from the trade unions. The idea itself was not new, but enhanced resources and an enhanced professionalism were applied to this important area which had previously been successfully developed by other Shell sites in the United Kingdom. The full participation of employees nominated by the site trade unions reinforced the independent and discrete

role that the unit had to play. In addition to a line management focal point, each employee leaving Carrington had, therefore, an RDU 'counsellor' allocated to help him find an alternative career outside Carrington. The assistance offered was both intensely practical and emotionally supportive. The unit marketed itself forcefully to its 'clients' and to external employers who might be able to offer employment to Carrington's surplus workforce. A series of booklets, leaflets, handouts and a video gave the unit a profile and a credibility which was crucial to the well being of many employees faced with the certainty of imminent job loss.

Carrington Now—The Realization of Change

The change programme, involving a 57 per cent reduction in manpower, was supported by almost the entire workforce as the best hope for the future of the site. The programme has throughout proceeded to its published tight schedule and training of the new multi-skilled technicians is nearing completion. Site manpower was reduced to the target level of below 500 by the end of 1986. Of the 500 staff that were laid off by the end of April 1986 some 76 per cent were helped to find alternative work outside Carrington by the Redeployment Unit, 42 per cent have also undergone some form of additional skill training which might help them find alternative work. A further 13 per cent chose not to continue working after leaving Carrington. The remainder of the surplus staff, some 200, had left the site by the end of 1986, and it is anticipated that a similar percentage of redeployment will be achieved.

The new Carrington is operating within its tight budget and the site is meeting its new profitability targets. The management believe that attitudes have really changed and that there is a new site culture, geared towards beating the competition amid the harsh realities of a highly competitive business world.

Planning for a Rapidly Changing Environment in SAS

Olle Stiwenius, Senior Consultant, SAS Management Consultants, Sweden

The author describes how Scandinavian Airlines achieved a turnaround from unprofitability and loss of market share. The creation and development of a corporate culture revitalized personnel and initiated a new management role, business-oriented rather than administrative. Punctuality became a specific goal and won for SAS the reputation of being Europe's most punctual airline. The change process is likely to continue into the future and the new internal management systems will change to meet these needs.

The dramatic turnaround of SAS probably owes more to changes in people and organization than to anything else. There is no doubt that the changes in profitability are exciting. However, once we have carefully studied the annual reports they are merely historic facts. The major transformation was from a production-oriented airline to a market-oriented service company. The management of SAS realized they had to become customer-oriented—simply to start working as a service company. One of our directors pointed out that 'the battle for the air will have to be fought on the ground'. The change has also emphasized the role of the manager in corporate renewal and the adoption of an explicit business philosophy in order to gain commitment and involvement.

Something had Happened Out There

For a long time SAS had lived in a steadily growing market very much protected by the international air line agreements. The business was managed to profitability by generally economizing and reciprocally dividing the markets.

As the market grew 'automatically' we were simply taking orders. Profitability was reached by keeping down costs and protecting our investments in

The author is Senior Consultant, SAS Management Consultants, Sweden.

aeroplanes and other assets. And we did very good business, focusing on technical improvements and selling our aircraft—very successfully (Figure 1).

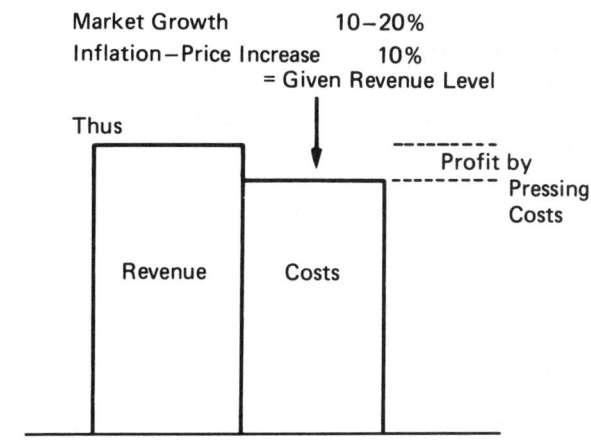

Figure 1. We could calculate profitability

Unfortunately, the more we cut costs the more we cut back our service and consequently lost market share. We got into some kind of vicious circle (Figure 2).

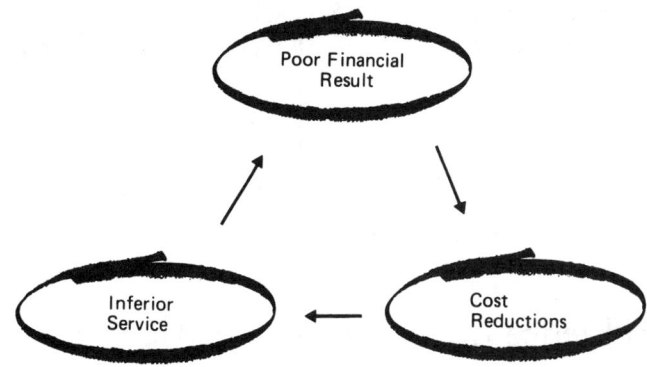

Figure 2. The vicious circle

Then many things changed: increased fuel prices, rising costs, price wars, dwindling demand and liberalization of air-transport competition. SAS lost money at the rate of £7000 per hour (Figure 3).

117

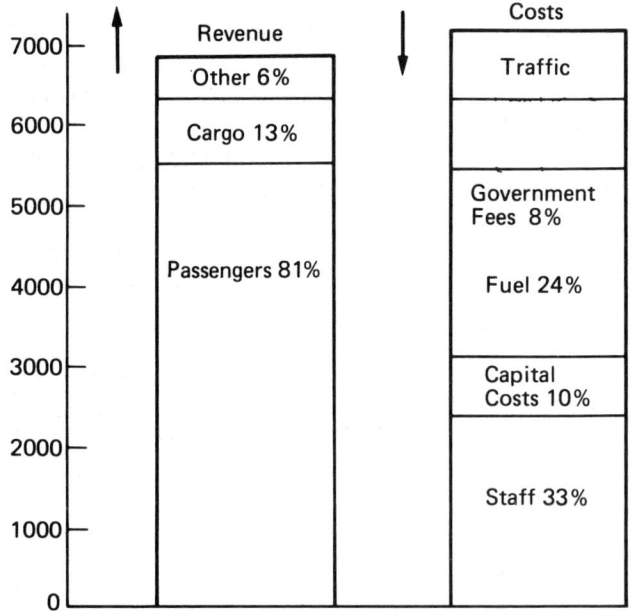

Figure 3. Revenues and costs 1980/1981

It became apparent that a competitive market called for an entirely new corporate philosophy, and our deteriorating service was having disastrous consequences.

Now, an airline like business can adapt to any level of market-share, but cannot live on with a falling trend. So we had to make a quick pull-up and to work together on becoming the world's best service airline. To master the accelerating deficits, caused by the vicious circle, we had to act and act fast (Figure 4).

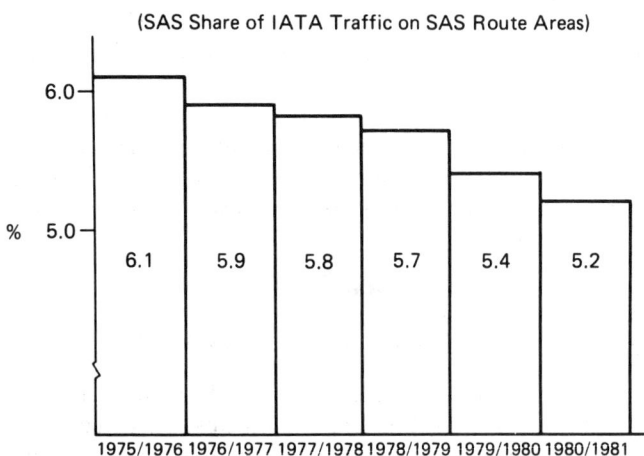

Figure 4. SAS market share

Influence on Organizational Culture

The aim was to adapt to the market preferences. This meant that we had to become attractive to our passengers by meeting their demands.

As our President pointed out

We can have as many beautiful aircraft as we like and still not survive if we don't have passengers who would rather fly SAS than our competitors.

Because the only ones who are willing to pay our cost next year are the satisfied customers of today

This also meant that we had to look upon our costs as a potential basis for income and to generate income by market-orientation.

Obviously the staff closest to the market tend to notice market-changes first, but our organization was not arranged to pick up the signals fast enough. Thus we might have been a bit late in adapting to the new environment.

The major reason for our former slowness was unquestionably that we had put too many restrictions on the behaviour of our front line employees, who account for roughly 50 per cent of our personnel. Living by the detailed rules and regulations did not allow our 'front soldiers' to give the service our customers demanded.

Who is in the best situation to adapt to the market's needs? Who has the most frequent contacts? Who is able to initiate better service and who knows the market's need the best? The Front Line of course!

With our 'Front line personnel' we already had all the knowledge we always tried to buy in market surveys. So we 'classified' all other human resources as 'support troops' or 'support functions', who are supposed to look upon the 'Front line' as their primary customer.

These basic circumstances called for a reorganization in order to achieve the greatest possible market contact and the greatest possible delegation of responsibility and authority to the 'Front line'.

In fact, no instructions or regulations whatsoever, could possibly 'direct' our annual 40–100 million individual passenger contacts to create customer satisfaction. It called for an entirely new view on 'the customer in focus' (Figure 5).

Towards a New Corporate Philosophy

The SAS turnaround had to be directed towards the reality that the only thing that counts in a service company is a satisfied customer.

Our company's philosophy and its organizational structure were based on the same prevailing ideas as industrial society. It was created to satisfying growing market needs by effective use of production resources, i.e. primarily managing investing capital—to keep installations profitable.

Many corporate reorganizations during the 1970s tried to bring about profitability by planning from their own production resources out to the market (Why don't they buy our super-product?). All

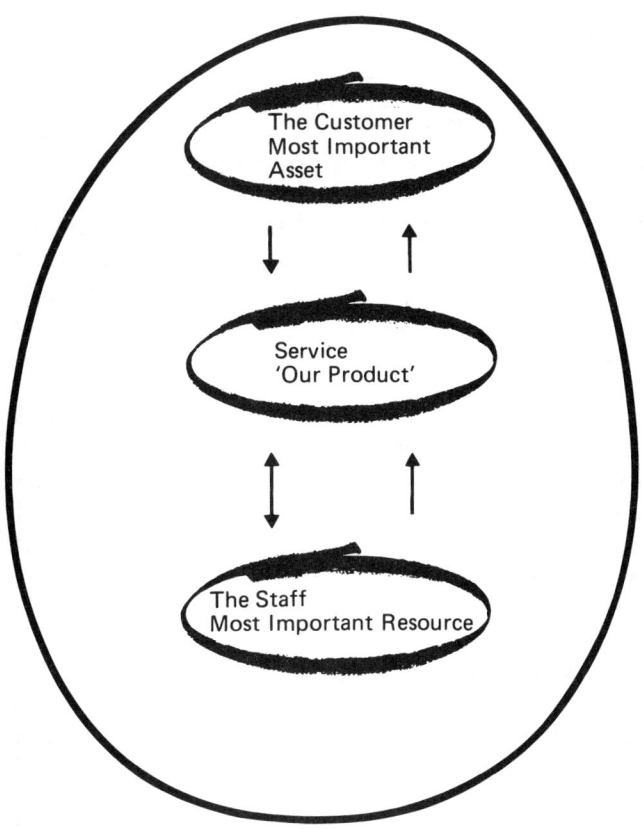

Figure 5. SAS concept

business education aimed at handling cost-cutting programmes, and the salesman's job was just to sell what the company produced.

SAS also fell into that trap. Specialist functions and specialists were created for every conceivable task—functional organizations were supposed to look after the assets, but rather they tended to preserve the investments already made. And manuals were produced abundantly with the aim of making us produce even more effeciently. The bitter truth however was that we were putting more and more restrictions on our employees' methods of working (Figure 6).

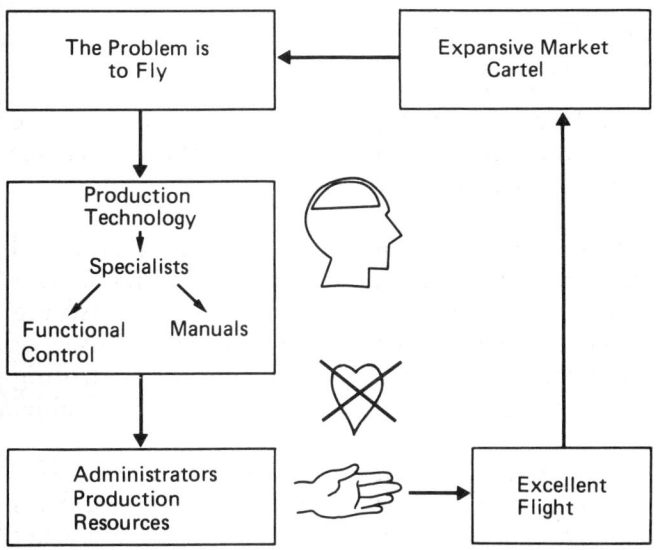

Figure 6. Old SAS

This belief in one 'right' course of action worked very well for a long time. But looking around in the world of uncertain income SAS management realized we had to start with the market, not with our resources. Product development and planning called for reversing our strategic approach.

As the growth in sales slowed down we started to look upon market development as our major challenge (Figure 7).

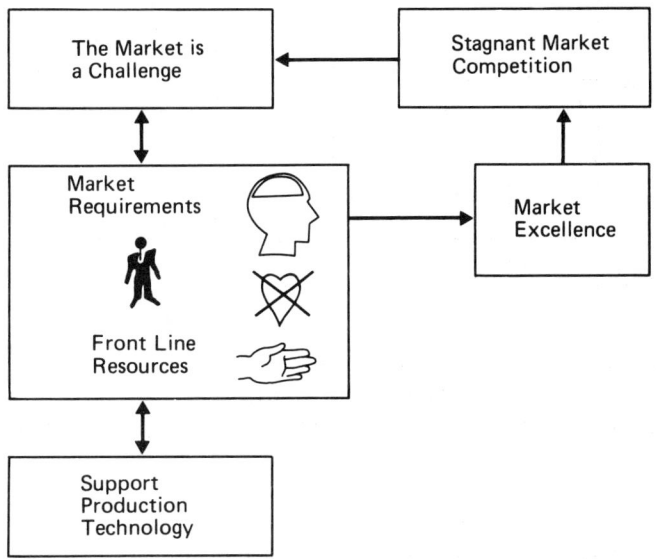

Figure 7. New SAS

Our strategic decision thus became firstly, an offensive directed towards market-segments we singled out. And secondly, we marshalled our resources to the needs of those markets, i.e. strengthening the 'Front Line'. Our corporate philosophy was reformulated thus:

> In a stagnating market, where competitive forces are set free, a company can achieve profitability only by adjusting and aggressively investing to meet customer needs better than the competition.

SAS Enters 'The Virtuous Circle'

One of the basic facts in business is that a deficit will arise if costs are higher than revenues. So to reverse the situation, you either have to reduce the costs or increase your income.

SAS decided to do both at the same time.

Our strategy meant that we had to bring our resources into line with their revenue-making potential. In other words simply cutting costs across the board would not be the solution to meet customer needs. Our President gave an expressive illustration of this, pointing out that:

> you have to set a car moving before you apply the brakes. Otherwise no other change may occur but the obvious risk that you may step through the floor and damage the car.

In practice we worked hard on helping our staff to understand what they should expect. The entire change process was supported by clear and simple information (brochures, videotapes, debates, in-house magazines, etc.) on our course of action. The introductory information on our new strategies was published in a brochure called 'Let's get in there and fight'.

This communication produced an increase in motivation, like all understanding does, and this was further reinforced by 'service-training'. Our third basis for the virtuous circle was an extensive management training programme to increase the organization's ability to act according to our new philosophy.

In short we created consciousness, knowledge and desire to change to the new approach.

Organizational Structure and Service Management

We had to adjust our organization to the fact that income is created by offering the customers those products they are prepared to pay for (basics in a market-orientated organization as opposed to a technology- and production-orientated one). Clearly, market segmentation is nothing new. On the contrary, it seems so evident that many industries have overlooked it in their struggle for production efficiency.

In the case of SAS we created the 'businessman's airline', in which we offered the business traveller a product to suit their needs.

Now, what about the costs? Certainly we focused on those as well, but we decentralized the initiative to managers closer to the market than our head-office. And this is where the service concept is so important.

Costs are largely incurred in the 'delivery system' of a company's structure, i.e. primarily in the human resources. We realized we had to improve our performance in these areas, to the concept of service, where you engage yourself in solving the customer's problems.

So we moved staff from the back office to more needed functions closer to the customer/passenger, to provide peripheral services (booking, checking, waiting, comfort, attentiveness, etc.) in the front line 'delivery-system' and we trained them for the new tasks.

We are now organized in relatively small, result-oriented and independent functions. We have discarded the old military organization where hierarchies tend to disrupt the communication patterns, thus delaying vital decisions close to the customer/passenger (Figure 8).

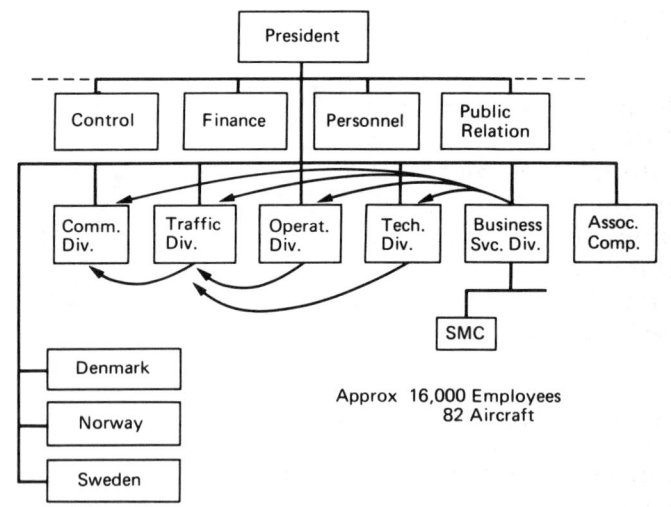

Figure 8. SAS organizations

Strengthened Market-Organization

The new SAS organization is adjusted to market-demand and based on wide spread delegation. It could be viewed as a wheel, where the customer/passenger constitutes the hub.

This kind of structure encourages the customer-orientation and flexibility. It opens up possibilities for competent personnel to develop quickly and take responsibility for results without direct supervision. The organization form also emphasizes communication, co-operation and co-ordination. And it is supported by a very ambitious programme of personnel and management development.

The Significance of SAS 'Cultural Patterns'

A corporate culture is the pattern of habits, goals, concepts, ideas and behaviour that are found within a company. It is strongly influenced by the formulas which management develops to the benefit of the company. In a successful enterprise the culture reflects the market situation. It develops differently in a situation of growth than in a stagnating market.

Thus, the corporate culture should harmonize with the commercial environment. When this changes, the culture has to change as well, if the company is to survive.

This change took place and is still taking place in SAS. In fact our organizational market-orientation meant a new Corporate Culture. We believe that in order to maintain SAS as an excellent service company we have to have the same basic values shared among all our staff. We are convinced that a satisfied customer continues to fly SAS rather than simply to fly, and is therefore the result of a market investment. Our values also suppose that customers want to be treated as individuals, they want personal service, to feel at home and to be taken care of by SAS.

We have described this culture by concluding that 'SAS lives with its customers' and 'a satisfied customer is our only real asset'. We also try to treat our own staff as individuals. We have created a culture where our customer is in the centre and creates opportunities for individual initiative and commitment that invests in market segments and 'backs winners'.

Open Attitudes

A major transformation calls for radical structural and cultural changes. And changing an obsolete success formula, deeply embedded in the minds of key company personnel, also calls for strong action. Probably, before meaningful changes can be carried through, it is imperative to demonstrate dramatically that the former, well-proven formulas are no longer valid.

The SAS way of doing this has been to provide generous and open information to create new attitudes towards the customer and to colleagues. For example the consequences of market orientation had to be clearly formulated and communicated. The new SAS philosophy states that 'change is a condition for survival and thus provides security'. So we focused very much on our view that the only way to survive is through a continuous process of change in people and organization.

We also made it our responsibility to give information fast, and to back it up with concrete initiatives. As we openly declared that 'our staff is our foremost resource' we made it our policy that 'everyone is responsible for making sure that we have satisfied customers' and 'seek the information you need so that you can assume your responsibility'.

When Something Goes Wrong . . .

There are always reasons when things go wrong. But we made it acceptable to risk mistakes. One of our most important messages from Management was that 'Mistakes can be corrected, but lost time can never be regained'. So we had to allow our staff to make decisions so that the customer's needs were satisfied immediately. The normal procedure would be *not* to refer the matter to a superior, who primarily has a supporting function and the responsibility to develop the quality of staff.

In the 'New SAS' the philosophy is rather to allow oneself a few misses now and then by testing new ideas instead of spending excessive time to be absolutely certain that the decision will be a complete success.

When things go wrong, information must immediately be given, internally and externally, explaining what has gone wrong.

The reasons why the problem occurred and the current position must be clearly formulated. The opposite, to emphasize uncertainty by total silence, will only result in confusion, scepticism and irritation. This is the core of SAS's new, open attitude.

New Supervision and Leadership

To focus so much on the employee requires supervision and leadership to support those who provide the customer-service. It also requires that product planning and the product itself are arranged so that the contact between personnel and passengers is positive.

All the components work upon each other, thus enabling every employee to provide a service to the individual customer/passenger, which creates positive feelings—the 'Moment of Truth' for SAS.

New Goals and Strategies

To support the individual in his decisions, our philosophy includes providing goals and strategies that are so easy to understand that all staff can help according to their abilities. The framework, set by management, has to allow our departments to change operations on the basis of market demand instead of keeping to detailed internal requirements. Thus, during the change process we have lived roughly with only one goal:

> to create such a profit by 1990 that we can favourably finance the need for new aircraft by then.

And we regard all costs as potential resources for the market. Even our own support functions have defined their 'internal markets', because services produced internally have 'buyers', who can define their need, volume, quality, etc. just like other purchasers (Figure 9).

Our main strategy is to develop 'The business traveller's airline', and as many resources as possible were directed towards this task. We also produced complementary strategies like marginal-, concentration-trading- and transformation-strategies. Of these none was allowed to influence our 'Main strategy'. Thus everybody was focused on serving our business travellers in all situations.

The Change

The most important feature of our transition was maybe the strategy of speed. The organizational restructuring was carried through in approximately 5 months. It was probably our 'crisis-awareness'

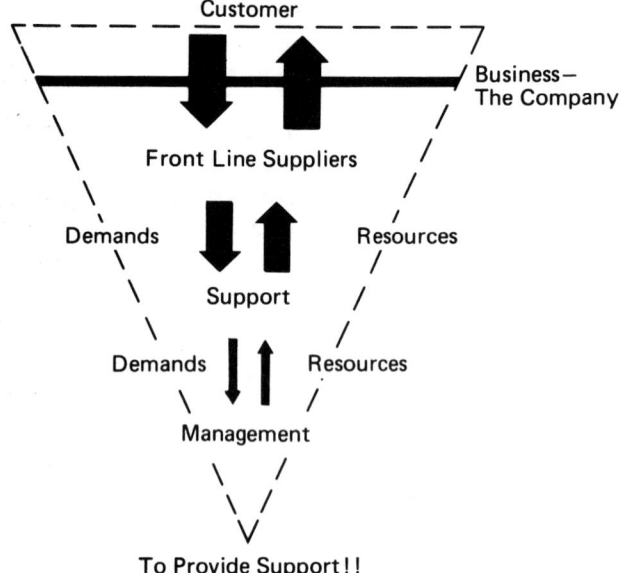

Figure 9. What is the purpose of the 'organization'?

that triggered the start. Everyone came to understand that our heavy deficits called for something to be done. Thus all of the staff wanted to change things (Figure 10).

Also, the direction of change was carefully communicated. At an early stage we gathered around the slogan: 'Let's get in there and fight', which clearly pointed out our strategy. It was formulated in a booklet sent to each employee's home which outlined SAS's goals, philosophy and course of development.

Popularly it was referred to as 'Carlzon's Little Red Book' and it was very helpful for working out decentralized strategies and change-programmes, which were achieved within 2 months.

One of the most interesting messages our President presented was 'to become 1 per cent better in a hundred details rather than 100 per cent better in one detail'. The change was heavily supported with an extensive information-plan, internally, to help the staff to understand what was happening and to encourage them to participate in changing their way of working.

Creation of Credibility

To build up a belief in communication a detailed programme of activities was worked out and carried through.

To realize our business strategies we invested $20m in 150 projects to become more customer-orientated, like e.g. 'business-traveller's airline, Euroclass and First business class'. This orientation towards market potential involved most of our staff in work to create 'a new SAS' instead of becoming too problem-oriented.

Simultaneously we carried through a comprehensive Management Development programme for approximately 2000 'key-persons' among upper and middle management. And in addition we offered all our 10,000 front line staff a 2-day course in 'Personal Service through personal development'. There is no doubt that this programme brought about a remarkable change in attitudes among our employees.

Emphasis on Training

The reason for the SAS success is that we were able, through training and combined information efforts, to create a new, creative and market-sensitive 'climate'. Our organization with very

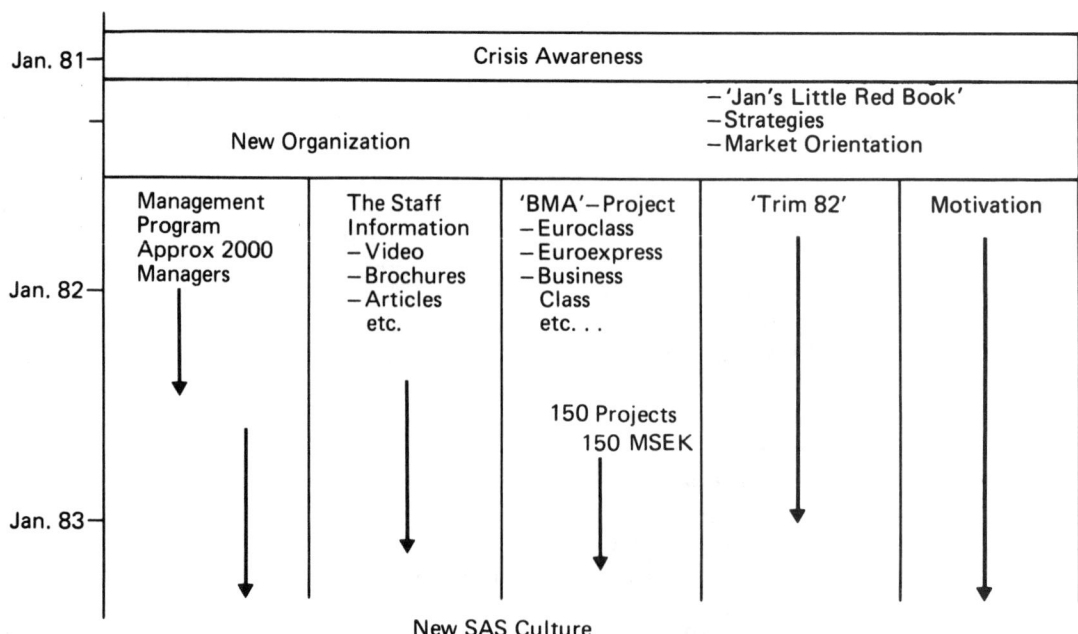

Figure 10. Plan of activities for the SAS change

open channels for communication has become more venturesure through this intensive programme of spreading our philosophy.

The basic programme has now been completed by bringing more middle managers, supervisors and foremen into training. As everything is aimed at changing our 'corporate culture' the subjects have included strategy finance and service management.

Market-Value Analysis

A vital element in the change-process was to relate resources to needs. This was carried through in the form of a decentralized value/activity–analysis, performed by each new division.

By holding a serious discussion between internal service functions (support-functions) and the receivers of this support (mainly front line personnel) we were able to define our 'over-capacity', i.e. services nobody was prepared to pay for. As a consequence these resources were transferred to other activities, where a shortage of resources could be found. This strengthened the front line organization by offering better service to our 'key-staff', meeting our customers in numerous 'moments of truth'.

New Management Role

This also means that a completely new management role has been recognized in SAS, that is the task of maintaining the continued development of our 'Corporate Culture', where will-power, energy and ability to push through a new policy might be decisive for success or failure (Figure 11).

From	To
Production Orientation	Marketing Orientation
Cost Responsibility	Result Responsibility
Centralization	Decentralization
Administrators	Businessmen
Instruction	Information
Force	Freedom
Reaction	Action
Problem	Possibility

Figure 11

It requires a business-oriented and participative leadership to imbue a team-spirit and to revitalize personnel attitudes. Thus management must be supportive and inspirational, setting goals and guidelines and delegating operational responsibility in a strong and clear manner.

In addition there is a strong emphasis on being result-orientated, where it is the result which is assessed and judged rather than the course of action that led up to the result.

In this result-orientated organization, department heads are expected to be businessmen rather than administrators, to cause action instead of reaction and to give information rather than instructions.

In other words the new leadership in SAS means that a manager's primary responsibility is to develop the quality of his or her staff.

The Future

We are pretty sure that our markets will undergo substantial changes in the future and that these changes will occur very swiftly. We also recognize that it is frequently difficult for existing management to review an earlier market-situation and radically question, re-orientate or reject former activities. Therefore we will probably be faced with the continuous re-organization of our business in order to formulate new demands, new goals, a new management philosophy and new strategies to achieve these goals.

We must also be prepared to draw up new internal management systems to change our company's culture and revise the modes of thinking among 'key personnel'.

Such changes are already taking place. We are now organizing for a 'Total Travel and Service concept' in order to adapt to new market requirements, and the change process goes on, or rather a new one is already emerging.

So, now that we have been successful in making a quick pull-up, we are building for the 1990s.

Leadership

No doubt the turnaround of SAS has been greatly inspired by the new type of leadership that Jan Carlzon represents. Some key characteristics could be noted:

☆ SAS staff at an early stage were made aware of the clear vision of the future that our President held, i.e. ideas about probable changes in the market-situation.

☆ He believes in the individual's ability to take on greater responsibilities given the opportunities.

This is of course a supportive management philosophy, executed by Mr. Carlzon and many others which clearly challenges people to be more adventurous and entrepreneurial.

☆ He has communicated very skilfully during the entire change. In a very simple and understandable manner our weak and strong points have been described. And through visual communication our staff has been encouraged to handle the business in an unorthodox way.

☆ Knowledge is also vital to carry through major changes. As Mr. Carlzon had experience of managing a successful domestic airline—and other travel businesses—he could act very confidently and this gave other people confidence in carrying out his decisions.

Changing the Corporate Image

The actual change in SAS service was quickly noticed by our passengers and aroused much interest from the media. Also our image as 'the businessman's airline' was projected in a number of brochures and advertisments, distributed to our customers and to our own staff. The distribution was based on the idea that 'you should not inform your customers better than your own employees'.

The presentation of the company's image is so vital in a change process that SAS management decided to change the firm's 'brand image'. We changed our logotype, colours, uniforms and made a complete redesign of our aircraft and office interiors. Not only did this signal an important change in the eyes of customers and employees, it was also intended to prolong the economic life-time of our assets.

We chose 'punctuality' for special attention as a central part of our image. For an airline employee 'punctuality' is the one thing everyone can easily do something about. Our President put up a TV monitor in his office so at any time of the day or night he could check our punctuality. And he had this particular priority projected to customers and employees. Thus we could all see how important 'punctuality' was to the new SAS.

The Role of Project Teams

SAS management believes in the effectiveness of project teams in solving specific problems and consciously uses them in the change process. The best example is probably the goal 'to become the most punctual air line in Europe'. A project team was asked what it would cost SAS to reach that goal. After a short time a comprehensive report was presented. Management, however, was primarily interested in the cost—estimated to some million Swedish kronor. They decided that 'punctuality' was worth that amount, and they gave the project an immediate 'go-ahead'.

In less than 3 months SAS was the most punctual airline in Europe, and our President summarized his conclusion in these words:

> We became Europe's most punctual airline. It didn't cost millions. It cost a fraction of the estimate, and we don't know how the money was spent.

If the project team had been given detailed instructions on how to make the airline more punctual, it would probably have spent the millions to find out they could not carry out the task.

It is this freedom of action which now guides all our project teams at SAS.

Changing the Corporate Culture of Rank Xerox

Paul Chapman

Since the introduction in 1986, by a new Managing Director, of an integrated team management philosophy and with the support of an advanced office systems technology, Rank Xerox has increased sales each year and management profits have more than doubled. The major strategic objective has been to exploit the opportunities in the office systems market by demonstrating the power that the right technology can have in turning a business around.

When David O'Brien joined Rank Xerox (UK) Ltd as Managing Director in early 1986, his major strategic objective was to exploit the technological opportunities offered by the company's office equipment range of products, particularly its multi-function workstations and Xerox network services, by becoming a key player in the emerging office systems market. While this market offered enormous potential growth it was (as yet) not dominated by any single supplier.

For many years Xerox Corporation had been able to develop concepts and products at the leading edge of technology through its world famous Palo Alto Research Centre (PARC)—in fact Xerox researchers had developed many techniques to support the use of technology in the office ranging from Ethernet local area network and document management architecture through to WIMP technology (windows, icons, mouse, pull-down menus) and the working desktop view concept—but had never really commercially exploited these products and ideas.

O'Brien analysed the challenge facing him into two main areas, the first concerned the company's strategy (see Figure 1) and its marketing, and the second its organization and management processes.

Strategic/Marketing Challenge

The historic strategy, organization and culture of Rank Xerox had evolved to optimize the selling of 'copiers' as stand-alone boxes. The copier/duplicator products which had made the name Rank Xerox famous, represented a 'replacement' market, and one which had been aggressively attacked by Japanese competitors. Such a market did not offer Rank Xerox the prospects for growth latent in the office systems market-place. Most marketing actions were, in spite of quality improvement and a good record of product innovation, tactical and reflected the intense competition:

☆ Aggressive pricing

☆ Selling features and price

☆ 'Box' selling

☆ Cost reduction programmes

☆ Product focus.

To help achieve Xerox/Rank Xerox's world-wide corporate revenue and profit growth target, David O'Brien had been tasked to develop the office systems revenues of Rank Xerox (UK) to a half of total revenue within 4 years. O'Brien's previous experience in the systems business told him that an entirely different set of skills, marketing programmes and strategic objectives would be needed to succeed in the office systems market, in particular:

☆ Account management

☆ Selling solutions

☆ Executive awareness and

☆ Customer focus.

The development of this approach and the associated skills could also have a positive effect in the more 'traditional' areas of the business, particularly as the technologies of the copier/duplicator and

Paul Chapman is Director of Business Management Systems at Rank Xerox (UK) Ltd.

```
┌─────────────────────────────────────────────────────────────────┐
│                ┌─────────────────────────────────────┐           │
│                │  INFORMATION TECHNOLOGY STATUS      │           │
│                └─────────────────────────────────────┘           │
│                         Many Executives today                    │
│              do not believe they have gained the full value of   │
│                 their investment in Information Technology        │
│                    despite the growing awareness of the          │
│                      strategic value of information              │
│                                                                   │
│            ┌──────────────────────────────────────────┐          │
│            │  OFFICE AUTOMATION VS OFFICE SYSTEMS     │          │
│            └──────────────────────────────────────────┘          │
│       Office Automation has applied technology to the automation of discrete activities │
│                                                                   │
│       Office Systems applies technology to the support of overall processes in the office │
│                    ┌──────────────────────────────┐              │
│                    │  THE TRUE OFFICE ENVIRONMENT │              │
│                    └──────────────────────────────┘              │
│            Requires support for both Unstructured and Structured Activities │
│                               involving                           │
│                       Office Systems Technology                   │
│                              as well as                           │
│                       Data Processing Technology                  │
│                                                                   │
│            Office Systems Technology can only be effective if it is built │
│               on an architecture designed to support the true office │
│                             environment                           │
└─────────────────────────────────────────────────────────────────┘
```

Figure 1. Rank Xerox's view of office systems

office systems market-places began to merge: facsimile on the net, electronic reprographics etc.

Organization/Infrastructure

Until Japan Inc's entry into the market, Rank Xerox had had the lion's share of the copier/duplicator market although it faced, and continues to face, tough competition from other technologies (e.g. offset printing at the 'top end' of its product range). IBM, Kodak *et al.* had begun to play in specific market areas as the Xerox patents expired but without denting Xerox's share to any great extent —and its structure and culture reflected that position. Strong, functional directors with a clearly demarcated territory, geared to consolidation of the company's (and their) position, internally focused with large staff groups concentrating on internal issues.

The company's systems and processes were geared to 'box selling' and were functionally owned. With the new strategic business dimension of office systems being added, these systems and processes needed a fundamental review to cope with a highly competitive business environment in which resource efficiency and competitive edge are paramount with the added complexity of the integrated systems product range (see Figure 2).

The classic approach to this situation would have been to replace the executive directors whose

experience had been predominantly in the copier/duplicator market-place with tried and tested executives, experienced in the systems business in order to drive the company towards achievement of its enlarged strategic objectives. However, there was a large ($300m turnover) copier/duplicator business to run. The company continued to innovate to retain product leadership in its copier/duplicator core business and the returns from this 'traditional' business would need to fund the investments needed to succeed in the office systems market.

O'Brien therefore adopted a different approach. He retained intact the Executive Board, with all of the 'operational' functions still in place: sales, marketing, finance, service, personnel and legal, and appointed two new directors as 'facilitators':

☆ Director, Strategic Business Development, to facilitate the changes required from a Strategic and Marketing viewpoint

☆ Director, Business Management Systems, to facilitate the changes required from an Organization and Infrastructure point of view.

The organization of the new board is shown in Figure 3.

Having put the broad organization in place, the next key step was to develop the 'vehicle' to deliver the strategy. One jewel which shone through the mist of issues was the company's own Leadership Through Quality Programme.

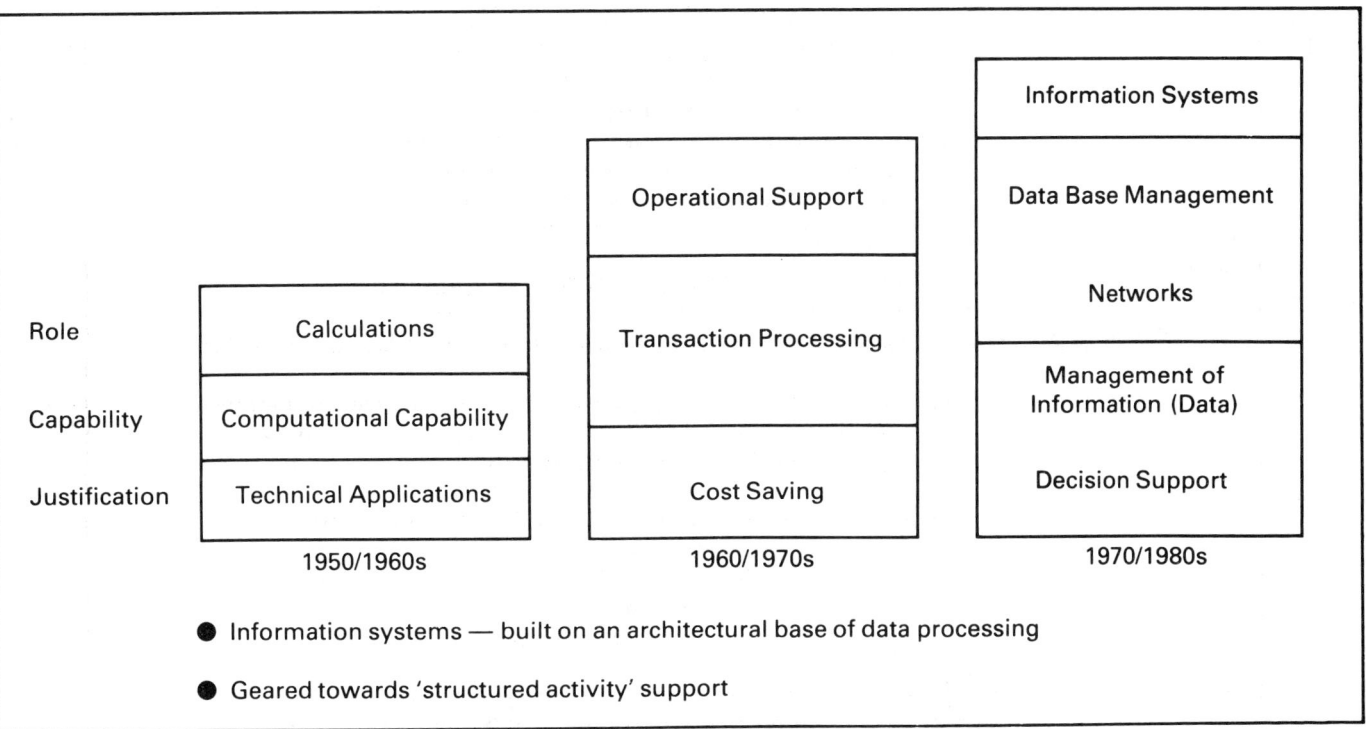

Figure 2. The impact of information technology 1950s–1980s

The Leadership Through Quality Programme was an initiative that had been started by David Kearns, CEO of Xerox Corporation. Kearns had recognized that much of the entrepreneurial spirit which had led to the spectacular growth in the Corporation in the 1960s and 1970s was becoming stifled by the growth of a cumbersome, bureaucratic, internally focused organization as the company 'matured'.

The inspiration for the programme, in common with a number of programmes introduced in the 1980s by Xerox to underpin its successful fight to

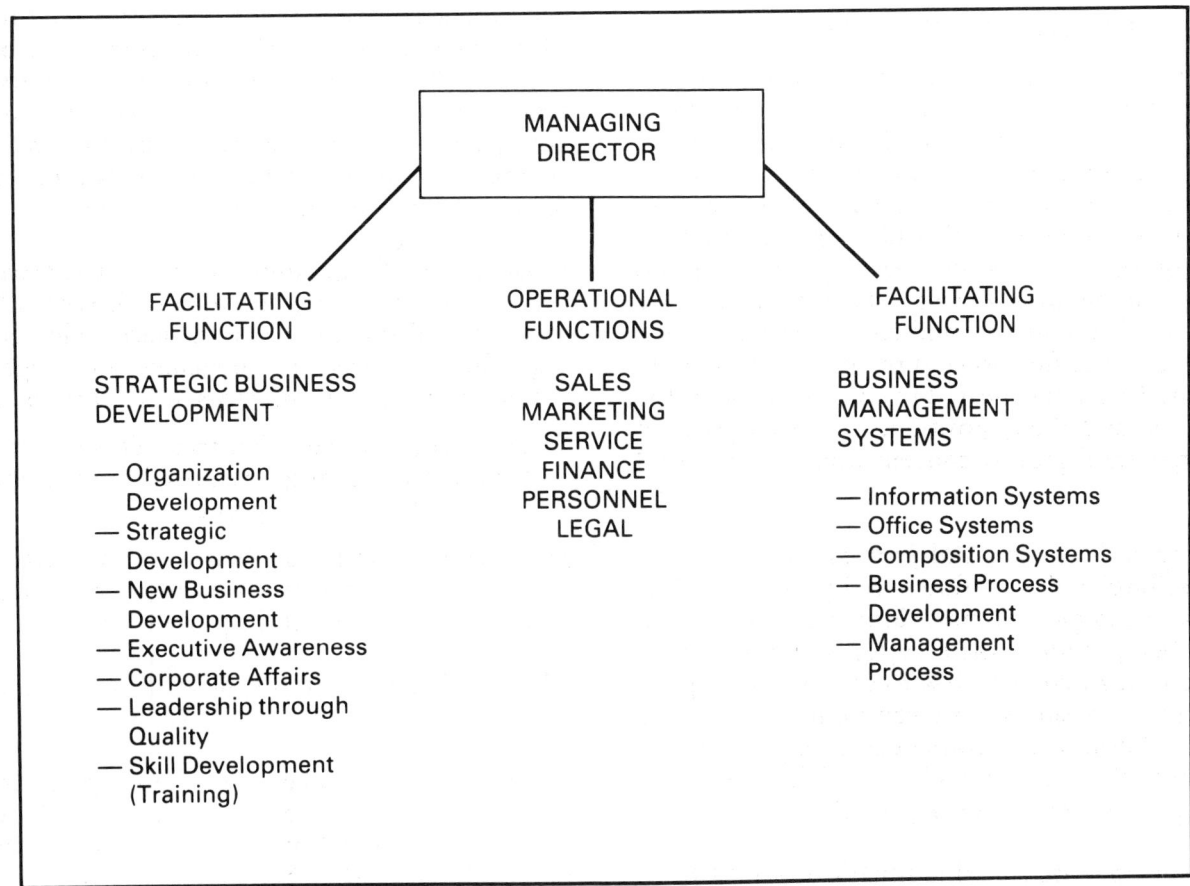

Figure 3. The new board arrangement

regain market share from the Japanese competition, was Fuji Xerox a 50:50 joint venture between Rank Xerox Ltd and Fuji Photo Film Company of Japan (see Figure 4).

Therein lay the problem. The Xerox definition of quality was 'conforming to customer requirements', and the Leadership Through Quality Process was clearly focused on identifying who the customer was (internal or external), determining his requirements, and then developing plans to satisfy those requirements. This was very much an 'oriental' approach to business problems, and in many ways clashed with the traditional 'occidental' managerial approach which was based on establishing objectives and achieving them via action plans.

A good illustration of the 'clash of cultures' is a story relating to Ray MacDonald, CEO of the Burroughs Corporation whose autocratic approach to his employees extended to his relationships with customers and suppliers. Visiting Tokyo to review a joint venture Burroughs had established in Japan to market its products, MacDonald was convinced that the executive offices were on the fourth floor, as were his own offices back in Detroit. Having informed the lift operator of his destination, his Japanese hosts, not wishing to disagree with the 'customer', suggested 'Fourth floor very good, but fifth floor may be better'.

The implementation of the Leadership Through Quality Programme in Rank Xerox (UK) with its emphasis on the customer had led to some severe organizational strains. The statement 'I am the customer, satisfy me' threw many of the traditional problem-solving processes into total confusion and led to substantial resources being dedicated to satisfying non-essential requirements.

Clearly what the process needed to be effective, was a framework in which to operate. During his time as Sales and Marketing Director at Burroughs, O'Brien had introduced a process called Business Development Planning, used successfully by his account teams, sometimes with customers, to determine the key strategies and objectives within an account. Facilitated by an external consultancy, Cambridge Associates, he introduced a similar process, but one tailored to the distinct requirements of the new situation in Rank Xerox, and developed a comprehensive approach to implementing an integrated management process.

Although the actual processes used in the Business Development Planning approach and Leadership Through Quality were very similar, their focus was entirely different. Taking each methodology at the appropriate 'organizational responsibility' level, he was able to implement a comprehensive and fully integrated planning approach. The step between Business Development Planning and Leadership Through Quality, the Business Systems Requirements Review, used the same methodology as Business Development Planning but focused on rules (policies, procedures, and guidelines), systems requirements, management processes and resources required to deliver the objectives defined from the Business Development Planning Output (see Figure 5).

Throughout the whole process, the emphasis was on teamwork. At the root of all the methodologies now incorporated under the banner of 'Leadership Through Quality' was the emphasis on true consensus and team commitment, on a cross-functional basis. Although initially decisions seem to take longer within this kind of process (and indeed the whole process outlined above took many months, with senior management locked at close quarters, often for week long sessions) this is only due to the initial investment required in training and understanding. As the functional barriers break down and individuals see the process as a 'natural' way to conduct their business, decision-taking speeds up and the *quality* of the decisions shines through.

The methodology and philosophy can best be illustrated with some examples of the results to date. Quite obviously, the major effects of such an approach are long term, but already the organization is beginning to see the benefits.

- **Unique Joint Venture:** Xerox, Rank Xerox, Fuji Xerox, Modi Xerox

- **Total Revenues:** ca £9bn, £6bn + Office Systems, £2bn Rank Xerox

- **Employs:** 125,000 World-wide, 26,000 Europe, 8 000 U.K.

- **Business:** Office Systems, Document Management Focus

- **Investments in R & D** £500m pa
  Human Interface — Workstations
  Communications — Networks/Electronic Printing
  AI   — Understanding

Figure 4. Xerox Corporation: key facts

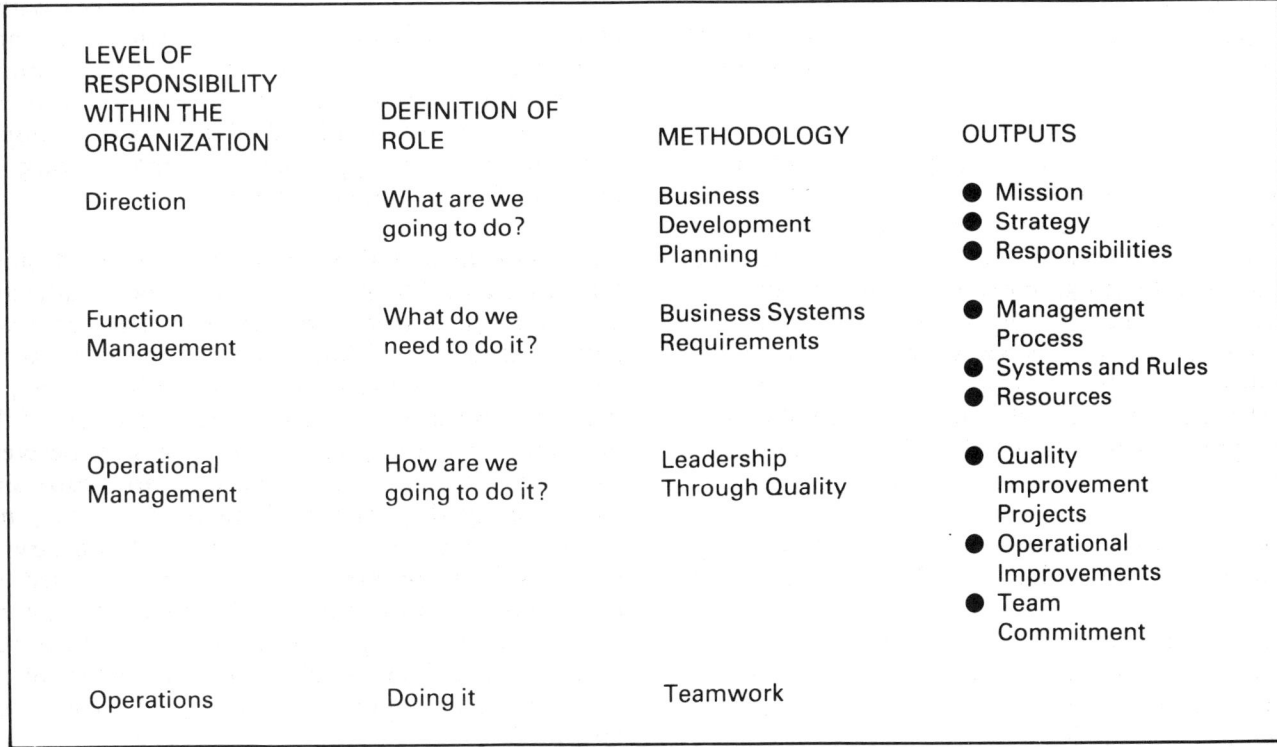

LEVEL OF RESPONSIBILITY WITHIN THE ORGANIZATION	DEFINITION OF ROLE	METHODOLOGY	OUTPUTS
Direction	What are we going to do?	Business Development Planning	● Mission ● Strategy ● Responsibilities
Function Management	What do we need to do it?	Business Systems Requirements	● Management Process ● Systems and Rules ● Resources
Operational Management	How are we going to do it?	Leadership Through Quality	● Quality Improvement Projects ● Operational Improvements ● Team Commitment
Operations	Doing it	Teamwork	

Figure 5. The Business Systems Requirements Review

From the Business Development Planning sessions, roles and responsibilities and objectives were established for every function, duplication and conflicts resolved, and a management process developed which cut down the number of senior executive monthly management meetings from eleven to three core meetings.

From the Business Systems Requirements Review, which involved more than 70 senior managers for week long sessions, over 1200 major defects in information, policies, guidelines etc. were identified and a strategy developed and approved which would benefit the profit line by over six times the investment required ($5m) over 3 years.

The Leadership Through Quality process is used now in many areas as a way of life. Over 3000 people (out of a total of 4500) have been fully trained in the process and by mid-1988 every employee will have been trained. The process is being used to solve many hundreds of problems large and small; from how to use the Company couriers more cost effectively to how to improve profitability on office systems—and every project has a payback!

Just one final illustration of how decision-taking speeds up once people are familiar with the processes and philosophy. When I joined the company in August 1986, as Director, Business Management Systems, one of the first major problems I confronted was the state of the order processing systems. The I.S. function had produced outline specifications for a new system and I was told that the operational functions had stated it was to take

240 weeks to agree the specifications! By using the Business Development Planning Process, with a cross-functional team of eight people, the specifications were agreed in 4 days and design of the system started the next day.

With a clearly defined methodology and management philosophy in place, the planning process could easily be developed (see Figure 6).

The new methodology was still resource intensive, however, and the next step was to look at how technology might be applied to the process, both to use internally and to articulate to customers and prospective customers how they could apply the philosophy, methodology and technology.

The basic elements of any management process are:

● ACQUIRE (acquire information)
● UNDERSTAND (build understanding)
● COMMUNICATE (communicate conclusions).

The understanding process is an iterative and interactive exercise of exchanging views, opinions and thoughts. Through the technological developments in the 1960s and 1970s most companies had acquired some level of capability in acquiring information via basic information systems, and some level of capability in communicating via networks and publishing systems. However, this is not where the majority of management cost and resource is expended. Case studies have shown that 20 per cent of the cost is in acquiring, and a similar percentage in communicating, leaving 60 per cent of the costs in the understanding area.

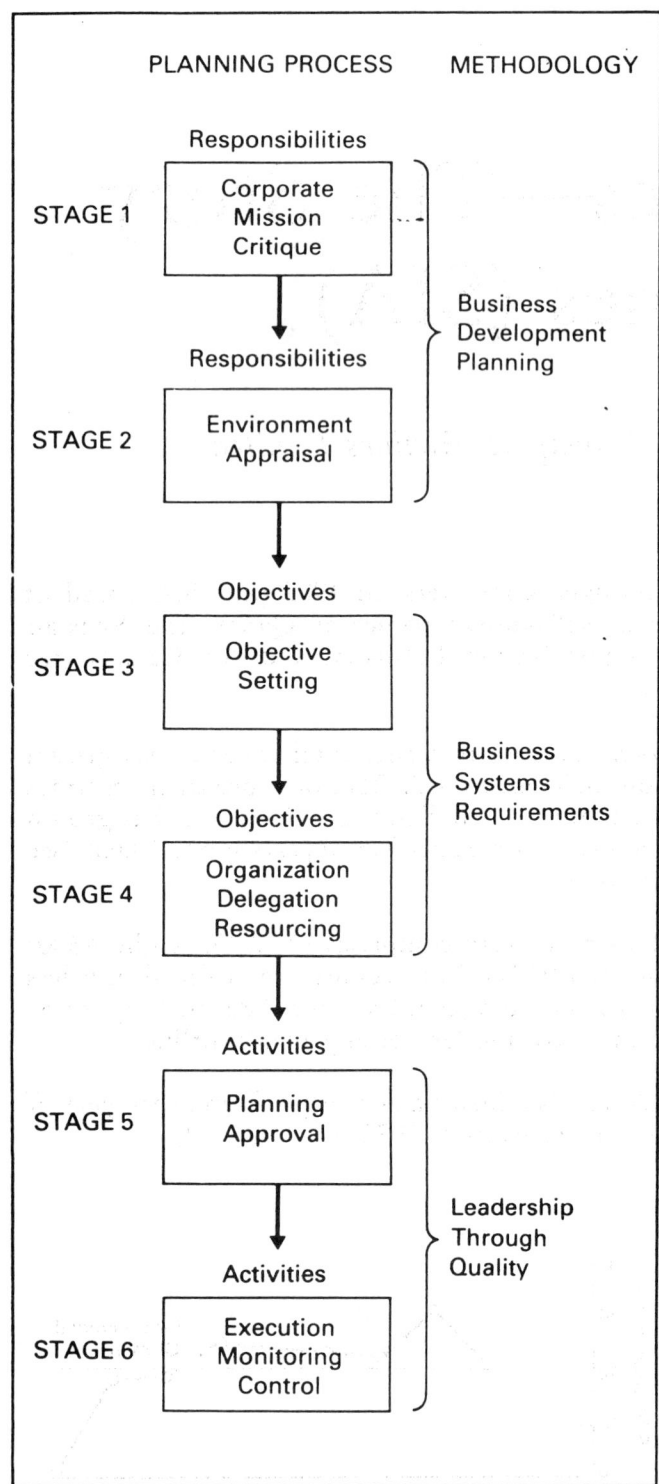

Figure 6. The Rank Xerox planning process

Clearly, therefore, this is where technology could achieve the maximum cost benefit. Also, the

understanding element of management is the key differentiator between companies; it is the area where management adds value to the business.

Even within the process of understanding, the three basic elements—acquire, understand and communicate—can be found, but this time dealing with thoughts, not data. Office systems technology is ideally suited to this part of the process with its capability to handle unstructured processes, data and information, and to communicate the resultant conclusions through publishing or composition systems.

Within the Rank Xerox range of products, there were all the necessary elements to create the necessary office systems technology, via multi-function workstations, the integration capabilities via networking and the communication devices via laser printers, fax etc.

The value that management adds to the business is its ability to facilitate understanding, the processing of thoughts, not just facts and conclusions. By developing and implementing an integrated team management philosophy and by supporting this with Rank Xerox's own office systems technology, O'Brien has been able within 18 months to make the U.K. arm of Rank Xerox the shining star in the Xerox world. Revenue is up 20 per cent year-on-year—the first time since the 'glory' days of the 1960s and early 1970s—and management profits have more than doubled.

In the process, he has begun to fulfil his major strategic objective, to exploit the opportunities in the office systems market by demonstrating the power that the right technology can have in turning a business around. This has already resulted in some major successes, for example a 200+ workstation network ordered from Logica, the systems house, the largest network order for Xerox ever outside of the United States; and an order for £3.2m worth of electronics printers from Lloyds Bank, in direct competition with IBM.

The opportunities for business and organization development offered by this approach to the application of office systems technology supported by a full Leadership Through Quality philosophy of management possibly herald the start of the next stage of the 'technological' revolution.

Successful Strategies—The Story of Singapore Airlines (SIA)

Karmjit Singh, Company Planning Manager, Singapore Airlines Limited

This case study describes the growth and development of Singapore Airlines from a small national carrier serving the Malayan States to an international airline with a network extending to 27 countries. Its strategy is simple: quality service at a competitive price, made possible by high investment in equipment and in staff training.

Introduction

SIA is the national air carrier of the island–state of Singapore. SIA's roots can be traced back to early 1947 when a twin–engined Airspeed Consul under the Malayan Airways insignia first started scheduled services between Singapore, Kuala Lumpur, Ipoh and Penang.

By 1955, international services were added using DC3s to Jakarta, Medan, Palembang, Saigon, Bangkok, North Borneo, Sarawak, Rangoon and Brunei. The airline underwent several fleet changes whilst additional destinations were added.

In 1963 it was renamed Malaysian Airways. In 1966, the governments of Malaysia and Singapore acquired joint majority control of the airline and in 1967 it was again renamed, this time to MSA (Malaysia–Singapore Airlines). MSA started to expand beyond the region with a chartered B707 operating to Sydney in the same year.

SIA was born on 1 October 1972 when MSA ceased operations and SIA took to the skies as Singapore's own national airline. The 'new' airline retained the B707s and B737s and continued to serve the entire international network formerly served by MSA. Today, SIA has grown to be among the top 10 international air carriers in the world. Its production of 18,081 million RPKs (revenue passenger kilometers) in 1982 puts SIA ahead of such well-known names as Qantas and Swissair and just behind Lufthansa and Air Canada (see Figure 1).

Over the past 10 years, total revenue has grown from S$389m to S$2,621m or more than six times (see Figure 2). Staff strength, however, has grown at a slower rate from 4906 10 years ago to 10,655 (see Figure 3)

SIA's fleet today comprises 17 B747s, eight A300s and two B727s. The average age of this fleet is less than 3 years old (as at October 1983) making it one of the most modern of any major airline.

SIA has also shown a decent profit in every year of its operations since 1972 (see Figure 4).

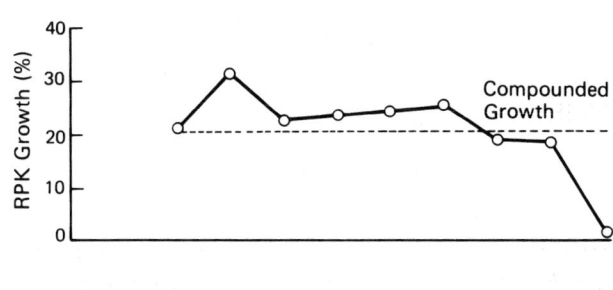

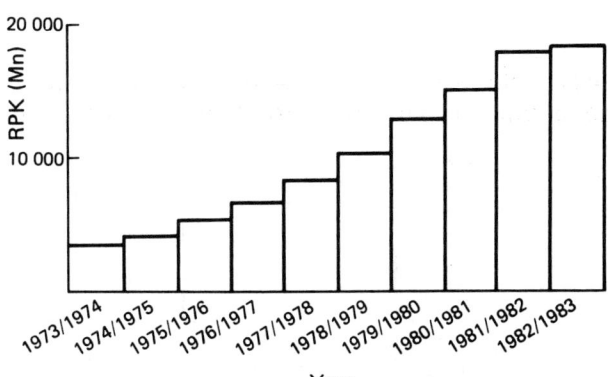

Figure 1. RPKs and growth rate

The author is Company Planning Manager with Singapore Airlines Ltd., Airmail Transit Centre, PO Box 501, Singapore 9181.

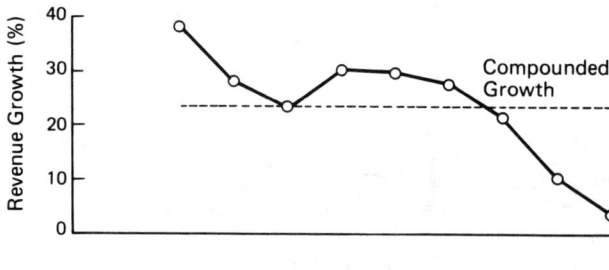

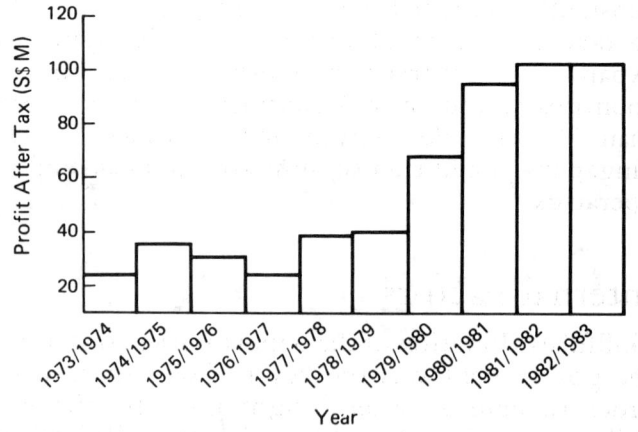

Figure 4. Profit after tax

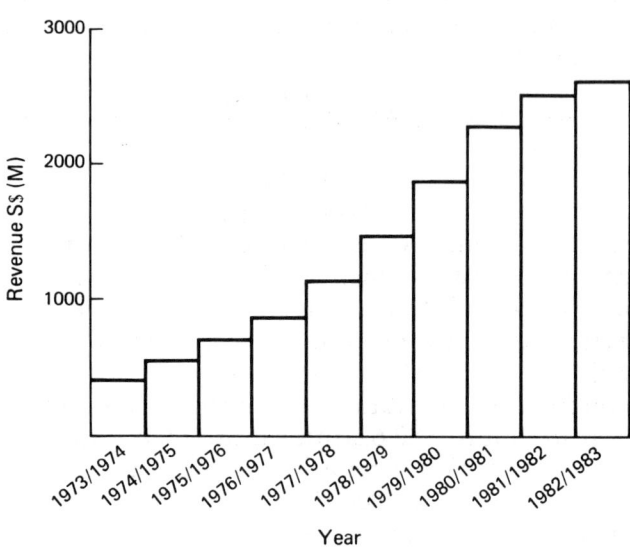

Figure 2. Revenue growth

Reasons for SIAs Success

What, one may ask, accounts for the enviable success of an air carrier from a tiny developing island-state half the size of Los Angeles with a population of only 2.5 million inhabitants and ill-endowed with natural resources other than its people?

Both external and internal factors have played equal and complementary roles in accounting for SIA's prosperity.

External Factors

Singapore straddles the Equator and is strategically located at the crossroads of one of the world's busiest sea and air routes. More importantly the airline's homebase is increasingly becoming the hub of the ASEAN hinterland with its thriving economies. It is also centrally located in the fastest growing region in the world—the Intra-Orient-Pacific Basin.

Hard-work and pragmatic government policies have turned Singapore into a modern and efficient metropolis, making it the most prosperous country in Asia after Japan. Its free enterprise ideology has attracted many Fortune 500 companies to set up regional headquarters in Singapore. Singapore today is the second largest port after Rotterdam and has the third largest oil-refining centre in the world after Rotterdam and Houston.

Liberal visa rules, good hotels and infrastructure and the promotion of Singapore as a shopping paradise have also helped to attract visitors by the thousands. Singapore now handles the largest number of foreign visitors among the Asian countries including Japan and Hong Kong.

The government also welcomes airlines from all over the globe to land at Singapore either as a terminating or transit point. To entice more of them to do so, airport and ancillary activities are

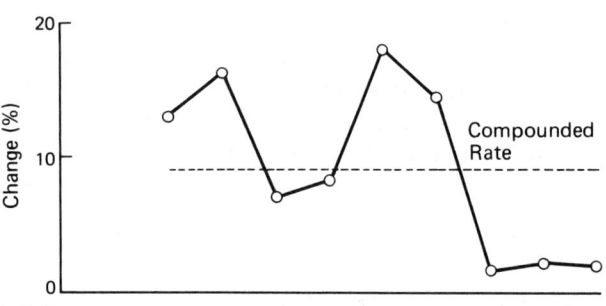

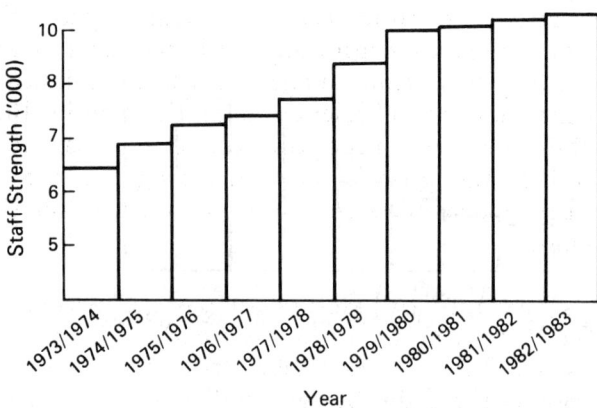

Figure 3. Staff strength

constantly upgraded. Consequently, SIA was able to take advantage of reciprocal traffic rights to expand. (Its current network extends to 27 countries spread over 4 continents.) Now, more than 30 scheduled international airlines call at Singapore in addition to numerous non-scheduled operators.

Internal Factors

Skillful exploitation of the opportunities created by the government was the key to SIA's success. In order to gain a better insight into the airline's ability to exploit its strategic location, and other advantages, we must return briefly to its inception stage.

Though almost wholly government-owned, the Airline does not receive any subsidies (which is taboo for all government-owned industries in Singapore). SIA is run along purely commercial lines—i.e. to make a reasonable profit for its shareholders. The airline is taxed like any other business and pays dividends yearly to its shareholders. SIA even has to pay fees to the government in return for guarantees that may be required by some banks on loans for aircraft purchases. The airline is constantly reminded that Singapore can exist without an airline since it is already well connected by air to all corners of the globe. Thus SIA fully recognizes its fate should it not make good in the marketplace.

Fleet Re-Equipment Decisions

SIA started with only five B707s and five B737s. To this were added four more B707s in 1972. After careful evaluation, the fledgling carrier decided to take a quantum leap into the jumbo league by ordering two B747s for delivery in 1973. This was not a hasty decision. Detailed studies had shown that this aircraft had the lowest unit operating cost. This was the first of many bold fleet re-equipment decisions. Thereafter the airline started to grow rapidly. More B747s were acquired in 1974, 1975, 1976 and 1977 as SIA's route network expanded to more European cities. Passenger response to the new aircraft and the inflight service was encouraging. In 1976 orders were also placed for three B727s. This order was then expanded to six in early 1977. These aircraft were needed to strengthen SIA's regional services and to replace the older B737s and B707s.

In late 1977 two more advanced versions of the B747 and five DC10s were ordered to service the TransPacific services.

In 1978 SIA shocked the world by announcing the then largest commercial aeroplane order ever placed, valued at U.S.$900m for 13 B747s and another six B727s. A few months later two more DC10s were ordered from McDonnell Douglas.

In 1979, it ordered six airbuses with options for a further six. Another huge order worth U.S.$1·6bn was placed in December 1981 comprising eight B747-300s with the stretched upper deck and eight more A300s. May 1983 saw yet another large order of aircraft—six more B747-300s plus six A310s and four B757s. Technologically obsolete and fuel inefficient aircraft were meanwhile retired. (See Table 2 for Summary of the Aircraft Deliveries and New Orders.)

By April 1988 SIA's fleet will consist of the following:

9	B747-200B
14	B747-300SUD
6	A310
4	B757

What was the justification for all these purchases? Firstly, SIA was able to exploit its traffic rights through skillful marketing. This, in turn, helped to stimulate traffic enabling the airline to expand at a rate of about 25 per cent a year in the 1970s.

Secondly, to support SIA's high service standards the airline decided to invest in the latest technology. It has since been part of SIA's strategy to maintain a youthful fleet with the lowest operating costs. The two fuel crises in 1973 and 1979 vindicated these 'bold' decisions, since the new aircraft proved to be an excellent hedge against fly-away inflation.

Thirdly, the major purchases were made at the bottom of the business cycle; best deals were therefore struck. With the carefully phased-out delivery of these aircraft, SIA could take advantage of any upturn in the economic cycle when demand for additional capacity was strong.

Service

From the start SIA understood that superior service, especially the standard of inflight service was paramount in order to establish itself. To provide a service 'that even other airlines talk about' became the unofficial motto for SIA's employees beginning with its cabin staff. According to Fortune magazine 'the combination of gentleness and efficiency helps the airlines lure customers from competitors on routes that now span half the globe'. The unceasing pursuit of excellence continues in the air as well as on the ground.

SIA's passenger load factors have been consistently above 70 per cent for the greater part of the past 10 years (see Table 1). Accolades from the trade and customers too have borne out SIA's belief that a superior quality of service is paramount under conditions of open competition where carrier's network, frequency and capacity are generally equal.

Table 1. Load factors by year (%)

	Passenger load factor	Overall load factor
1973/1974	71	63
1974/1975	67	60
1975/1976	68	64
1976/1977	71	66
1977/1978	74	68
1978/1979	73	70
1979/1980	74	71
1980/1981	72	69
1981/1982	75	72
1982/1983	73	69

While the inflight service has been highly visible, the airline has also spared no expense to raise its standards on the ground. Ground services are reviewed continually to match the standard of service provided in the air. With the passenger foremost in mind, SIA has invested millions of dollars in computers to link its reservations network worldwide to provide instant access on schedules and seat availability.

Owing to its high inflight standards and charming cabin crew SIA has managed to capture the mystic of the Orient in its 'Singapore Girl' advertising theme. The 'aura' created by the Balmain-clad girls has made the stylized yellow bird logo of SIA instantly recognizeable everywhere. Advertising recall of SIA advertisements is generally one of the highest wherever polled. This evergreen theme has also won some of the most prestigious awards in the advertising industry including the 1983 Clio award for the best International Television and Cinema category. SIA has also won Clio awards for the best television commercial (1975) and best overall print campaign (in 1976 and 1977).

Human Resources

Because Singapore lacked natural resources it has had to rely on its human resources to upgrade itself. Recognizing this, investment in human resources has been one of the cardinal facets of SIA's game plan.

Recruitment

During the recruitment phase, the best available personnel are sought. The new recruits are exposed to various departments and on-the-job training. High priority is given to staff training and development in diverse forms, both in-house and out-house, locally and overseas. Total expenditure in this area of staff development and training ranges between U.S.$15m and U.S.$20m annually.

This huge investment has been well spent. For example, its engineering staff can do almost all the maintenance on the latest generation of aircraft and engines. Hitherto, a greater part of the maintenance was contracted out-house at higher cost.

As mentioned earlier innovation and creative ideas are highly regarded and rewarded. Staff are continuously encouraged to send in ideas which save costs, increase revenue or productivity or upgrade service. Numerous ideas have been recognized, rewarded and implemented. Not long ago S$50,000 was awarded for an idea which saves the company about S$1·5m a year on fuel. It is through such schemes that employees are encouraged to give of their best.

Innovations

The innovative spirit also gave the travelling public the first slumberettes on B747 upper decks, jackpot machines to relieve boredom and Round-the-World fares. SIA also became the first airline, apart from British Airways and Air France, to operate the Concorde which cut travelling time, between London and Singapore, to $9\frac{1}{2}$ hours. This not only fulfilled SIA's goal to provide total service to the public but also enhanced SIA's reputation and image in the industry.

Behind the service standards lies the corporate philosophy supporting it. Among the attributes ingrained into employees are teamwork and the pursuit of excellence. The smallest possible units are created to carry out required tasks. Authority is delegated down to the lowest level consistent with accountability and efficiency. Decentralized decision-making enables fast reaction from the man-on-the-spot and especially the sales staff in the field. Executives are encouraged to progress to 'problem-solving' and on to opportunity-finding. Training and retraining remains the unwavering object of the company.

Productivity

Productivity is SIA's catchword in its drive for excellence. Staff recognize that survival in today's harsh competitive environment rests on raising their own productivity. With assurances from management that retrenchment is not the objective in seeking productivity gains, employees have been forthcoming with suggestions with improvements. SIA's employee productivity measured against the number of CTKs produced, ranks amongst the highest in the airline league (see Table 2).

Table 2. CTKs/employee

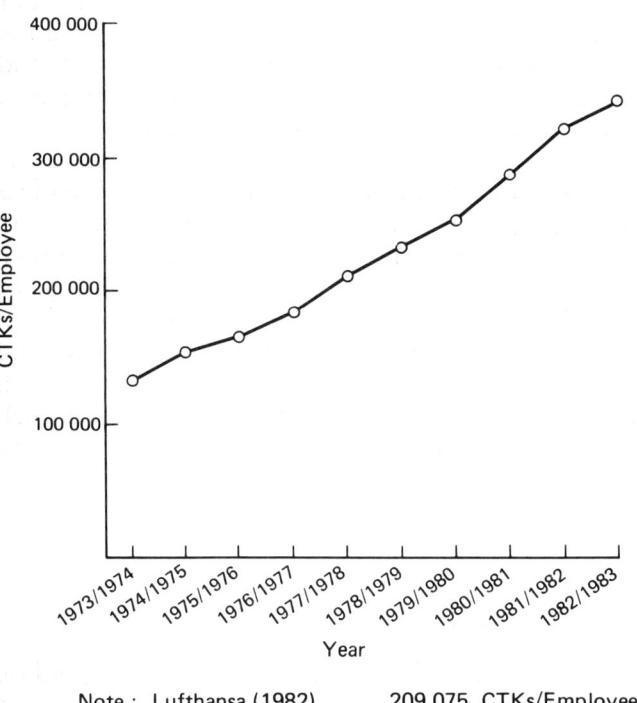

Note : Lufthansa (1982)　　 209,075　CTKs/Employee
　　　 Swissair　(1982)　　　 170,221　CTKs/Employee
　　　 KLM　　　(1982/83)　　256,120　CTKs/Employee
　　　 SIA　　　 (1982/83)　　339,232　CTKs/Employee

SIA intrinsically believes in being slim and trim. Staff recruitment is tightly controlled and is closely related to capacity growth rates. Staff made surplus through technology are either retrained or redeployed or induced to leave through generous redundancy schemes.

Industrial Relations

Because of the huge investment in human resources it is not surprising that Management and Unions try to co-exist for the good of the airline. Most industrial relations problems are solved amicably.

The cordial Management–Union atmosphere enables Management to concentrate on its task of running the airline instead of being preoccupied with 'public relations battles against criticisms and fighting for support of government and unions'.

Quality of Management

Of all the major and well-established airlines in the world, SIA has one of the youngest management teams. The average manager is in his late 30s with executive directors only 3–4 years older.

The young and dynamic team has been able to react quickly and decisively in decision-making. Luckily

for SIA the government does not interfere in day-to-day affairs and quick decisions can be made and actions taken.

Financial Conservatism

Management also believes in prudent financial management. New aircraft, for example, are depreciated over 10 years. This policy of accelerated depreciation reflects the rapid and continuing increase in the cost of new aircraft. Start up costs of aircraft are also written off fairly quickly. This has enabled SIA to finance a huge portion of its aircraft and other capital expenditure from self-generated funds. Because of SIA's credit standing, it has been able to tap the market for funds at the finest rates.

The Role of Corporate Planning

When SIA was expanding at double digit growth rates the Company Planning Department was preoccupied mainly with fleet planning. Over the last 2 years, with both capacity and traffic growth showing modest growth, the Company Planning Department became actively involved in identifying and establishing Corporate Objectives and Corporate Goals. To support the accomplishment of Corporate Goals, the Company Planning Department acted as a facilitator and catalyst and got the Divisions to establish their respective Divisional Goals. Consequently the smallest department in the Company was functionally linked in one way or another to the broader Corporate Objectives and Corporate Goals. In this way staff at various levels were motivated to do their best since the goals were well defined and measureable. The Company Planning Department monitored the progress of the goals, monthly, on behalf of management.

More importantly, in the realm of strategy formulation, the Company Planning Department consolidated the 'Environmental and Resource Analysis' inputs from all the departments and prepared an 'Issue Analysis'. Essentially this 'Issue Analysis' provided the kernel for management response and strategic thought and eventual functional strategy development. Implementation was, of course, decentralized.

Strategic Issues for the Future

The Company, historically, experienced capacity growth rates close to 20 per cent per annum. This was possible thanks to the systematic exercise of attractive traffic rights. Most of the relatively attractive traffic rights have now been used up. Meanwhile the global economic recession has served to heighten protectionist sentiments in several airline quarters. The prognosis is that we have to live with modest to low capacity growth rates in the future.

Strategically, we are now preoccupied with issues such as how to maintain profitability in the face of slow growth and rising costs. Also, in a low growth regime, how do you keep improving productivity continuously? There are other issues; and these feature prominently in the search for suitable strategies.

Conclusion

Through sheer hard work, innovation, bold and pragmatic decisions and huge investment in the staff SIA has grown from its humble origins to serve 36 cities in 27 countries. Its strategy is quite simple. It believes in giving the customer a quality service at a competitive price while earning a small return. This has been made possible by the high investment in the most up-to-date equipment and facilities and in staff training and development.

In short, SIA's success is founded on the prudent practice of sound and well-tried business fundamentals rather than any earth-shattering or new corporate strategies.